The Experience of Being Called

Thank you N. Smith Publishing,

For bringing such an inspiring resource to me, I am grateful to you and your dedication in the religious life promotions. The questions that you gave me are in my mind to see for myself the guidance inside this book filled with the virtues of devotion, trust and gladness of zeal living with the Eucharistic Heart of Jesus. I will gladly share with you the knowledge that our Father shows me within this book of hope in assurance. Peace be with you and God bless!

Your sister in Christ,

Lindsay

Thanks N. Smith Publishing,

I've been accepted as a postulant at Holy Trinity Abbey. I just got the news Saturday from Fr. Cummings. It has now been over a year since my observership there. I'll need several months to transition. I hope, God willing, to be at the Abbey by August of this year. Thank you so much for everything. I'll continue to stay in touch during this transition time. God bless you and the work you do.

Yours in Christ,

Arno

Dear N. Smith Publishing,

Please allow me to say "congratulations" on the success of "The Experience of Being Called."

Peace,

Richard

Dear N. Smith Publishing,

The outline of the book sounds ideal. I'm sure it's well worth the cost. You defined things very clearly. Thanks for your work and your interest. May you receive an unexpected blessing.

In Christ,

Anne Marie

The Experience of Being Called

A Guide to Knowing if You Have a Religious Vocation

Br. Gerlac O'Loughlin O.C.S.O.

N. Smith
Publishing

Coral Springs, Florida

Acknowledgements
Special thanks to:
Typists
Kelley Fivey
Sara Rogers
Editorial Assistants
Charlotte McCobb
JoAnn Curatolo

Published by
N. Smith Publishing, Inc.
6311 NW 47 Ct.
Coral Springs, Fla. 33067

Telephone: 1-866-548-3463 / 954-340-5705
Fax: 954-344-9231
Visit us at: http://VocationsPlacement.org/books.asp?bookpage=true
Customer Service E-mail: NsmithBookOrder@AOL.Com
Printed in the United States of America

Library of Congress Control Number 2005903682

ISBN 0-9769197-0-2

TABLE OF CONTENTS

DIVISION II

UNIVERSAL RELIGIOUS MAN'S EXPERIENCE OF BEING CALLED

DIVISION IV

THE CALL TO THE VOWED RELIGIOUS LIFE

DIVISION V

THE CALL TO GROW AS A VOWED RELIGIOUS

INTRODUCTION TO THE TOPIC

My interest in looking more deeply into the question of "vocation" was aroused a few years ago when a few of us were talking about religious life and someone raised the question, "What do we really mean when we talk about being called?" After the discussion I tried to put some of my thoughts down on paper. The general trend was as follows:

> Vocation is a call but it may be, partially, a call from within. It may be my conscious perception of the need to fulfill my inner potential. It may be the seed of destiny that has been planted within me asking for water and nourishment so that it can grow to fruition. The earth that is packed around a seed is both the barrier through which the growing plant will have to force its way and the source of the nourishment which will make growth possible. So in my life, the germinating seed will have to force its way through several layers of fear, inhibitions, prejudices and selfishness. But it will also have to find its nourishment in my interests, abilities, ideals and talents.

These thoughts aroused my interest in vocation as a human phenomenon. In the experience of vocation, what part is played by my interests and abilities? What part is played by my background and environment? How do these interior and exterior elements interrelate? Are there some conditions under which I may not be able to experience a call, and other conditions under which such an experience is more likely? What happens if I don't care to respond to the call? These are some of the questions I propose to study.

The term "vocation" is derived from the Latin "vocare" meaning "to call." The dictionary [1] gives three meanings:

1 a: a summons or strong inclination to a particular state or course of action; esp. a divine call to the religious life
  b: an entry into the priesthood or a religious order

2 a: the work in which a person is regularly employed: occupation
  b: the persons engaged in a particular occupation

3 the special function of an individual or group

The first definition: "a summons or strong inclination to a particular state or course of action; especially a divine call to the religious life" is the meaning I will be mainly concerned with in this book. The experience of vocation does not seem limited to a religious context though the term "call" may have its origin in religious experience and literature.

It may be helpful to make a preliminary distinction between vocation and motivation. Vocation seems to be a special form of motivation. It is an attraction that will have far reaching effects in my life. The attraction may not be as intense as some other forms of motivation but is more enduring and attracts me on several levels of my being, not just the instinctual, emotional or intellectual. The experience of vocation carries with it an implicit obligation to give it a respectful hearing though I may feel considerable resistance to doing so.

[1] Webster's New Collegiate Dictionary (Springfield, Mass.: G.C. Merriam Co., 1975).

2

When I graduated from high school my main concern was not so much what to do with my life but which college to go to and what classes to take. Physics interested me more than any of the other possibilities so I chose that. What I would do after college was still uncertain. I had no really clear specific interest as far as the future was concerned.

I had some slight interest in monastic life in high school but it was more of a daydream than something that I considered as a real possibility for myself. It was like a young boy admiring major league ball players, identifying with them, picturing himself as a player, but not really making any practical efforts toward realizing his ideal.

The interest had first been stirred by a novel [2] about Brother Nicholas, a Cistercian monk in Germany during the time of Hitler. He and his community were expelled from the monastery and he began working for the local bishop smuggling papers and money across the German border. He was captured by the Gestapo and sent back to the monastery which had been converted into a prison. Since he knew every inch of the buildings he could have easily escaped but decided to stay and carry on his former way of life as best he could.

What fascinated me most about the book was the simple, laborious life of the monks before they were expelled and the love of Brother Nicholas for his monastery and the life he had lived for so many years.

---

[2] Thomas Kernan, <u>Now With the Morning Star </u>(New York: Charles Scribner's Sons, 1944).

3

That simplicity seemed so lacking in my own life. I felt the world to be a much more complicated place than it need be with many obligations to do this or that because it was what was expected, what one did, or something that the previous generation wished they had had the opportunity to do. Most of the middle class standards around me did not have much appeal and I was refreshed to read of the simple, silent, laborious life of the monks. They were not busy trying to improve their status or keep up with the family next door. They had what they needed and kept themselves unencumbered. My interest, however, seemed to be a passing one. I recognized some of my ideals in the monastic values but it did not seem like a real possibility— more like a fairy-tale existence.

A few years later I came across another book on monasticism. Again the strange fascination was felt but this time there was the opportunity to follow up on the feeling by reading a few other books that were ready at hand. The interest grew into something more than a daydream as I began to realize that there were still monasteries in the world, even in America, and entering one of them was not an impossibility.

For the first time the new interest began to show some effect besides fascination in my life. Physical work became somewhat enjoyable as a way of "playing monk". Religion took on a new importance and meaning. Things that would have to be given up if I were to enter a monastery, like sports and dancing, were still enjoyable but not as important as before.

The interest became more intense in my first year of college as I found myself having to study hard for no apparent reason except to attain the middle class standards that had been set for me. I did not enjoy studying and it became more and more absurd to spend four years doing something I did not like in order to be qualified to spend the rest of my life doing things I liked even less. Monastic life appeared as an alternative. The less meaningful college became, the more I was attracted to monastic life. Still, I continued on in school.

At the beginning of my second year of college I told a friend that I thought I was just passing time until I entered the monastery. Still, I had made no contact with any monastery and had made no move in that direction. It was as if I were just waiting for "it" to "happen".

The second year of college was not nearly as bad as the first. I was attending a different college and the atmosphere was much better. After a couple months of school I wrote to Gethsemani Abbey and made arrangements to make a retreat over the Thanksgiving vacation. When the reply to my letter came; it was like getting something from another world. I stood on the porch with the letter in my hand trying to realize that this letter had really come from the monastery and had been written by a real live monk. There was his name written with his own pen inside the monastery. I tried to picture him sitting at his desk writing it. That letter made the monastic life much more real to me.

I set off hitchhiking happily for Kentucky. I did not mind the snow or the cold, the long periods of walking, the fact that on Thanksgiving day I had only breakfast and a candy bar. Those things did not bother me. I had my heart set on something else and those things did not really matter at all.

5

I found, in my weekend at the monastery everything I had hoped for. I felt no doubt that this was what I wanted to do, and should do, with my life. Monastic life appeared to be more than just desirable. The values of the frugal, simple life stood out so clearly that I felt obliged to respond to them. Could I sincerely continue to say that I esteemed them if I did not respond to them when they presented themselves? The possibility that I might not be accepted never entered my mind. In fact, when I was ready to leave home and enter the monastery shortly after Christmas I had not yet received notification of acceptance. Without giving the matter a thought; I left for the monastery as if there were no question or reason for doubt.

I found very little encouragement for my venture from my family and friends. My family was generally opposed, especially my parents. I was, surprisingly, indifferent to their opinions or, at least, not very affected by them. I just took it for granted that they were wrong since it was so obvious to me that this was the right thing for me to do. Once the decision was made, and it was hard to say just when it was made, I did not talk very much about it to anyone – just made my preparations and left. It never seemed to occur to others that I would stay; it never occurred to me that I wouldn't.

Reflections on the Experience

Looking back on this experience after twenty years I might question whether the person described really had a vocation at all. That, of course, depends on what is meant by vocation – which is what this book is to be about. In the

6

description there was not much mention of a call or any indication who was calling. Naturally, when I was thinking of entering the monastery I was thinking and speaking in terms of "having a vocation". But did this terminology spring spontaneously from the experience or was it a concept which I had learned about and had imposed on the experience as a way of understanding and justifying it? To a great extent the latter was probably the case.

Still, while the experience could certainly be described as a "strong inclination", to use the dictionary's terms; it also had something of the flavor of a "summons". It was not just something that I wanted to do but something I <u>should</u> do. Who says I should? The only experiential answer seems to be that the experience itself says that I should. It is not as if the experience provides a certain amount of data from which I draw the conclusion that I should enter a monastery. Rather, it is as if the obligation is a part of the data given in the experience.

Other forms of motivation such as movements of anger might also appear to bear their own authority in that they may say, all too loudly, "Do this!" But such a movement would not be likely to perdure, apparently unnourished, over a period of two or three years, as did my experience. Neither would such an emotional experience carry with it the implicit message, "This is something I <u>should</u> do." Nor is there anything particularly mysterious about the source of such motivations.

My attraction to monastic life did not seem to originate as a solution to any particular problem but when particular problems arose— such as dissatisfaction with college - the attraction presented itself as an alternative. Yet, when my second year of college proved less problematic than the first, the attraction did not diminish. It seemed content to bide its time but never missed an opportunity to nourish itself.

Thus there were many elements that went into the composition of the experience. There was the realistic attraction to the values of the simple, uncomplicated monastic life. There was the alternative to the meaningless work of college and middle class life. I was fairly conscious of these elements but there were other reasons for the attraction which only became apparent much later. It was only after several years that I realized that monastic life was partially the answer to a search for a "secure" life in which everything was mapped out for me, that it was an escape from guilt feelings by identification with a "holy" model – the monk. Superficially, all these motives had seemed to fit together nicely and were experienced as a strong attraction to the monastic values. Only later would I realize that seeking to take refuge in such a shallow security or to escape from feelings of guilt were motives that were incompatible with dedication to the monastic values. Though some of these elements would later have to be rejected, they contributed at the time to the intensification of the attraction and made it possible for me to give up other things such as sports, marriage and family. In other ways the attraction allowed me to make explicit some needs that I had hitherto not recognized or admitted such as the need for community.

My attraction to monastic life seems to have passed through three recognizable stages which were not, of course, mutually exclusive. First there was the stage of fascination in which I saw the monastic life as something of an idyllic existence which was interesting to read and think about which had no real practical relation to everyday life. At best, it strengthened my admiration for the monastic values but I made no effort to incorporate them into my everyday life. The second stage – "playing monk" – seems to have been a timid step toward taking these values seriously enough to experiment with them without committing myself or risking anything. The third stage consisted of the gradual commitment of myself to the monastic life. This is an ongoing process in which elements of the first two stages are evident. Each new step in the direction of commitment brings with it the realization that some of my understanding of true values has been idyllic and self-centered. Along with that disillusionment some new aspect of their true nature is revealed to me and demands a response. Each such revelation results (or should result) in some initial, uncertain, attempts to express my esteem for those values. These attempts make the values more real for me and encourage further commitment.

Components of the Experience

1. I am attracted to a particular state or course of action in which I see the possibility of realizing the values I esteem.

2. I freely assent to the attraction and commit myself to a positive response to it.

3. I express my assent to the attraction in my attitudes, decisions and actions.

These three components are not three stages in a linear process. Rather they appear as a continual series of cyclical movements by which I perceive, accept, and incorporate each new aspect of the attraction.

The third component is not a full-fledged response to the attraction but a process of concretizing the attraction itself, making it real, trying it on for size. With the second component I have accepted it as an attraction to which I am open and receptive, one with which I am willing to experiment.

Such movements are the elements out of which a vocation grows. At one point in my life it may be confidently said that there is no indication that I have a vocation. Some years later it may seem apparent that I do. But the transition point between these two situations is not usually easy to specify any more than a person can specify at what moment he reached maturity.

Statement of Purpose

It is my purpose to study thoroughly the human elements that are involved in the experience of vocation. With these as a basis, the specifically religious vocation will be examined. I hope to learn not only about the nature of the attraction but also about the dynamics involved in its growth and development. The part played by the personality, values and background of the individual who undergoes the experience will be considered as well as the influence of his social milieu.

Statement of Limits

I intend to study the phenomenon of vocation in the sense mentioned in the introduction as a "summons or strong inclination." The "summons" aspect seems essential. The person must experience some type of obligation to respond while remaining essentially free to refuse or decline.

Thus, "vocation" in the sense of occupation, career or profession will not be specifically considered. Neither will the vocation to marriage be given particular consideration since the topic is sufficiently broad to require a book of its own. However, human love will occasionally be used to demonstrate the dynamics of human attraction and response.

I will limit myself to the study of the way the experience of vocation usually comes about. This is not intended to deny that extraordinary manifestations may occur.

Method of Research

The material presented in this book will be taken from a variety of fields of study, philosophy, psychology, sociology, biographical and autobiographical writings and general literature. The method to be followed will be that developed within the Center for Study of Spirituality of the Institute of Man.

Having presented the views of a particular writer I will reflect on them in the light of my own experience and relate them to the opinion of the writers. Throughout the book I will attempt to unify the various perspectives, filling in gaps when necessary, to integrate the material into a single description of the experience of being called.

This book is ultimately concerned with the vocation of a member of a Catholic religious order during ongoing formation. It will begin by building a foundation, which will consist of several layers. First I will consider the experience of vocation on the natural human level without any religious connotations at all. I will then proceed to study the implications for the experience in a man whose vocation is specifically religious, though pre-Christian. Following that, the vocation to embrace and live a Christian life will be studied in the light of the foregoing chapters. The findings will be applied to the vocation to the vowed religious life and especially to the situation of the professed religious.

DIVISION I

THE HUMAN EXPERIENCE

OF BEING CALLED

INTRODUCTION

The experience I have described illustrates the way I came to find the meaning of my life. It involved an attraction to which I gave my assent and which I expressed in my behavior. With each new assent and expression the attraction grew more intense and the sense of obligation to follow it became stronger. The cycle of attraction, assent, and expression continues daily as I come to know more explicitly the unfolding meaning of my life.

The ambiguity of the term "vocation" seems to justify some further clarification of the way in which I will be using the word.[3] My way of using it is not, of course, the <u>only</u> legitimate use of the term.

A teacher might specify his vocation as "enhancing the intellectual growth of mankind." He might also say that his vocation is "teaching chemistry at the high school level." The first description points out his aims and ideals. The second tells

---

[3] The distinctions in this section are based on William K. Frankena, "The Philosophy of Vocation", <u>Thought</u>, LI (December, 1976), pp. 393-408. Frankena is dealing with the <u>concept</u> of vocation from the point of view of moral philosophy, rather than the <u>experience</u> of vocation.

13

the everyday means which he is using to realize those ideals. Which is really vocation? [4] For my purposes I shall include both elements. Thus I might be more inclined to say that the teacher's vocation is to enhance the intellectual growth of mankind by teaching high school chemistry. That includes both the ideal and its expression in everyday life. But that still does not quite pinpoint my topic. I am speaking of <u>the experience of being called</u> to express some ideal in everyday life.

Another question concerns the relationship between the ideal and its expression. Is teaching high school chemistry only one of many ways in which the teacher expresses his ideal? Or is it the primary way – possibly even the exclusive way? For my purposes, I am interested in the situation in which the expression is the <u>primary</u> way in which the ideal is lived out in daily life. Also, the particular expression is chosen primarily <u>in order to</u> live out these ideals. In the above example, teaching high school chemistry would not be just a way of making a living but an activity which has been chosen <u>in order that</u> the person concerned may be enabled to give expression to his ideals. Ideally, making a living and expressing ideals should coincide as they do in this example. A less ideal case might be an artist who has to dig to make a living. [5]

---

[4] Philosophical works, when they treat the topic at all, tend toward the more abstract, ideal use of the term. See Johann Gottlieb Fichte, <u>The Vocation of Man</u> (New York: Bobbs-Merrill, 1956), pp. 93-99. Fichte speaks of vocation in a sense that is applicable to all men. More practical works speak of the vocation of the particular individual but usually refer to vocation as merely the job or career in which the person is involved. See Donald Super, <u>Vocational Development; A framework for Research</u> (New York: Bureau of Publications, Teachers College, Columbia University, 1957).

[5] Certainly social restraints such a poverty or prejudice may impede the living out of ideals in everyday life. Abraham Maslow speaks of a hierarchy of basic needs and growth needs. A brief account of his theory can be found in Frank Goble, <u>The Third Force</u> (New York; Grossman Publishers, 1070), pp. 36-51.

Vocation, as I am viewing it, would involve a fairly long-term commitment. To express my patriotism by joining the army for a few years would not be considered a vocation but to devote my life to military service might be.

In this book I will be presupposing an essential view of man as a subject who is necessarily involved with the world around him. [6] Our modern, scientific minds prefer precise definitions and razor sharp distinctions. But manifold variables and ambiguities that occur in the relationship between man and his world urge me to adopt Aristotle's advice:

"We must be content, then, in speaking of such subjects and with such premises to indicate the truth roughly and in outline, and in speaking about these things, which are only for the most part true, and with premises of the same kind to reach conclusions that are no better. In the same spirit, therefore, should each type of statement be <u>received</u>..." [7]

---

[6] For an explicit development of this view of man see William J. Luijpen, <u>Existential Phenomenology</u> (Pittsburgh; Duquesne University Press, 1969), pp. 54-88. For a comparison of the existential view of man with the positivist and rationalist views, see Adrian van Kaam, <u>Existential Foundations of Psychology</u> (Garden City, NY; Image Books, 1969), pp. 15-23.

[7] Richard McKeon, ed., Nicomachean Ethics in Introduction to Aristotle (New York: The Modern Library, 1947), p. 310.

15

In Division I, I will deliberately bracket the religious dimension of the vocational experience and consider the experience as it might occur in the life of any person. The division will be divided into three chapters, the first dealing with the attraction to a particular state or course of action, the second dealing with the assent that maybe given to the attraction and the third with the expression of that assent in everyday life.

CHAPTER I

I AM ATTRACTED TO A PARTICULAR STATE

OR COURSE OF ACTION

The first stirrings of a vocation are usually experienced in the form of an attraction. In my experience it was an attraction to monastic life. All the other students in the class read the same book and, far as I know, none of them found such a life the least bit attractive. It was a particular person with a particular background and in a particular situation who was attracted. The nature of the experience is influenced – but not totally determined – by the subject who undergoes it.

The experience is also influenced by the "object" [8] to which he is attracted. In my case, the object-pole of the experience was monastic life as presented in a novel.

The attraction results from the dynamic relation between the subject-pole and the object-pole of the experience. Each pole contributes to the attraction but the attraction itself is more than the sum of them. Each pole may also bring its own limitations. I may have a completely false estimation of my own abilities.

---

[8] The term "object" is not to be understood in the sense of "thing", but in the sense of "objective"; that to which I am attracted. For further understanding of the way in which existentialist thinkers use the terms "object-pole" and "subject-pole", see William A. Luijpen, <u>Existential Phenomenology</u> (Pittsburgh: Duquesne University Press, 1969), pp. 35-45, 83-86.

I may also be presented with an unrealistic picture of the object and find myself attracted to something that does not really exist. Or I may have some difficulty in responding properly as a result of past behavioral patterns.

This chapter will examine the vocational attraction from four angles: the influence of the personality and background of the subject who feels the attraction, the implications of the state or course of action to which he is attracted – the object-pole, the dynamics of the interrelation between the subject-pole and the object-pole and, finally, some of the difficulties that may arise and prevent the attraction from developing into a vocation in the full sense of the word.

Before discussing attraction on the human level, I will present a prefatory analogy in the form of a brief discussion of magnetic attraction.

Francis Bitter [9]
Magnetic Attraction

Nearly everyone is familiar with the simple bar magnet, a straight piece of steel that attracts and holds small pieces of iron. The magnet has a "North" pole at one end and a "South" pole at the other.

---

[9] Francis Bitter, Magnets: The Education of a Physicist (Garden City, N.Y.: Doubleday Anchor Books, 1959). All quotations from this work will be followed immediately by page references in brackets.

If two such magnets are brought near one another we see that a magnetic north pole is attracted by a magnetic south pole; north poles repel each other, and south poles repel each other. An attempt to separate the two poles of a magnet by cutting it in half results only in two smaller magnets, each with its north and south pole since "... magnetic forces are due to <u>dispoles</u> [italics in the original], or pairs of poles of opposite polarity that cannot, for some reason, be separated." [p. 42]

An invisible field of magnetic forces surrounds a magnet. The pattern of this invisible field can be observed by placing a sheet of paper over a magnet, scattering iron fillings on the paper and tapping the paper gently. The forces of the magnetic field will cause the fillings to align themselves as in Figure 1. Not only can the poles of a magnet not be

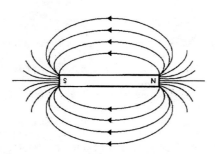

Figure 1. The magnetic field lines do not converge at a point at either end of the magnet.

separated, they cannot be accurately located:"... the fields of a magnet indicate that the magnetic poles are <u>always</u> [italics in the original] spread out, that they are smeared out over the ends of a magnet,...." [pp. 46-47]

In an ordinary, unmagnetized bar of iron each atom is a tiny magnet with a north and south pole. These atoms are bunched together in small clusters called magnetic domains. All the atoms in a domain have their north poles pointing in the same direction, thus each domain is also a small magnet. But the poles of the domains are pointing in random directions. When the iron bar is introduced into a magnetic field, the domains are "twisted" by the force of the field so their north poles point in the same direction. This has the effect of making the bar into a magnet, at least for as long as it is under the influence of the magnetic field. Thus it is seen that a magnet does not just attract a piece of iron, it makes the piece of iron into a magnet like itself. Nothing new is added to the iron; its inner patterns are merely rearranged.

Reflection

Like the magnet, human life seems to have a bipolar element about it. Each time I am attracted to something I am also attracted away from some other possibility. Often I will try to build the attraction up by rejecting that which I will have to give up. I used to marvel at how my sister's former boyfriend immediately sank to the category of a "real creep" the minute she found someone new. The opposite seems to be true too. Being involved in a task that I find boring seems to breed a plethora of new interests and desires. As I sit looking at this computer and wondering if I'll ever get this book finished, I recall that I am long overdue to write some letters, I need a book from the library and this is such a nice day for a walk. I haven't practiced playing my recorder for a couple weeks. There is no end to the list. When I say "Yes" to one attraction I always have to say "No" to another.

The attractions I feel are seldom as clear and simple as I would have them be. I simplify them when I try to understand and articulate them, but, like the magnetic pole, my motivation is always "smeared out" into areas of which I am quite unconscious and perhaps very unwilling to face. Domains of magnetism might be compared to what we often refer to as mixed emotions. At some level of motivation I may be drawn towards a particular course of action and, at the same time, repelled at another level. The more "domains" of motivation [10] that are tending in the same direction, the more all-embracing the attraction will become. Nothing new is really added to me. It is just that my various energies are being unified in a single direction. If a piece of iron could feel, what would be its experience when brought into the influence of a magnetic field? It would probably not feel pulled all at once towards the magnet as if it were being pulled or pushed from without. Rather, it would feel its "innards" churning slightly as one, then another, then a few more of its magnetic domains turned towards the magnet under the influence of its field. Finally, nearly all the domains are reoriented and the piece of iron, now a magnet itself, feels only the irresistible tendency to move in the direction of the magnet which has affected it.

---

[10] A very detailed analysis of motivation can be found in Alexander Pfander, <u>Phenomenology of Willing and Motivation and Other Phaenomenologica</u> (Evanston, Il1: Northwestern University Press, 1967). [pp 12-40]

21

So it is with the human attraction. I am attracted to something outside myself but the attraction is known in its effects within me. The difference, of course, is that I can take a stand in regard to the attraction. I can lessen its influence by resisting it or I can enhance its effect by giving my assent to it. I am responsible for what I make of the attraction.

I will return to the analogy between magnetic attraction and human attraction throughout this first chapter. It is now time to turn to the subject of the attraction to examine the ways in which his personality and background affect the experience.

I: THE SUBJECT-POLE

Donald Super [11]
The Role of Self-Concept

Donald Super, a vocational psychologist, uses the term "vocation" interchangeably with the terms "career", "occupation", "job", "work". He states that "In choosing an occupation one is, in effect, choosing a means of implementing a self–concept." [p. 196]

---

[11] The material in this section is taken from Donald Super, The Psychology of Careers (New York: Harper and Brothers, 1957). All references to this work will be followed by the appropriate page numbers in brackets. Relevant material can also be found in Anne Roe and M. Siegelman, The Origin of Interests (Washington: American Personnel and Guidance Assoc., 1964, (G.B Simons, "An Existential View of Vocational Development", Personnel and Guidance Journal XLIV (1966), pp. 604-610, C.F. Tageson, The Relationship of Self Perceptions to Realism of Vocational Preference (Washington: Catholic University of America Press). A very brief summary of these works and others can be found in the first chapter of Luigi M. Rulla's book, Depth Psychology and Vocation: A Psycho-social Perspective (Chicago Loyola University Press, 1971).

Super sees adolescence as a period in which a person is in the process of moving from the subculture of youths to that of adults, learning the ways of adults and adopting their mode of behavior. But there is much more involved than this.

The adolescent brings a great deal to this world himself: he brings his <u>self</u>. What he sees, what he tries, how well he likes it, and how well he succeeds at it, depend upon his self as well as upon the culture. [p. 81, italics in the original]

The child is born with certain temperamental characteristics which favor the development of some abilities and traits and make others more difficult. From early in life these characteristics interact with the environment of the child. Some of his behavior is favored by his parents, some is disapproved of. Much of his behavior is an attempt to imitate them. Gradually he finds out that he is like others in many ways, but he is also different, "...he begins to develop a concept of himself as a distinct person, as self rather that as other." [p. 81] Some elements of the self-concept may be realistic while others may be false. Possibly there is a conflict between two elements which are not compatible with one another. Through trial and error, a change in circumstances, insight or counseling, one of the elements – hopefully the false one – is altered and brought into conformity with the rest of the self. Otherwise, conflict and anxiety will set in and normal personality integration will be hampered.

By the time the person reaches adolescence, then, much of his self-concept has already been formed. Over the years he has experienced a gradual increase in the number of possibilities open to him and the number of responsibilities he should take upon himself. He has some idea what can be inferred about a person from the type of work he does, what kinds of occupations he himself finds most satisfying

23

and how well he does them – in his own opinion and in that of others. This exploration of himself and exploration of occupations usually takes place without a clear awareness of what is happening. In adolescence, the process becomes more explicit:

> Therefore adolescent exploration is not so much a process of developing a new picture of one's self as of putting it into words and thus developing a basis for finding out what sort of outlets there are in society for a person who seeks to assume a given kind of role, and then of making modifications in the self-concept to bring it into line with reality. Adolescent exploration, then, may be viewed as a process of ascertaining and testing reality. [pp. 84-85]

Choosing a career is an attempt to implement a self-concept, and self-concept is fairly well formed by adolescence. It would seem, then, that high school students would have a fairly good idea of what career they want to pursue, and their future work would, in fact, prove to be consistent with these aspirations. Experiments have been performed to study the degree of consistency between the vocational aspirations of high school students and the actual occupations they later adopted. The findings of the various studies conflict with one another but Super is clearly of the opinion that there is a relatively high degree of consistency. [pp. 90-91] [12] This conclusion is in keeping with his theory that choosing a career is an attempt to implement an already formed self-concept.

---

[12] Super is somewhat unconvincing at this point. He refers to three studies done by Lehman and Witty, Schmidt and Rothney, and Sission [p. 90] which indicate lack of consistency between high school aspirations and careers actually undertaken. He then mentions two studies, one done by Porter and the other by Hartson which show a relatively high consistency. Pointing out that other studies have shown that the form of the question asked often determines the realism of the answer, Super concludes: "It thus seems likely that the questions in studies like those of Porter and Hartson were so phrased as to obtain more realistic responses than were those used in studies such as those Lehman and Witty, Sission and Schmidt and Rothney" [p.91]. He seems to take consistency for granted and judge the reliability of the tests by whether or not they produce the desired results.

In studying the development of vocation, Super deals with the implications of the person's aptitudes, interest and personality traits, his disabilities, and his family and economic background and situation. The really important thing seems to be that the individual have a fairly realistic estimation of these factors. "Here, then, is a major goal for education: the development of clear, well formulated, and realistic self-concepts." [p. 111] He adds, however, that "self-understanding... is not easily achieved and is usually limited at best." [p. 113]

Reflection

Super is not speaking specifically of the experience of being called. He is saying that the self-concept I have developed over the years – my idea of what sort of person I am – has much to do with the type of activity I will be attracted to and how satisfied I will be with that activity. My self-concept includes my own awareness, unawareness or distortion of my interests, abilities, limitations and needs. [13] It is only one of the things I bring to the experience of being called but it is an important and unifying factor.

---

[13] For more complete discussion of self-concept, see Brian Wangler, "Spirituality and Self Concept", Unpublished Master's Thesis, Center for the Study of Spirituality, Institute of Man, Duquesne University, Pittsburgh, 1978.

How was my self-concept influential in my vocational experience which I described in the general introduction? I certainly thought of myself as a person who was not interested in the complexity and status seeking of middle class society or in the race to keep up with the rest of the world. I thought of myself as one who enjoyed and appreciated a simple life lived close to nature, a quiet and unobtrusive life without a great deal of dependence on modern technology. This view of myself has not changed much.

I did not think of myself as a particularly independent person, one who would pack up his bags and calmly leave home when he found a life that seemed to suit him. But the description of the experience as well as a number of experiences since that time, indicate that I was and still am independent in many ways. This was and area of reality that was not included in my self-concept.

I thought of myself as an easy-going and fairly gentle person who didn't anger easily or harbor resentment. I have learned since that this part of my self-concept was unrealistic.

That my lack of interest in a complicated middle class life should help nourish an attraction to a simpler type of life is reasonable enough and presents no problems. My unawareness of my independence did not raise any serious obstacles either. The independence was there and at my disposal whether I knew it or not. I wasn't denying or repressing it. When the time came I exercised it and was a little surprised at myself – but pleasantly surprised, not shocked or ashamed. The anger and resentment were repressed and unconscious. They no doubt acted unconsciously to urge me to get away from all the things that I resented but they were not visible to me at the time so that I might see them as obstacles.

This does not, of course, explain the attraction. My self-concept did not cause the attraction. But it did influence the attraction; it is part of the situation out of which the attraction grew. An attraction always requires two elements – the one which is attracted and the one to which it is attracted. Each element contributes something.

This was seen to be true in the analogy of the magnet. The piece of iron placed near the magnet is not just "there". A block of wood might be just "there" without being affected by the magnet. There is something that the iron contributes to the situation, and must contribute, if there is to be any attraction at all. It is partially because of the nature of the object to be attracted that the attraction becomes possible. So in the vocational experience, it is partially because of the nature of the person to be attracted that there can even be an attraction at all.

Super has spoken of how one's past life and present situation are bound up in his self-concept [14] and how this may affect his vocational attractions. He has spoken of the subject-pole of the experience. [15] We must now turn to the considerations of the object-pole: that to which one is attracted.

---

[14] For a phenomenological discussion of how man's past (and future) are tied up with his present see William Luijpen, Existential Phenomenology (Pittsburgh: Duquesne University Press, 1969), pp. 237-244.

[15] Another theory of vocation which emphasizes the subject-pole of the experience can be found in Carl G. Jung, The Integration of Personality (London: Routhledge and Kegan Paul, 1940) pp. 281-305. Jung speaks of vocation as "...an irrational factor that fatefully forces a man to emancipate himself from the herd and its trodden paths." [p. 291]. "Who has vocation hears the voice of the inner man: he is called." [pp. 291-292] All men, according to Jung, have vocation but it is stronger, more immediate and compelling in the great personality and somewhat distant and less distinct in the lesser personalities, often being absorbed into the voice of the group. It is "my" vocation only in the sense that it affects me, not in the sense that I have anything to say about the constitution of it; I can only follow, or refuse to follow.

II: THE OBJECT-POLE

Dietrich von Hildebrand [16]
The Call of Values

In describing my vocational experience I spoke of being attracted to the monastic values, to the monastic life. How do values attract me? For that matter, what are values?

Von Hildebrand bases his study on the data of experience, the "immediately given" [p. 2] and asks the reader to withhold judgment in terms of familiar theories. [17]

---

[16] The material in this section is taken from Dietrich von Hildebrand, Christian Ethics (New York: David McKay Co., 1952). All references to this work will be followed by the appropriate page numbers in brackets. In using the term "Christian ethics" the author means "...the one, true, valid ethics." [p. 453] Much of the book is concerned with the ethical values without any direct reference to religion and it is from these sections that this material is taken.

[17] This does not mean that all familiar theories are untrustworthy and must be rejected. But neither should they be considered infallible. Each new datum of experience should be approached with an uninhibited openness that will allow it to manifest itself as it really is. This should be done even though the new datum may seem to be at variance with some well-established system or with other data that seems self-evident.

Importance. The term "importance" is used by von Hildebrand to designate that character of an object [18] which allows it to motivate my will or to become the source of an affective response. Objects may have a positive importance or a negative importance, that is, they may be desirable or undesirable. Negative importance is not just the absence of positive importance but its very antithesis. [19]

There are three general categories of importance. There are, first of all, those things that are merely subjectively satisfying. I may enjoy smoking or taking a drink, but there is nothing "wrong" if I don't smoke or take a drink. It is merely a question of my subjective satisfaction.

There are other things that "ought" to be done – acts of kindness, generosity or forgiveness. In a situation which "calls for" such an act we recognize immediately that there is something "wrong" if the appropriate response is not forthcoming. These acts are said to have an intrinsic importance. That which is intrinsically important is what von Hildebrand calls "authentic value". He would include such things as the beauty in nature or in the art as well as the splendor of some great truth.

---

[18] Here, again, "object" does not simply mean a thing. It refers to anything to which I can relate as a subject, whether it be a thing, an act, a quality or even a person other than myself, though in the context of another person von Hildebrand is usually more specific.

[19] Anything which does not present itself as a source of motivation is considered to be neutral importance, though, from a metaphysical point of view, even it may be said to have some importance. [p. 25].

Von Hildebrand describes the call of authentic values and differentiates it from the attraction of the merely subjectively satisfying in the following words:

> Besides the merely subjectively satisfying and the authentic value, there is a third category of importance. It covers those things that are objectively good for the person. This differs from authentic value but presupposes it. Thus the love of another for me, besides having the authentic value of any true love, also has a special importance for me, it is "...something conducive to my true interest." [p. 50] It may also be subjectively satisfying.

Authentic Values

It is in authentic values that von Hildebrand is most interested. We cannot change the call by our wishes, nor is it "... left to our arbitrary decision or to our accidental mood whether we respond or not, and how we respond." [p. 38] The call of values is an attraction and an invitation to respond; it imposes an obligation to respond but it does not cause the response. The response must issue from my free spiritual center. It is the value concerned, however, that "takes initiative" and dictates the terms of the response. Thus it appears that von Hildebrand places most of the emphasis on the object-pole of the experience.

It would be misleading, however, to think that he ignores the subject-pole altogether. Not only does man have "... a sensitivity to values just as man's intellect has a receptivity for the nature of other beings." But:

> It is indeed a deep characteristic of man to desire to be confronted with something beyond self-centeredness, which obligates us and affords us the possibility of transcending the limits of our subjective inclinations, tendencies, urges, and drives rooted <u>exclusively</u> in our nature. [p. 37] [20]

Reflection

When I first began thinking about the topic of vocation, I was wondering if the question could be approached from the point of view of a polarity between invention and discovery. Do I <u>discover</u> my vocation; is it something that is "already there" and I either discover it or miss it? Or do I <u>invent</u> it; do I arrange and order my activities and surroundings according to some plan or idea that I have? [21]

---

[20] This desire for transcendence might be compared to Adrian van Kaam's ideas of "spirit" and "emergent self" described in <u>The Dynamics of Spiritual Self Direction</u>, (Denville, N.J.: Dimension Books, 1976), pp. 10-14.

[21] The relationship between the meanings of the word "discovery" and "invention" is far more complicated than the above presentation suggests.

Von Hildebrand would quite definitely lean towards the idea of discovery. He would say, as I said in the description of my experience, that I discover values – I see them embodied in some situation or act – and I respond to them. The values existed before I was aware of them and gain nothing from my perception of them or from my response to them.

This description seems to correspond to my own experience. The monastic values of silence, simplicity, and solitude had existed long before I came on the scene. I may have been, as von Hildebrand states, so designed as to recognize what is important in itself and to respond to it. But my recognition and response did not in any way appear to me to co-constitute the values. [22]

Was I, perhaps being too idealistic in my interpretation of the call? Was I hiding from myself, and trying to hide from others, the fact that many aspects of my attraction to monastic life were selfish? Quite possibly. But that does not argue against the existence of authentic values; it only states that I was, to some extent, attracted to them for the wrong reasons.

---

[22] William A. Luijpen in <u>Existential Phenomenology</u> (Pittsburgh: Duquesne University Press, 1969), pp. 206-217, presents other possibilities. One is the view of Jean-Paul Sartre that there are no objective norms or values. He paraphrases Sartre's view in the following words: "In absolute autonomy man must create values, invent norms, and choose his morality," [p. 208] Luijpen replies that general laws are not useless but, on the other hand, are not sufficient for genuine morality. "What has to be done here and now cannot be deduced from general norms, for these norms say nothing about the character of <u>this</u> deed and <u>this</u> situation." [p. 214]

Von Hildebrand's theory of authentic values gives an explanation of the "obligation" to respond that the subject of a vocational experience feels. But he speaks of values that call to <u>all</u> <u>men</u> and in the <u>same</u> way. This does not contribute much toward the understanding of an individual vocation except to indicate that there are probably some authentic values involved in the object-pole of a true vocation. Von Hildebrand does not go into the question of how certain values may interrelate in such a way as to attract one person and not another, or how the differences in persons may result in an obligation on the part of one person and not on another. He points out that one may err in his estimation of a value or be afflicted with value blindness resulting from pride and concupiscence [p. 46], but he is not entitled to accept or reject values on his own authority. He is like the woman in the art museum who, when she expressed a distaste for the painting, she was told by the attendant: "Madam, you do not judge these paintings; they judge you!"

In terms of the magnetism analogy, von Hildebrand is talking about the magnet (that which has power to attract) more than he is talking about the piece of iron which is attracted. A magnet is of a particular size, and has a particular magnetic field around it. If the piece of iron that is being attracted is larger or smaller it will be more or less strongly attracted but that is beside the point. The point is that the magnet had the capacity to attract iron whether it is actually doing so or not.

Super, the psychologist has shown that the subject brings with him to the experience a self-concept which influences the way he will respond to the world. Von Hildebrand, the philosopher, has shown that the values that present themselves to the subject confront him with an invitation and obligation to respond in a certain way regardless of his self-concept. The findings of both theorists seem to correspond to experience. How do the needs of the subject-pole and the demands of the object-pole interact?

III. THE DYNAMIC INTERACTION

Viktor Frankl [23]
Search for Meaning

Viktor Frankl, the Austrian psychiatrist and founder of Logotherapy, does not speak explicitly about phenomenon of vocation. However, his "search for meaning" theory offers a good framework in which to unite the subject-pole and the object-pole of the attraction we have been considering.

Frankl sees a man as living in three dimensions, the somatic or bodily, the mental, and the spiritual. The spiritual is what makes a man specifically human, that is, distinct from the animal world. It is in this dimension that he "locates" the will-to-meaning, the self-transcendence that he considers to be the essence of human existence. [D&S, p. x; MM, p.21] Man is characterized by his constantly reaching out, and having to constantly reach out, for meaning in his life. [MM, p. 21]

---

[23] The material in this section is taken from three works by Viktor Frankl: Man's Search for Meaning (New York: Simon and Schuster, 1962), The Doctor and the Soul (New York: Vintage Books, 1973) and "What is Meant by Meaning?", Journal of Existentialism, VII, No. 25 (Fall, 1966), pp. 21-28. All references to these three works will be followed by the appropriate page numbers in brackets. The three works will be noted by the initials MSM, D&S and MM respectively.

34

This is not a movement towards an ultimate equilibrium or tensionless state called, in biology, "homeostasis." Frankl declares:

> What man needs is not homeostasis but what I call "noo-dynamics," ie, the spiritual dynamics in a polar field of tension where one pole is represented by a meaning to be fulfilled and the other pole by the man who must fulfill it. [MSM, p.105]

Meaning appears to have an objective existence independent of man. Frankl insists frequently that meaning is to be "discovered" or "found." This, he affirms, represents a higher form of development than "projecting", "conferring" or "inventing" meanings. [MSM, pp. 98-99; D&S, p.62; MM, pp. 24-25] He explains this "objective existence" differently than von Hildebrand would:

> There is, therefore, no such thing as a universal meaning of life, but only the unique meaning of individual situations. However, we must not forget that among these situations there are also situations which have something in common, and consequently there are also meanings which are shared by human beings throughout society and, even more, throughout history. [MM, p. 22]

It is these"... meaning-universals which crystallize in the typical situations a society – humanity – has to face" [MM, p. 22] that Frankl is referring to when he speaks of values. There is no reason for a conflict of values since "The experience of one value includes the experience that it ranks higher than another." [MM, p. 22]

How does man, the subject, relate to these values? Does not meaning always involve an interpretation on the part of the individual? Is it not therefore subjective? Not so, says Frankl. The perspective through which we observe the world is subjective but "What is <u>seen through</u> the perspective, however subjective the perspective may be, is the objective world." [MM, p. 24]

35

Life continually confronts man with the question, "What is the meaning of this particular situation?" Man is free to answer but he is also "...responsible for giving the right answer to a question, for finding the true meaning of a situation." [MM, p. 25] There is, then, only one true meaning to be found just as there is only one true answer to the question "How much is seven plus seven?"

The world of values is therefore seen from the perspective of the individual, but for any given situation there is only one single perspective, which is the appropriate one. Accordingly, absolute rightness exists not in spite of, but because of the relativity of individual perspectives. [D&S, p. 42] [24]

But how does man go about finding "the true meaning" of a situation? He is led and guided by conscience, which Frankl defines as "...the intuitive capacity of man to find out, to scent out, as it were, the meaning of a situation, that Gestalt [25] quality that is hidden in the situation." [MM, p. 26] By conscience one manages to intuit the presence of traditional values in a situation. But conscience is creative as well as intuitive. It may recognize values that have never been known and appreciated in the culture or, having once been known, have been lost sight of.

[24] The comma following "perspective" in the first sentence of this quotation is a little confusing. Apparently Frankl means that there are several possible perspectives but only one of them is appropriate; only one corresponds to the objective values that are available in the situation. He does not seem to mean that the appropriate perspective is the only possible perspective (as the punctuation suggests).

[25] Gestalt is defined as "a structure, configuration, or pattern of physical, biological, or psychological phenomena so integrated as to constitute a functional unit with properties not derivable from its parts in summation."

The individual meanings of each unique situation remain even if universal values should disappear – a state which Frankl feels we are approaching today. Universal meanings are being lost and many people without the "full capacity of conscience" cannot find meaning in their lives. They are caught in a feeling of aimlessness which Frankl calls an "existential vacuum." [MM, p. 26]

"Conscience is a definitely human phenomenon", Frankl insists. It is not just the result of conditioning. But it is not infallible. Man must follow conscience even at the risk of error and can be whole-hearted, even though only half-sure, says Frankl in quoting Gordon Allport. [MM, p. 26]

Reflection

Though Frankl does not speak about vocation, his observations fit well into the attraction-assent-expression cycle in which I am considering the experience of being called. I do not find meaning "once and for all" but only one moment at a time. Meaning is not something that has the independent, objective existence of von Hildebrand's authentic values. Frankl's "meaning" corresponds more nearly to von Hildebrand's third category of importance: that which is objectively good for one person. The trans-cultural character of some meanings is due to the fact that they are generally esteemed by people over a long period of time. [26]

---

[26] For a phenomenological study of the concept of meaning see Luijpen, pp. 39-40, 63-83. Frankl's insistence that there is one true meaning for each situation is difficult to deal with from and experimental point of view. It is reminiscent of Frankena's observation that "one's true vocation is the vocation one should have or have had, ... It is one's ideal vocation, however this is to be determined." Frankena, [p. 397] The big question, of course, is: Just how is this to be determined? Can it be determined? If not, how much value is there in talking about it? When the possibilities are unlimited, it seems slightly presumptuous to conclude that because one plan worked out well it was the best.

How do Frankl's concepts apply to my own vocational experience? A certain amount of silence, solitude and simplicity seem to be values that have a degree of universality. Everyone needs some of them in his life, but not everyone needs the same amount. The amount I need is related to the perspective through which I see the world. Perhaps it would be better to say that various meanings in particular proportions correspond favorably to my particular needs. At any rate, it is a whole situation which confronts me. Not just an individual isolated value or meaning. The same situation confronting another person might be experienced by him as quite repugnant. This does not necessarily imply any value blindness on the part of either of us. What I see as value-for-me must not be pursued at the expense of some higher value such as truth, honesty or courage – the level of values of which von Hildebrand seems to be speaking.

Perhaps von Hildebrand's and Frankl's thoughts can best be integrated as follows: von Hildebrand's "authentic values" are fundamental norms which call out to all men for recognition and respect in all situations. They appeal to his ethical or moral conscience. Frankl's "meanings" are these same values embodied, or potentially embodied, in some partial and incomplete way in daily life situations.

They appeal to what might be called man's practical conscience; his intuition of what is the best thing for <u>him</u> to do in <u>this</u> particular situation.

My experience was seen (and felt) to have a long-term meaning in some vague way at first. I was attracted by this meaningfulness without understanding the attraction. I explicated it for myself in terms of the values involved. The values are generally recognized as such by thinkers of all times. To say "yes" to these values as attractions, does not mean to deny the value of the other things which must be fore gone. It means, rather, that as seen through my particular perspective, certain values – or a pattern of values in some particular proportion and relation to one another – appear as more important. My "perspective" includes my past, my present condition and the situation around me, my plans for the future and, of course, my self-concept. I thought of myself as a generous person rather than a greedy or self-centered one. I would see the values somewhat as von Hildebrand does: good things to which good people respond. I would be less aware of the other benefits that would come to me at the same time – security, freedom from guilt or from responsibility. At the time it appeared to be the <u>one true</u> meaning of the situation. It still appears to have been the one right meaning <u>for me</u> even though I now recognize that I misinterpreted many of my own motives.

As the constituents of the vocational attraction become more and more specifically human the analogy of magnetic attraction becomes weaker and weaker. It may be true that the magnet has a "meaning" for iron that it doesn't have for wood or aluminum. But the iron cannot change its sensitivity to magnetism.

Perhaps the best we can do with the analogy is to tamper with the circumstances by placing both the magnet and the piece of iron on a large iron plate which will affect the magnetic field. Another possibility would be to heat the piece of iron so the magnetic domains and 'atomic' magnets would be agitated and not line up according to the influence of the field.

We have seen some of the elements that go into the constitution of a vocational attraction. The subject of the experience brings his own personality, background and needs to the experience. The world in which he lives presents him with elements that manifest a value to him and seem to deserve response. One of the ways in which these two sets of elements interact is by bringing new meanings into the life of the individual. [27]

Differentiating the elements in vocation is useful but can become mechanical and unreal. Therefore, we will now look at a comprehensive theory, which includes the subject-pole, object-pole and interactions, but describes vocational attraction in more holistic terms.

---

[27] For a literary example of a person finding meaning in her life see Chaim Potok, <u>My Name is Asher Lev</u> (Greenwich, Conn., 1972), pp. 18-26, 47-51, 151-155. Asher Lev's mother falls into a deep depression when her brother is accidentally killed. She puts much of the blame for his death on the local Rabbi under whose direction he had been working to relieve the plight of persecuted Jews. Eventually she sees the possibility of devoting her life to carrying on her deceased brother's work.

Emmanuel Mounier [28]
A Personalist Framework

Personalism, according to Mounier, the late French existentialist thinker, is a philosophy but not a system. Systematization is excluded from his thinking since the centering of his thought on the existence of free, creative persons introduces a principle of uncertainty that is fundamental. This is not just a concession to individual differences but a taking account of creativity and personal responsibility. The person cannot be known from outside but is "the reality that we know, and that we are at the same time fashioning, from within." [p. xvii] He is not an object that can be isolated and examined but a center of re-orientation of the universe. His activity, if it is to be truly <u>human</u> activity, is not just adaptation to the world around him. Adaptation is, indeed, a first step. But at a certain point man must "deny nature as it is given affirming it as a task – a task which is both personal and the condition of all personality." [p. 12] Man's task is not to reign tyrannically over nature nor become a slave to his own technical progress; it is "to open up, before the creative liberty of an ever increasing number of men, the highest possibilities of human being." [p. 12]

The fundamental nature of the person in terms of experience is not "originality or self-knowledge nor individual affirmation. It lies not in separation but in communication." [p. 17]

---

[28] The material in the section is taken from Emmanuel Mounier, <u>Personalism</u> (Notre Dame, Ind.: University of Notre Dame Press, 1952). All references to the work will be followed by the appropriate page numbers in brackets.

Others do not limit the person, they enable him to be and to grow. [p. 20] Social relations do not tend toward a mutual fusion but towards a love which "is creative of distinction; it is a gratitude and a will towards another because he is other than oneself." [p. 23]

In this context a person is constantly faced with innumerable surprises rising out of his unconscious, his own creativity and spontaneity and that of others. Each of these renews the question of his identity which is neither self-evident nor given all at once:

> One has to search oneself to find, amongst the litter of distracting motives, so much as a desire to seek this living unity, then to listen patiently for what it may whisper to one, to test it in struggle and obscurity, and even then one can never be sure that one grasps its meaning. It resembles, more than anything, a secret voice, calling to us in a language that we would have to spend our lives learning; which is why the word 'vocation' describes it better than any other. [p. 41]

Personal life and growth consists in "concentrating in order to find oneself; then going forth to enrich and to find oneself again; concentrating oneself anew through dispossession;..." [p. 41] This continual reinterpretation of identity and vocation disrupts all short-term goals and objectives and allows no opportunity for the person to become embedded in any particular external form. There will always be an element of unpredictability "even though his every action be one of commitment or devotion." [p. 42]

Man can never be inventoried; he is always the need and desire for more, the constant tendency to transcend what he already is. "A reality that transcends another is not one that is separated from and floating above it, but a reality that is superior in the quality of its being." [p. 65] The values which the personalist seeks to realize are not usually seen as existing apart from man and in some way "above"

42

him. They are personalized values whose value cannot be proved but "verification is manifested in the fullness of the personal life." [p. 68] Some examples would be happiness, knowledge, science, moral values and artistic values.

Reflection

With Super and von Hildebrand we look at some of the elements in man and in his world that may act as influences, if not determinants, in the vocational attraction. Frankl offered a framework in which to understand how the various elements fit together to make a whole. The implication has been that if all the elements involved were studied thoroughly, the whole matter of why I am attracted to some particular way of life might be understood – with, perhaps, a small margin of error to allow for limited human freedom.

Mounier begins with a different emphasis. Man is free and creative. His freedom is not just something that is "left over" after all the determinants have been taken into account. It is at the heart of man's subjectivity. His personal characteristics and temperament, if they are seen as limitations, are limitations to be faced, challenged and transcended. The same is true of the world he lives in. Man must approach life with an energetic, almost aggressive attitude, determined to open up the maximum possibilities for personal development. His task is to personalize the universe, not merely to adapt himself to it or find a meaningful life within its limitations. Such limited ambitions may represent his first attempts; they may be the way he understands his vocational attraction. But while his self -concept and his recognized values may be put forward as the reasons for his attraction, there is also the deeper, fundamental need for more life, deeper life, fuller life at work. This need will never settle for adaptation but will immediately say "Ah, I have grown...but now I must grow some more."

The continual reinterpretation of my vocation involves an ever changing perspective as new depths of my creativity are liberated. I cannot predict, or place clear <u>a priori</u> limits on the direction in which my vocation may develop. In the description I gave of my experience, it sounded as if much of the motivation was in the direction of adaptation. Perhaps that was true, but that does not prove (or even indicate) that there were not other elements involved that escaped my consciousness. Unconscious motivation is not always unauthentic and sinister. If adaptation and immersion in a comfortable way of life had been the totality of my motivation and I would have long since died of boredom or, more probably, fled the monastery for a more interesting life. It seems, however, that I had creative needs that saw in monastic life the opportunity for personal expansion and development. Perhaps a certain amount of adaptation was needed for me in order to find my bearings. Maybe I needed a little security in order to find out where I was at the time. But there must also have been the implicit realization that I could transcend the temporary embeddedness, that there was "more" to monastic life than just a problem-solving state.

What does it mean to transcend something? Mounier has already pointed out that it does not mean "float above it." Etymologically, the word means to climb across or climb beyond. To do this I must maintain contact with that which I am transcending, using it as a basis for my climbing or reaching. I will be using the word in the sense of <u>growing</u> beyond, rather than moving beyond. When I grow physically I continue to be what I was before but I become more than I was. Real growth affects, and takes place in, my whole being. A swollen ankle may increase my volume slightly but it would hardly be considered growth. Nor would I have grown just by putting on platform shoes. Only by assimilating material and transforming it into the living organism that I am is real growth possible. Hunger and the attractiveness of good food may appear on the surface to be a periodic need which must be satisfied to maintain a comfortable equilibrium. But there is a growth-oriented dynamic at work beneath the surface. Eating has a short-term goal which is pretty obvious. But it has a deeper meaning which is at work as long as I am providing balanced nourishment. Growth is a slow generally imperceptible process. I can interfere with it but I cannot accelerate it. If I satisfy the daily hunger with food that offers no nourishment I will not grow. But I will not remain embedded in my present condition either. I will deteriorate and suffer the symptoms of malnutrition.

Psychological growth is similar to physical growth. A balanced "diet" of challenge and achievement, personal relationships and social contacts will allow me to develop a healthy ego. They do not <u>cause</u> the development. Neither are they merely uninvolved conditions for growth. I grow by participation in, and assimilation of, the world around me. Psychological growth is more easily disrupted than physical growth. While there can be obstacles, the digestion and assimilation of food takes place somewhat "automatically." Psychological growth can much more easily be inhibited. My attitudes may impede my participation in any number of ways. But when I overcome an inhibiting attitude I may seem to make more rapid progress and make up for lost time.

The growth of the human spirit makes a further step. It is not independent of physical and psychological growth but it goes beyond them. The human spirit is that dynamic tending of my whole being to grow beyond what it already is. It is not merely a potentiality for growth but a fundamental need to grow. Though I may concretize my goal in short-term aims, none of them can ever satisfy my need for spiritual development. The movement of the spirit is not goal oriented but growth oriented. The growth to which I have already attained does not diminish the spiritual need and allow me to "coast." Rather, it gives me a broader, stronger basis for further growth; it liberates me from some of my former limitations and opens new vistas for development. Mounier's words about the perfection of the embodied personal universe seem applicable to the perfection of the person as well; it is:

...not the perfection of an order, as it is in all the philosophic (and all the political) systems...It is the perfection of a liberty that is militant, locked in combat, subsisting indeed by the limits it overcomes. [p. 16]

What are the limits to my potential growth? Certainly, in a quantitative sense, there are limits to the number of areas to which I can dedicate my life. It is not essential that I develop all my potentialities; some may have to be sacrificed for the sake of others. But what about the degree to which I may develop – is it limited?

46

It seems that the ultimate limitation of human development would be humanity itself. As I develop I become more human, not less human. And as long as I am human I am a potentially for transcendence. I still have room and capacity for further growth. The term "human" always seems to imply a certain lowliness. We say, "He's only human" to explain a person's limitations. We also say, "He's so human," in reference to someone whom expected to be a little cold and distant because of his profession or excellence in some field. There is, somehow, the feeling that one becomes superhuman when he does great things; he is now a little too good to be called human. The popular singer John Denver expressed this when he said, "I can do anything. One of these days I'll be so complete I won't be a human. I'll be a god." [29] For a man to succeed to the extent that he is no longer human but some sort of a god is for him to fail as a man. Human transcendence does not mean rising above humanity but immersing oneself more deeply in it, accepting its limitations and realizing its potentials.

Any attraction that is to develop into a vocation must have room for this human lowliness. It cannot be just ambition or a self-centered desire for adaptation – Frankl's "homeostasis." It must have an element of responsibility about it; I am answerable in some way for the use I make of my life, for the use of the world, for my relationship to others and for my attitude towards their rights. In other words, I experience my call in the context of my whole world.

---

[29] Maureen Orth, "The Sunshine Boy" Newsweek (December 20, 1976), p. 68.

It may often happen that my attraction proves problematic in some way. I may feel an attraction on one level and repulsion on another. Or I may feel attracted to a life that does not seem to correspond to my abilities at all. Or, perhaps, there is no realistic expression of my attraction possible in the world in which I live. Some possible explanations of these phenomena are offered by the findings of modern psychiatry.

IV: PROBLEMATIC ATTRACTIONS

Karen Horney [30]
Inner Conflicts and the Idealized Image

Karen Horney, as a psychiatrist, is naturally concerned mainly with neurotics - by which she means "a person to the extent that he is neurotic." [p. 27] She begins her book, however, by pointing out that "it is not neurotic to have conflicts." [p. 25] Conflicts are common and normal in the life of the healthy person. Often our conflicts are not with others or with the environment but within ourselves - conflicts between desires, values or principles.

While such inner conflicts are to be expected, there is the possibility that the person concerned may not be aware of them. In that case he will not be able to resolve them consciously by a clear and intelligent decision. He may subsist in a state of indecision without knowing what is wrong.

---

[30] The material in this section is taken from Karen Horney, Our Inner Conflicts (New York: W.W. Norton, 1945). All references to the work will be followed by the appropriate page numbers in brackets.

He may procrastinate until circumstances force one choice or the other upon him. This will not really solve the problem since the desire that has not been fulfilled has never really been given up or renounced.

In order to be able to recognize the elements of an inner conflict and decide between (or among) them four things are necessary. We must be aware of what our wishes and feelings are and we must have developed our own set of values. Further, we must be willing and able to give up one of the contradictory desires and, finally, be willing and able to take the responsibility for the decision. [pp. 25-26]

Horney seeks to trace all inner conflicts back to a basic conflict. She finds the source and underlying pattern of all conflicts in the way the child tries to cope with his "basic anxiety," his feeling of being "isolated and helpless in a potentially hostile world." [p. 41]

There are three main ways in which the child may respond to his anxiety. He may, in Horney's words, "move toward people" [p. 42] in an attitude of dependence seeking to find security in their love and approval. Or he may "move against people" [p. 42], taking their hostility for granted and opting implicitly to rebel and fight to protect and avenge himself. Finally, he may find neither of these strategies satisfactory and simply "move away from people" [p.42] by dissociating himself from them and seeking to build up his own little world independently of them.

Whichever of these movements the child employs, if it proves successful, may become his predominant attitude toward others. It represents the behavior with which he feels most comfortable. The other two tendencies do not disappear when one is emphasized. They are seen to represent unsatisfactory modes of behavior and are repressed but still find indirect expression. This basic conflict among incompatible attitudes is seen by Horney to be the core of neurosis. Beginning with our relationships with persons, it gradually spreads to permeate our attitudes towards ourselves and the world.

To the normal person the three movements may be quite compatible depending on circumstances. "One should be capable of giving in to others, or fighting, and keeping to oneself. The three can compliment each other and make for a harmonious whole." [pp. 45-46] One who feels they are incompatible may experience a certain feeling of unity by overemphasizing a particular movement and repressing the others but he diminishes his potential in the process.

A further attempt at disposing of the conflicts within consists of the creation of what Horney calls an "idealized image." The image is always flattering and unreal though it exerts considerable influence on one's life. The person may be convinced that he actually is what he imagines himself to be. Or he may be self-critical at his inability to ever live up to this ideal. A third possibility is that he will drive himself mercilessly to live up to his image. "In contrast to authentic ideals, the idealized image has a static quality. It is not a goal toward whose attainment he strives but a fixed idea which he worships." [p. 98]

Besides substituting for the realistic pride and self-confidence that has never been allowed to develop, the idealized image provides a sense of superiority over others. It acts as a substitute for genuine ideals and covers up most blatant faults and shortcomings or even converts them into virtues. Finally, it brings conflicting movements into apparent harmony providing a sense of unity.

However unreal the idealized image may seem to be, it still usually contains elements of the person's real ideals and potentialities and gives an indication of what his real needs are.

Among the disadvantages of the idealized image is the fact that it makes the person highly vulnerable and dependent on affirmation from others. It alienates him from himself and involves him in a life of endless pretense and rationalization and intensifies his disgust with his true self.

Reflection

Seldom is anything as simple as it looks. Vocational experiences are usually described many years after they have occurred. References to the anguish and confusion that was felt at the time lose some of their impact over the years. Many of the little problems that have been worked through are forgotten – perhaps they were hardly even noticed at the time – and the picture appears to be one of continual growth. Perhaps it is a process of continual growth, but growth in Mounier's sense of continually confronting and transcending obstacles and challenges.

When the obstacles are internal they are more difficult to explicate clearly. Added to this is the difficulty that one is not a good judge in his own case and the fact that some material may be repressed and not available to recall. Thus, when I try to apply Horney's theories to my own case I may come up with some pretty unreliable results and her theories themselves show why. My conflicts or my image keep me from seeing some important things about myself.

If this is true when I am reflecting on my vocation it must be even more true when I am trying to discern it in the first place. If I am the type who tends to move "away from" people, life in a monastery may appear very appealing. It may fit my image of myself as one who is independent of the trivialities of life and somehow "above" the type of life that most people live. Again, I may be strongly inclined to move "toward" people in excessive dependence and think of myself as a most co-operative member of society. In a monastery I can be freed from the oppressive burden of personal responsibility.

If it is not particularly abnormal to have conflicts, we may reasonably suppose that they are present and operative when I make my vocational choice. What if I am attracted to a state or course of action that appeals to me primarily as an escape from conflicts or an expression of an unrealistic idealized image? Can such an attraction possibly develop into a vocation in which I can grow and find personal fulfillment? Is it not doomed to failure from the start?

If such undertakings usually fail it does not necessarily mean they are doomed from the start. Perhaps in following up on such an attraction I may find a little respite from my conflicts and be able to grow to the point where I can confront them as challenges. Even if the attraction does not develop into a long-term vocation I have made some progress and the venture seems to have been worthwhile. It has not been a failure – perhaps just a fortunate mistake.

In following a particular way of life I must always give up some other possibilities. In responding to a false attraction I may realize for the first time that I am running away from some things that I really need, some things that are important for my personal development. Again, an educational mistake.

If worst comes to worst (as it occasionally does) and I stubbornly insist on following the attraction which is based on illusions about myself I may at least come to face, however reluctantly, my limitations. I may learn some new modes of behavior in the process and get some good advice that will prove helpful later. In all these cases it seems better to have taken the attraction seriously and tried to follow it.

There is another question that must be raised and left unanswered. How do we know that such false attractions do not really grow out of a genuine attraction? All too often we speak as if the true vocation is what will be left after the dross is purged away. Is it not possible that the true vocational attraction was there first? Maybe my first attraction arises out of deep intuitive grasp of my potentialities, values and needs. I may hardly recognize this movement and the picture it presents may seem like a dream world. It has no power to move me to action. Yet its influence remains as something of a dim beacon in my inner mind lighting up a possible path for the future. When various conflicts, problems and needs appear to me, this path is always there as a potential way to go. If it proves to be a possible solution to enough difficulties and the possible source of enough satisfaction, the desire to follow it will grow stronger. From this point of view, the genuine aspect of the attraction would provide the illumination and the false motives would provide the gradually increasing urgency that finally moves me to act. They would carry me along for a while as I grew in self-knowledge and in my real appreciation of the genuine values involved. Gradually I would see that this motive was selfish, that one was an obstacle to realizing some values, the other motive made life difficult for those around me. They would decrease in intensity and the genuine element in the attraction would have room to grow.

This seems a more positive and constructive way to explain the presence of selfish or unrealistic motives in a vocational attraction. The fact that it is more positive and constructive does not, of course, mean it is true. Nor does it mean that the attraction cannot be undermined by selfish motives or lack of self-knowledge.

At any rate, the attraction is only the first element in a vocation. It gains strength when I give my assent to it and becomes more concrete when I express it in my outward behavior. The last two elements, assent and expression, remain to be considered.

CHAPTER II

I FREELY ASSENT TO THE ATTRACTION

However strong the attraction I may feel, I am still free to accept, resist or refuse it. Ordinarily the first stirrings of an attraction are not enough to elicit a commitment of my whole life. At first I may only entertain the possibility of responding positively. Even this can be an implicit assent which allows the attraction room for growth. Eventually it will require a conscious, wholehearted and habitual acceptance if a true vocation is to develop.

The dynamics, implications and difficulties of responding to the attraction by taking a stance toward it and making an effective decision form the subject matter in this chapter.

There are a number of responses that are open to me when I experience a vocational attraction. I may sit back and picture myself living the life to which I am attracted. I may wish, rather than will, to live that life. I do this by finding satisfaction in forming detailed mental images of how well I would carry out my duties. But at the same time I may really do nothing effective about embodying in my life the values I claim to esteem.

Another possibility is that I will feel the attraction but simply dismiss it as something that I could never do – "It's just simply beyond me so why bother thinking about something that I could never do anyway?" At the opposite pole from the will-less attitude, I may give my assent in an overbearing way and approach the new life as if all depend on my iron will. All opposition, whether from other people, circumstances, even from my own feelings and limitations, must be "bulldozed" out of the way. This willful approach is as much a distortion of true willing as is the will-less attitude. [31]

Finally there is the possibility of authentic willing which takes into consideration the rights of others, the demands of the situation and my own potentialities and limitations. It is this type of willing that leads to wholehearted commitment which is the proper response to a vocational attraction. These various possibilities will be treated in the order in which they were presented above.

Silvano Arieti [32]
Wishing

"The individual says to himself, 'I want to do this,' and he does it." [p.31] Thus Arieti begins his treatment of the relation between wishing and willing. He proceeds to point out that the simplicity of this expression is deceptive due to the many complex mechanisms involved in human action. Though these mechanisms are not fully understood, we at least know that any mature willing presupposes some kind of thinking and choosing.

---

[31] The terms "willful" and "will-less" are taken from Adrian van Kaam, <u>Religion and Personality</u> (Garden City, N.Y.: Image Books, 1964), pp. 112-122.

[32] The material in this section is taken from Silvano Arieti, <u>The Will to be Human</u> (New York: Quadrangle Books, 1972). All references to this work will be followed by the appropriate page numbers in brackets.

Animals are bound to the patterns of their instinctual behavior but man has an immense number of possibilities open to him at any particular moment. Why is it that, in spite of his intelligence and freedom, man often errs, makes choices that turn out to be bad for him?

Arieti gives several reasons for human error. The first is that we don't always know all the facts of the case. Even so, we usually have enough information available for our purposes. A second cause for error might be a mistake in logical judgment. Again, my judgment may be determined by fear of other people. Fear is a more important cause of error than a lack of information or poor judgment.

Another important reason for error is that "in choosing, man follows not his best judgment, but his wish." [p. 33, italics in the original] This can happen in two ways: through weakness or through deception. I may rightly judge one action to be in my best interests but be unable or unwilling to overcome my wish for something else that is incompatible with it. Or my wish for something may be so strong that it deceives me. I have become the victim of "what in psychoanalysis is called unconscious motivation." [p. 33, italics in the original]

The wish is distinct from, though often confused with, appetite, need, tendency, instinct, urge and will. The wish is a mental representation rather than a biologically based instinct, appetite or urge. It is not a choice or decision nor does it require any effort or attempt to obtain that which is wished for. In Arieti's words it is "a mental representation of something that, once attained, would give pleasure, which means that the representation has a significance and motivation inherent in it." [p. 36, italics in the original] Wishing is a specifically human phenomenon since animals cannot form images for themselves.

57

Wishing is a very important source of motivation, its power resting in the meanings given to the mental representations. Only in very exceptional cases is man driven to act by appetite without the meditation of wishing and willing. Of course, my wish may be based on an appetite; I may wish to satisfy my hunger or thirst. But I may also wish to abstain from eating when hungry. Human action presupposes willing and willing presupposes wishing.

Not every wish is followed by an act of will. There may be a conflict among wishes. Wishes do not merely exist side by side but strive for expression in action. The existence of two mutually exclusive wishes may, until resolved in some way, increase tension and anxiety. However, it is important to remember that "conflicts may also stimulate the emergence of new benefits, new points of view, unexpected syntheses, and unforeseen possibilities of choice." [p. 39]

Many wishes may, for one reason or another, have been repressed. Though the person is unaware of these wishes, they still may exert a strong influence in his life. They do not determine his behavior but they do influence him. They may enhance or interfere with his conscious wishes.

According to Arieti, then, all willing presupposes wishing of some sort, but not all wishing results in willing.

Reflection

Arieti's concept of wishing places it in a little better light than that in which we usually think of it. We usually think of it as an occupation to engage in when

58

what we desire cannot be attained by our own will or action: "I wish it weren't so hot" or "I wish I could graduate without writing this thesis." We do not usually think of it as a first stage of willing. However, that is Arieti's use of the term so we shall stick with it. His use seems to be the accepted one among psychologists. [33]

The element of wishing was fairly evident in my vocational experience. When I first experienced the attraction to monastic life I engaged in what Arieti has termed "wishing", producing a mental representation of myself living as a monk. This was far short of a decision to become one but was a prerequisite for any such decision according to Arieti. Dwelling on the attraction kept it alive, made it a little more real to me even if my idea of monastic life was not altogether accurate. It was only one of several wishes that were active at this time, some of which must have been in conflict with it.

My wishing I could be a monk or wishing I were one was, perhaps, the most positive and appropriate attitude I could be expected to show at the time. At that stage of the attraction it was a favorable response. A decision at the time, even a publishing of my feelings, might have been too much for the attraction to support.

---

[33] Rollo May in <u>Love and Will</u> (New York: Dell Publishing Co., 1974) speaks of wishing in similar terms; "Wish is the imaginative playing with the possibility of some act or state occurring." [p. 215] Later he distinguishes it from willing by pointing out that wishing is like "a mere hankering, as though will stirred in its sleep, but did not get beyond the dreaming of action." The latter statement is a quotation from John Macquarrie, "Will and Existence," <u>The Concept of Willing</u>, ed. James N. Lapsley (New York: Abingdon Press, 1976), p. 76. May seems to emphasize the emotional content of the wish more than does Arieti.

Like cake in the oven, the attraction has to have enough time. If cake is removed too soon on the grounds that it looks good or because I'm so hungry I cannot wait another minute, it will collapse. It wasn't "done." Likewise if I try to outrun my vocational attraction, to make a "mature" decision regarding an attraction that is not yet mature – and is not yet supposed to be mature – I may be building on a weak foundation. I may be making a premature decision that will prevent further growth.

On the other hand, when it is time for a decision one must be made. I cannot continue wishing forever. If cake is left in the oven too long it will become dry and hard. If the attraction doesn't get a fitting response what will happen? Will it lose its life and vitality and just fade away? Perhaps. But Arieti suggests another possibility. He mentions that a wish that remains over a long period of time may become a need. He does not explain this. One explanation might be that in the mixture of motives involved in the attraction some motives are more permanent, others less so. Perhaps the warmth, the energy and the generosity cannot be sustained as long without some ratification and expression. After a certain point they may look elsewhere for an outlet. But the need to implement my self-concept, to find a secure situation and the myriad other self-centered motives remain and may take control of the attraction. Then when I finally follow the attraction it is not for the sake of the values involved or for the good I can do; it is to fulfill a personal need. Like the over done cake, the attraction had become hard and dry, lacking the lightness, springiness and flavor it should have.

There is, then, a time when it is too early to make a decision and carry it out. The decision can also be delayed too long. [34] But when I give my assent to the attraction in an explicit way I may also allow distortions to enter into my attitude. Two such possible distortions and the characteristics of true willing will now be considered.

Adrian van Kaam [35]
Willfulness, Will-lessness, Existential Willing

Adrian van Kaam speaks of willfulness as one distortion of true willing. It comes to the fore in a man when "He separates his will, as it were, from the other elements of his personality," [R&P, p. 112] expecting everything in himself to be subservient to the dictates of his will. He ignores the power of his past life, his habits, his feelings and emotions. They will simply have to bow to his will. Any feelings that go contrary to his designs must be repressed. When he finds that he can succeed – or, at least, obtain results – by this method he will use it on the situations and persons around him.

---

[34] A similar polarity has been pointed out in relation to marriage. It is often said that the engagement period should be at least six months but not ordinarily more than two years. Apparently it is felt that it takes at least six months for the decision to establish itself and mature. But if it hasn't matured in two years time there is something wrong.

[35] The material in this section is taken from two books by Adrian van Kaam: Religion and Personality (Garden City, N.Y.: Image Books, 1968) and In Search of Spiritual Identity (Denville, N.J.: Dimension Books, 1975). All references to the two books will be followed by the appropriate page numbers in brackets. The books will be referred to as R&P and ISSI respectively.

This cuts off his own inner spontaneity and warmth and isolates him from the reality of others and from his situation. He develops a stereotyped approach to life and reacts automatically and blindly to situations rather than meeting them with an original response. [R&P, p. 118]

At the opposite extreme from the willful person is the one whom van Kaam describes as "will-less." This is the person who feels he has no power to determine the course of his life but is at the mercy of public opinion, circumstances or his own impulses. While the willful person tries to run the world by his will power alone, the will-less person lets himself be run by whatever forces happen to be working on him at the time. He, too, reacts to the situation. He does not distance himself from it or consider the various meanings it might have. [R&P, p. 122] This may allow him to feel free of the experience of personal responsibility, anxiety and guilt. But is also prevents the possibility of his making a true response. He cannot create from his own inner resources a behavior that is effective in this unique situation.

These two distortions of willing are contrasted with what van Kaam calls "existential will" or authentic will. It implies an openness to all the messages of reality. Authentic willing takes plans and previous commitments into consideration. It also considers feelings, moods, habits from the past, interests and abilities. Further, it makes provision for the world around the one who is willing. It is an openness to all reality with all my faculties.

When I am open I am receptive with my whole being, not only with my logical mind but also with my intuition, not only with my eyes and ears but also with my emotional sensitivity, not only with my imagination but also with my memory, for my past experiences enlightens me concerning the situation of the moment. [R&P, p. 128]

In the light of all the aspects of experience, the person gradually comes to a decision. He does not manipulate or repress any of the elements but allows each of them to exert its influence, to "have its say." Not all of them will be followed of course. Some will be left unfulfilled.

Once the decision has been reached it is put into effect. In the execution of a decision there may be indications that it was not really as wholehearted an act as it may have appeared. Van Kaam points out three such indications. The first is that the person practically never has any concrete theoretical or practical ideas about the things he claims to do willingly. Secondly, he may find it impossible to overcome the natural small resistance to getting started with his project or, finally, some nearly insurmountable resistance may appear when he is faced with carrying out his decision. [R&P, pp. 131-132]

These difficulties should not be attacked with will power as if they were enemies. They should be listened to respectfully as possible indications that some deep element was overlooked in the decision.

Many other obstacles and difficulties may arise that must be met and worked with in some practical way. True willing includes making plans and carrying them out amid difficulties. This aspect of willing van Kaam calls variously ego-willing, executive willing or managing willing. [ISSI, p. 187]

He distinguishes it from what he calls primary, transcendent willing or receptive volition. He illustrates receptive volition with the example of one who wishes to write a poem. He can go to a quiet place, free himself from distractions and dwell on the theme he wishes to express. Later he may type up the poem making a few changes. But the inspiration is not something he "does." It is something to which he can only be open and receptive. If he tries to will it into existence he will only interfere with it. He must receive it as a gift. [ISSI, p. 188]

Both these aspects of willing are needed for smooth human functioning. The tendency today is to over emphasize the managing aspect and ignore the need for receptivity. [ISSI, p. 187]

Reflection

It is somewhat tempting to think of willfulness as simply an exaggerated emphasis on the managing will and seeing this as a reasonable explanation of why one might try to follow an attraction before it has matured. On the other hand will-lessness might appear to be receptive volition carried to extremes with the possible effect of delaying the response to a vocational attraction.

This seems to me to be a neat, but over-simplified, understanding. The human being isn't that compartmentalized. If I pick up a heavy suitcase with my right hand my whole body has to accommodate the change. I lean to the left and extend my left arm to the side a little to keep my balance. My breathing rate increases to provide more oxygen and I take quicker, shorter steps. My whole body cooperates in the act. My members work together with one another taking the load and the terrain into consideration. If I have a blister on my foot I may feel the pain but go on anyway, favoring the other foot a little to keep the discomfort to a minimum. Suddenly I may feel that something is drastically wrong. I should not carry this load any further. I need to stop and rest. Why? I feel no particular pain but I know deep in my bones that something is wrong, fundamentally and seriously wrong. I may heed this warning or I may tell myself it is really nothing, and continue with my load. The result of the latter decision could be serious or even fatal.

I have decided to carry the load and to continue in spite of the discomfort of the blister. These decisions represent acts of the managing will. If I go in spite of the more serious warning from my heart or blood pressure I may be acting out of willfulness – "I'm okay, nothing's going to happen to me!" But it may also have aspects of will-lessness about it – "I offered to carry his suitcase; what will they think of me if I have to put it down and rest?" It might be said that my body is reacting against what I willed. This view takes will as the conscious decision, intention and effort.

A less compartmentalized but more satisfying view is implied by van Kaam when he speaks of exploring "what I really will in the depths of my existence." [R&P, p. 132] My will permeates my whole being. It is acting through my body, my emotions, my needs, my potentialities and my limitations. It is not – or should not be – a free-for-all in which the majority of tendencies get their way. Nor is it a free-for-all which can only be given order by my conscious decisions. My deepest will is a fairly well-ordered whole, a preconscious movement of my whole being. My conscious understanding of it may be quite inadequate or even inaccurate due to repressions, denials and false ideas about myself. But within the context of the limitations that my education and experiences have imposed on it, my will works as

65

a unit for the good of the whole. The plans and projects I come up with were being thrashed out within me long before I was aware of them. Everything was being put together and fitted into place. Several tries may be needed before a possible plan gets my conscious attention. Then I may catch only part of it. I may distort it somewhat to fit my conscious needs and desires. I may exaggerate some elements and overlook others. What I decide upon is <u>my understanding</u> of what my deepest will is.

This understanding is tentative and provisional. To try to defend it against all challenges from within or without will lead to willfulness. I must remain open and receptive to further information about the full meaning of my decision. In the case of an attraction to a way of life, I may well spend a lifetime learning all that was involved. There are also many new things becoming involved all the time since circumstances are constantly changing and I am constantly changing also. Functional decisions and willing are necessary but they must be nourished from my own depths and must be in dialogue with the external situation. Each new development of the attraction calls for a receptiveness that will allow the new experience to permeate my being so that it may influence future practical decisions.

Richard J. Westley [36]
The Will to Promise

In the overall development of a vocation the movement assent can be seen to pass through the three general stages of wishing, willing and commitment or promise. The assent to each aspect of the attraction seems to pass through these same stages on a smaller scale. It seems that in a healthy vocational development this cycle should continue indefinitely as new explications of my original attraction are revealed to me.

Having considered the implications of wishing and willing, it remains to say something about commitment and promise.

Richard J. Westley distinguishes promises and commitments from contracts. He defines a promise as "A unilateral and gratuitous verbal pledge of my person to another." [37] [p. 10] A contract is a mutual agreement in which each party expects something in return from the other. A promise is a free, unconditional gift. But this does not mean that it does not hope for some results.

---

[36] The material in this section is taken from Richard J. Westlye, "The Will to Promise", Humanitas VIII (February, 1972), pp. 9-20. References to this work will be followed by the appropriate page numbers in brackets. The same issue of Humanitas contains several other articles on commitment.

[37] While Westley defines promise in terms of interpersonal relations there is nothing in his findings that does not apply to committing oneself to a particular state or course of action.

A promise is always a response to the promising prospects which a man sees in his world and the people he lives with. He commits his person in the joyful hope of bringing to actuality the promise which he foresees as possible in his life. [p. 12]

The problem arises when the promising prospect that he has foreseen fails, for one reason or another, to come about. What then is to be done? Westley rejects the two extreme views that promises must always be unconditionally kept or that they are dehumanizing in the first place and should not even be made. These solutions try to circumvent the basic ambiguity that lies at the heart of man's being. [p. 18] When "a man feels strapped by promise once the 'promise' has gone out of them" [p. 11] it is understandable that he may feel tempted to give up his commitment. Some do give up but others remain faithful.

Those who aspire to fidelity, even after the original promise they sought goes out of the situation, remain faithful because their fidelity actualizes another kind of promise. They remain hopeful because they see some new promise in their fidelity, even after all other kinds of promise have vanished from it. [p.20]

They do not remain faithful to a dead cause out of a sense of obligation. Their fidelity itself has created new promise.

Ultimately, fidelity remains theoretically possible only for those more hopeful men who continue to see in fidelity a genuinely human response to life's promise. They are those among us who truly have the will to promise. [p. 20]

Reflection

For the sake of my reflections I would like to abbreviate Westley's definition of promise. I will be using the term to mean a unilateral and gratuitous pledge of myself. It need not be verbal nor need it be made to another person.

There is, as Westley points out, a fundamental ambiguity at the core of man's existence. I plan for the future but my plans may fail. I provide for the future but circumstances and needs change. So much of life is unsure, uncertain, unpredictable. Life, happiness, security are such fragile things. There is a strong tendency to "play it safe." Why risk the little I've got? If we get involved in theoretical discussions of the pros and cons of commitment [38] it is only to justify what we <u>want</u> to do prior to any theories as Westley points out [p. 19] Those who want to commit their lives do so because of the promise that life holds out to them. Their faith is, perhaps, not totally invested in the particular promise (attraction) that first appeals to them, but in life itself and the possibilities it offers for development of the human. This does not mean that I commit my life just in order to get something out of it. There are, as I have already pointed out, usually some less worthy motives mixed in with the best of intentions. There may be promise of some gratification on the biological level. There may also be a promise of satisfaction on the psychological level. Life may readily fail me on these levels. The level on which it will not fail me – though I may fail it – is the specifically human level. On this level

---

[38] Westley notes that an uncommitted life is an impossibility. "Camus' <u>Stranger</u> was religiously committed to his lack of commitment. Even Sartrean man is whole-heartedly committed to his own freedom." [p. 18, footnote 14] Charles A. Kiesler in "An Experimental Approach to Commitment" in the same issue <u>Humanitas</u>, pp. 79-96 points out that everyone is committed to <u>some</u> form of behavior. It is a question of just what one is committed to and the degree of commitment. He also refers to the dangers of commitment: polarization, narrowing of outlook, mistrust and lack of communication.

I experience not gratification or satisfaction but joy. [39] Unlike the two other levels on which fulfillment is found by receiving or taking into myself something which I needed, I experience joy by going out of myself. I rejoice in something else. Etymologically, the word joy is related to the Greek word "gauros" meaning proud. When I rejoice in something I am proud of it. More clearly this is the case when I rejoice in another person. The source of my happiness is entirely invested in the other, or so it seems. I am proud of the other because of his genuine goodness and not because of any advantage I gain from him.

However promising the goodness of the other person may appear, it too can fail me. What if he should fall from his present attitudes? What if he dies? Am I not then deprived of the joy that he had "promised?" So it would seem.

There is, however, another way of considering the question. When the other dies something in me dies with him. But something else lives on: the capacity for love that has grown in me as a result of the relationship. It was not purely and simply the other person who was the source of my joy, but my loving him, my being

[39] The use of the terms gratification, satisfaction and joy refer to fulfillment on the biological, psychological and specifically human levels respectively is based on the class lectures of Mr. Charles Maes, Institute of Man, Duquesne University, Spring Semester, 1977.

proud of him, my going out of myself to and for him. [40] While this particular love is no longer available to me in the same way, many others are. Loving has become a possibility for me in a new way. My friend has allowed me to open up to goodness in others. Where all the "promise" seemed tied to one person before, I am now able to see numerous other promising possibilities and to actualize the promise they hold out.

This may be all well and good when the other person dies, but what about the situation where he lets me down by falling from the attitudes or principles he first had? Should there really be a difference? I doubt it. If I only wanted the satisfaction (as distinct from joy) of being supported in some way by someone with certain attitudes and principles my disappointment may be complete. I never went beyond these surface qualities and when they evaporate so does all the promise that the other held out to me. If I did manage to go beyond them the other's change will be a source of grief to me; perhaps it will mean the end of the mutuality of the relationship, but its fruits may remain and grow. In either case there was, behind the promise of support, the promise of a loving relationship, which would free me from my dependence on surface qualities and make many other loving relationships possible for me. It is a matter of hoping beyond my shattered hopes, of having

---

[40] This is not to say that my love for the other is a greater value than the person himself. But it is only in and through my loving him that his true value is revealed to me. It is not just "him" and it is not just "my love for him" that is the source of this particular and unique experience of joy.

faith in life and in myself to believe that there are deeper meanings than I am able to see at the present and that I am capable of realizing some of those meanings in my life if I am willing to be patient, open and receptive in the midst of disappointment. [41]

What has been said of personal relationships is true also of a vocational attraction. My original attraction may be deeply influenced by a search for gratification or satisfaction. If I can see no further than these desires I will probably be in for a painful awakening. There is nothing wrong with gratification or satisfaction but they are not reliable in the long run. They come and go. Beyond them, however, are more human possibilities whether I see them or not. I can only see them if I am hopeful that life and my own human nature have more to offer. I hope for the more but I must also settle for the "good enough" or the "best I can do" for the present moment. I can only see a few steps ahead in life. Maybe I have no real light to go by except gratification and satisfaction. Perhaps the best thing I can do is give them a respectful hearing, trusting that they are only the surface aspects of some all-embracing good that is appealing to my deepest will for a response. When I have discovered, after a few such experiments, that such deeper meanings do exist I will be more ready to make promises, to commit myself, to make a unilateral and gratuitous pledge of myself and to see in fidelity a genuinely human response to the promises life holds out.

---

[41] Literature abounds in examples of promising friendships that collapse in bitter disappointment. One such is the description of the relationship between Hyperion and Alananda in Friedrich Holderlin, <u>Hyperion</u> (New York: Frederick Ungar Publishing Co., 1965) pp. 37-50.

My assent to the attraction passes through the cycle of wishing, willing and promising or commitment many times in the course of vocational development. But each time, the decision must be tested in the real world. Committing myself is not just a noble interior act of the will. It should be an act of the whole person. The best intentions may prove unrealistic either because I have not sufficient resources to carry them out or because there is no practical way that they can be expressed in the world in which I live.

CHAPTER III

I EXPRESS MY ASSENT

TO THE ATTRACTION

Man's existence is an embodied existence. His body and its relationship to the world and to others must always be taken into account. When I speak of vocation as the experience of being called it is always implied that one is called to something, to some state of life or course of action. The state of life to which I may be called is not just an idle status but a structure which suits me to do something. My assent to the attraction I have experienced must be expressed in my attitudes, decisions and behavior.

I have already spoken of the relationship between the ideal to which I am attracted and the expression that I give to it. [42] It may be worth repeating at this point since the matter is relevant to the material in this chapter. When I speak of expressing my attraction, I am thinking of the expression as being the primary way in which I live out my ideals, not just one of several ways. I am also thinking of

---

[42] See pages 14-15.

the situation in which the particular expression is chosen <u>primarily</u> in order to live out these ideals. It is also to be understood that a vocation will involve a fairly long-term commitment. [43]

The general pattern of this chapter will be similar to that of Chapter I. The influence of the subject of the experience, his potentialities and limitations, will be considered first. Next, the object-pole of the experience, the expression, and the world in which the expression takes place will be treated. An attempt will then be made to demonstrate the dynamic relationship between the subject and object poles. Finally, some difficulties that can arise in the process of giving expression will be dealt with and the question of a "lost" vocation will be briefly studied. A short concluding note will suggest a possible holistic approach to the whole question of vocation.

I. THE SUBJECT-POLE

<u>Chaim Potok</u>
<u>The Role of Talent</u>

Among the personal characteristics that may influence the way a person expresses his assent to a vocational attraction, talent stands out as one of the most important. A person may have several talents, some of which are incorporated into his expression, some of which are sacrificed. Occasionally there appears one whose talent is so integral a part of his personality that any attempt to sacrifice it seems destined either to fail or to destroy him as the unique person he is.

---

[43] Such use of the term may rightly be understood to indicate that not everyone has a vocation. I see no reason for broadening the term to the extent where it will include everyone. Presumably one can live a normal, happy life without having clearly had this experience.

The story of the development if such an outstanding talent is told by Chaim Potok in <u>My Name is Asher Lev.</u> [44] Potok portrays Asher, the only child of strictly religious Jewish parents, as a promising artist from his earliest years. There is no indication in Asher's background of the source of the talent but he recalls drawing at the age of four. His mother gives him some encouragement but his father is unimpressed: "You have nothing better to do with your time, Asher? Your grandfather would not have liked you to waste so much time with foolishness." [p.17] His father would have him – already at the age of five – showing some interest in Talmud and the plight of so many persecuted and underprivileged Jews throughout the world. It was to this cause that his father's own life was dedicated totally and heroically.

With what appears to be merely childlike simplicity Asher draws things as they are. To his mother's embarrassment he draws her falling awkwardly in a boat and is careful to add the beads of perspiration to her face. But soon this honesty takes a sterner character. When his mother falls into a deep and prolonged depression over the death of her brother, Asher draws a picture of his father

---

[44] The material in this section is taken from Chaim Potok, <u>My Name is Asher Lev</u> (Greenwich, Conn.: Fawcett Publications, 1972). References to this work will be followed by the appropriate page numbers in brackets.

talking angrily on the phone. To his mother's question whether it was a pretty drawing he replies, "No, Mama, but it was a good drawing." [p. 32] To her admonition that he make the world pretty he responds "I don't like the world, Mama. It's not pretty. I won't draw it pretty." [p. 32] She insists that the world is only "unfinished" and he should try to finish it. This leads Asher to an emotional crisis:

> To this day, I have no idea what happened then. There was a sensation of something tearing wide apart inside of me and a steep quivering climb out of myself. I felt myself suddenly another person. I heard that other person screaming, shrieking, beating his fists against the top of the table. "I can't stand it, I can't stand it, I can't stand it," that other person kept screaming. I remember nothing after that. Sometime later, I woke in my room. [p. 33]

When faced with the prospect of moving to Austria for a time for the sake of his father's work, Asher reacts strongly. "Something inside me says I shouldn't go." [p. 108] "I don't want to lose it again, Mama." [p. 103] "But I can't leave my street." [p. 109] His first drawings were of the apartment where he lived, the furniture, the trees, the street and the people outside. He reluctantly gets his passport but the local Rabbi and his teacher decide it is better for him to stay home. Later, under parental pressure, he does go to Vienna. He is sick on the way over, sick while he is there and sick on the way home. The entire affair lasts only a month.

At one point he steals some oil paints from a friend but cannot bring himself to use them. He returns them in secret - or so he thinks. His mother later buys him some oil paints "So you shouldn't steal the again..." [p. 167]

He and his father make mutual attempts to understand one another but invariably fail. At his father's request he tries to explain some concepts of art.

I began to lose him somewhere around planar structure and by surface control it was hopeless. He listened attentively to what I was saying. But there was nothing in his intellectual or emotional equipment to which he could connect my words. He possessed no frames of reference for such concepts. [pp. 290-291]

The rabbi appoints Jacob Kahn, a non-religious Jew, to guide Asher in his artwork. Jacob tells him that he is to paint his feelings, not a story, that if he hates a classmate he is to paint his hatred or not to paint at all and that he is responsible only to himself and to the truth as he sees it. Everything is to serve his art, even the guilt he feels for the trouble he has caused his parents – "Use the guilt to make better art." [p. 209]

The rift with his father widens as Asher's pictures include nudes and scenes from Christian tradition. The last straw comes when two pictures expressing the family's anguish portrays his mother fastened to a cross in the window of their apartment house. They are highly acclaimed by the critics but shock his parents and friends.

I should have destroyed them. Who needs them? What good are they going to do the world? I had painted them; wasn't that enough? No, it wasn't enough. They had to be moved into the public arena. You communicate in a public arena; everything else is puerile and cowardly. [p. 336]

Because of the pain he is causing to those near him, the Rabbi, respecting his gift but not entirely understanding it, asks Asher to go away to Paris. There he can go to school and develop his artistic gift without angering others so much.

Asher Lev,...You have crossed a boundary. I cannot help you. I give you my blessings. [pp. 347-348]

As he leaves the Rabbi's office Asher reflects on the powers of creation and destruction that pervade his gift:

Asher Lev paints good pictures and hurts people he loves. Then be a great painter, Asher Lev; that will be the only justification for all the pain you will cause. But as a great painter I will cause pain again if I must. Then become a great painter. But I will cause pain again. Then become a still greater painter. [p. 348]

The inevitable separation from his parents takes place and they watch sadly from the window of the apartment as he sets out alone to pursue his calling.

Reflection

At first glance, it might seem more appropriate to say that Asher Lev had a "mission," not a vocation. He was "sent" into the world with a talent that needed to be expressed. He was not "drawn" or attracted from a neutral stance toward some goal but was "pushed" towards one.

There is a certain truth in this last statement. But the "push" came from within Asher; he was not sent by anyone. The Rabbi's admonition to go to Paris was not a mission but an attempt to avoid further trouble at home. His words "I cannot help you. You are alone now" [pp. 347-348] testify to that. One is much more on his own in following a vocation than in carrying out a mission. Carrying out missions might be the primary way in which one implements or expresses his vocation [45] and a vocation might grow out of a mission, but the two are different. Vocation develops from the interaction of the subject and the object to which he is attracted. In mission a third party specifies the pole.

---

[45] An example of this would be Asher Lev's father who expresses his vocation to alleviate the sufferings of the Jewish people by carrying out dangerous missions for the local Rabbi.

Neither should it be said that Asher's talent is the <u>cause</u> of his vocation. It is, rather, a significant element in the ground out of which the vocation grows. The world around him is the atmosphere in which it develops. It takes nourishment from both. Thus it is not so surprising that Asher fears that he will lose his artistic gift if he leaves his street. [p. 131] Later he leaves his street in order to preserve the gift intact.

What was the objective of Asher Lev's attraction? It was not just painting. There was never much danger that Asher would end up as a commercial artist. He was attracted by the truth that the world communicates to man in the depths of his heart. He has a reverence for his own inner emotions and feelings. They may not always be reliable as norms for behavior but they are windows opening out to the truth. They are real. [46] He does not see why others do not understand and respect them. He must defend them against the attacks of others, he must give them form, body and permanence. They are too valuable to be lost, however painful they may be. He expresses them verbally. Often he cannot put them into words and is silent as when his mother asks him how he feels when he draws. [p. 104] He tries not to offend others and often withholds a reply but never denies his feelings.

---

[46] Asher's reliance on his feelings may be partially due to the fact that he had little else in his world. There were no other children in the family and there is no indication that he had any friends his own age. Frequently his father, and later his mother, were away and he was left with only the housekeeper.

But painting is the <u>primary</u> way in which he expresses his inner response to things. And he paints <u>primarily</u> in order to express his inner feelings. Everything is sacrificed to this one end: his parent's feeling, the convenience of living at home, the approval of his own people, even his external identification with his religion. One thing alone is not sacrificed – his own integrity. He cannot be untrue about his own inner feelings nor can he lie about the rights of others by using the stolen paints. He cannot say that all good paintings have to be pretty or that the world is always pretty. When he agrees to go to Austria against his better judgment his whole being rebels. His "deepest will" is to preserve and express his artistic gift.

Not everyone has an outstanding talent as did Asher Lev, but everyone has some talents. A certain amount of expression of these talents is necessary, even if it be only a symbolic expression. Since the talents are an element in the ground out of which the vocation grows, only an act of repression can keep them from influencing both the attraction and the means of expression. One with a lesser talent than Asher Lev might have been able to satisfy his needs in his spare time. He might have been a lawyer or salesman and done a few hours of artwork each week at home. Perhaps he could have been an engineer and integrated his talent into his work.

The important thing about talents and capacities that I bring to a vocational experience is not that they each get full opportunity for expression. The important thing is that they are not denied.

According to an interest test I took in high school, I am interested in mechanics and science. I don't recall that the test made any provisions for physical activity but if it had, I might have ranked high in that too.

Presumably I have a little talent for such things. We usually are not too interested in things for which we have no ability at all. [47] I may let these things drop into the background for a few years in order to study. Even so, I find I have to dig up something to tinker around with occasionally. If monastic life consisted in sitting in a scriptorium several hours a day copying manuscripts I would probably have lasted about two weeks – two pretty horrible weeks at that. But, fortunately, it provided a considerable amount of physical activity, some contact with machinery and occasionally an opportunity to apply what little scientific knowledge I had picked up by way of trying to figure out how or why something worked – or why it did not work. It might not have been enough for a mechanical genius, but it was enough for me.

When I express my assent to an attraction, it is best if it can be as much an expression of the whole person as possible. My present situation – having to tinker around in between studying – is not the ideal. It is a temporary expedient. It would be better if I were devoting the major part of the day to a meaningful task that fulfilled my own needs and gave me all the outlets for expression that I need. For a time I can do without that. But Asher Lev could not. He could not have given up painting for two or three years even for the sake of studying art in order to be a better painter. His need to express could not be suppressed. [48]

---

[47] There are exceptions to this. Karen Horney's theory of the Idealized Image has already been mentioned (pp.50-51 of this book). Willy Loman in Arthur Miller's <u>Death of a Salesman</u> (New York: Viking Press, 1949) is a good example of one who tried to live out a career for which he had very little aptitude.

[48] Suppressed – set-aside willingly until some more opportune time – differs from repressed which involves denial, <u>refusal to admit the existence</u> of the need.

So my expression must allow for my talents and gifts. The more central the talent is to my personality, the more central should be its place in the expression. But along with talents I also have limitations. There are some things I cannot do. These too have a place in the ground out of which my vocation grows. These too must be taken into consideration if my expression is to be realistic.

Emmanuel Mounier
The Limitations of Character

Some talents seem to be an integral part of the person's personality. Such was Asher Lev's. In other cases, a talent seems to have developed through practice resulting from circumstances. A person may feel no need or even desire to tinker around with machinery, but in some particular instance he may have to do so. He finds it pleasant, finds he is good at it, makes it a hobby, and finally pursues some related form of activity as a career. We might call him a "born" mechanic but perhaps he had no more innate mechanical skill (if there is such a thing) than the next guy who could figure out how to use a can opener.

Like talents, many limitations seem to be born along with us. Others are acquired along the way. To be without limitations would mean not being human. To refuse to take limitations into consideration might easily lead to willfulness. But to accept all limitations without question will lead to stagnation.

Emmanuel Mounier [49] presents a balanced view of the significance of character limitations for the question of vocation. He begins by pointing out that any kind of "laws" we can construct are only relatively close approximations to the causes and effect of behavior. They can never replace the uniqueness of an autonomous person in a particular situation. Such laws do provide norms which prevent arbitrariness and egocentricity from infiltrating into personal experience. [50] [p. 285]

The first "rule" that Mounier presents is: "Know yourself and accept yourself, because you will never be effective outside the paths and limitations that have been assigned to you." [p. 286] This knowledge is experiential rather than analytical or speculative. Many elements of secondary personalities surround my main personality. They are usually misrepresented to consciousness. To know them is always to react to them; they are known with a knowledge that is acquired by action and by opting for my real self. To attempt to apply will power to secondary or repressed areas may stabilize the very tendencies I am trying to combat. This may

---

[49] The material in this section is taken from Emmanuel Mounier, <u>The Character of Man</u> (New York: Harper and Brothers, 1956). All references to this work will be followed by the appropriate page numbers and brackets.

[50] Mounier, in this section is speaking specifically about character limitations as they affect moral life. But, as he points out, morality is for the sake of the development of the human spirit and if it "knows how to simplify its preoccupation and respect the freedom of the heart, it serves our vocations without restraint..." [p. 284] From this point of view the effects of limitations on vocation may be less immediate but more fundamental.

happen by focusing too much attention on them or by strengthening their resistances. Often a technique of distraction would work better.

A second "rule" is "You will never discover what you are (prospectively) except by denying what you are (statically)." [p. 289] That is: I must accept and know my whole self, including my potentialities that are, as yet, unrealized. I must know them through action. Just following nature is not enough since each virtue has its corresponding vice: "the man who loves gentleness usually lacks force, the generous are not prudent and the prudent not always generous." [p. 290] The solution is not to temper the virtues one has and end up in static mediocrity. Mounier suggests the possibilities of an "agiotherapy, or treatment of personality disorders by commitments of an ethical nature" [pp. 290-291] geared towards developing the virtues complementary to those that are natural to a particular temperament. He sums up his thoughts on the need for flexibility in the following words:

> Push each of your inclinations in the direction in which it will bring you the greatest richness and openness: disarm rigidity exclusiveness: try to harmonize your character by its contrary dispositions, but keep it firmly organized along one master line. [p. 292]

Attention to others is also a great aid to self-knowledge and self-acceptance. "Understand and accept the character of the other, for it is the only way to lead you to his mystery, to break down your own egocentricity and establish the working foundation of a life in common." [p. 293]

While it is true that the movements that expose me to myself are subtle and elusive it is also true that "the obscure voices of inspiration are only heard by those who have their hearts available to them: thus, in the last resort, it depends on us whether we hear them or not." [p. 296]

Reflection

Mounier, as usual, sets a high standard. He gives some general rules but emphasizes personal responsibility. I am responsible for guiding my life along one dominant path but I cannot let that dominant path become an exclusive path. I must accept my limitations while realizing that I may be misjudging their borders, that I may be able to stretch potentialities further. Do I have some strong quality that seems largely responsible for my success? I must nourish and develop the virtue that is complementary to it, the virtue which may all too often look like a weakness to me. I may not let the opinions of others distract me from my goals, yet I must be attuned to them and their reactions to my character.

But can this really be applied to someone like Asher Lev, for example? Before I try, let me try to practice what Mounier is preaching by explicating some of the limitations that are involved. First, there is no reason to try to fit Asher Lev into a mold of perfection. Perfect self-knowledge and self-acceptance are not essential in order for a vocation to develop. Second, I am not an artist and to a great extent I share Asher Lev's father's lack of "intellectual and emotional equipment" to understand the specifics of an artistic vocation. I mentioned previously that I am writing about the way vocation usually develops and I left room for exceptional cases. Perhaps Asher is one of these. But let us see.

It seems that self-knowledge and self-acceptance are at the very heart of Asher's vocation. He is trying to "paint his feelings" to give them body and permanence. Is this passion for truth and honesty accompanied by a lack of the complementary virtues – tact and consideration for others? He loves his parents but he does cause them pain. He tries to have the pictures of his mother removed from public display but it is too late. Had he succeeded it would have seemed to him a betrayal of his calling – "You communicate in a public arena." This same thought might have characterized his response to his father's accusations of "moral blindness" indicated by his apparent lack of concern for the sufferings of the Jews. Asher might have replied that all men, not just the Jews, are suffering and his job is to minister to them all. He is not just trying to alleviate the pain but to help them to face it, to see it as it is. They cannot bear to look at their own so he takes his and gives it to them to observe undefended and vulnerable. Perhaps they will be able to catch a glimpse of their own in it. His vocation has a very definite social element.

Asher's life does necessarily strike most of us as a little one-sided. Would a few other activities have necessarily interfered with the exercise of his talent? The attempts to take him from his one way of expressing himself were, for the most part, attempts to take him from it forever. In small amounts, other activities might not have been so threatening. They might have broadened his social experience a little and enriched his emotional life by contact with different types of people. This seems perfectly logical.

Perhaps it is even true. [51] But perhaps it is very, very false. To "broaden" Asher Lev might have been to "level" him, to move him toward the not-so-happy medium, to reduce "genius" to "very talented." The sacrifice of breadth may have been more than justified by the height he attained. The noteworthy point is that the expression is as important as the attraction and, like the attraction, is strongly informed by the subject of the experience. He is the soil of which it grows.

But, to carry on with the horticultural analogy, the expression also grows in an atmosphere also. Thus I consider the influence of the world. Both expression and surrounding world must be considered under the aspect of the object-pole of the experience.

---

[51] It is very dangerous to apply logic too strictly to human life. Mounier points out the need to consider the autonomy of the person and the uniqueness of his situation. Even the person himself is not in the best position to explicate his behavior. Mounier (p.26) quotes Melville as saying "As far as we can judge, blind moles that we are, the life of man seems only to move by mysterious suggestions: it is somehow suggested to us to do this or that. Truly any ordinary mortal who has somewhat considered himself, will never claim that even the least of his deeds or thoughts has its sole origin in his own well defined identity." Such a statement might be an admirable substitute for the entire first chapter of this book – if not for the whole book!

II. THE OBJECT-POLE

B.F. Skinner
Reinforcement

It is often said that in spite of his tremendous advances in technical skills,

man has not made much progress in happiness or in living at peace with his fellow

man. The implication – if not explication – is that man cannot succeed in life only by

manipulating the external world. He must change his attitudes, aims and ambitions.

B.F. Skinner [52] appears, at first to agree with this view of man's problems:

> The application of the physical and biological sciences alone will not solve
> our problems because the solutions lie in another field...New methods of agriculture
> and medicine will not help if they are not practiced, and housing is a matter not only
> of buildings and cities but how people live. Overcrowding can be corrected only by
> inducing people not to crowd, and the environment will continue to deteriorate until
> polluting practices are abandoned. [p. 2]

Skinner's solution is the development of a technology of human behavior.

He feels that human behavior is governed by laws as precise and determinative as

those that govern a falling body or a moving projectile. What man must do is to

discover those laws and apply them to his life in order to produce behavior that will

avoid the catastrophic results towards which man often seems headed.

---

[52] The material in this section is taken from B.F. Skinner, <u>Beyond Freedom and Dignity</u> (New York: Bantam Books, 1972). All references to this work will be followed by the appropriate page numbers in brackets. His earlier work, <u>Walden Two</u> (New York: Macmillan, 1948), was an attempt to present similar principles being put into practice in an imaginary commune.

Paradoxically, however, Skinner's solution consists precisely in manipulating the environment. It is my environment, according to Skinner, that makes me behave as I do. In ways that Skinner compares to Darwin's "natural selection," my environment encourages or reinforces some kinds of behavior. [pp. 15-16] The reinforcement is the important thing.

What is maximized or minimized, or what is ultimately good or bad, are things, not feelings, and men work to achieve them or to avoid them not because of the way they feel but because they are positive or negative reinforcers. [p. 102]

Skinner rejects "autonomous man" who is, by definition, not changeable at all. [p. 96] The concept of autonomy has only risen out of our ignorance to cover areas which science could not yet explain. Man must be dispossessed of this ambiguity if we are to deal with the real causes of behavior scientifically. [p. 191] Skinner says we must redesign our environment to produce behavior that will insure the survival of the race. We must decide what types of behavior are conducive to this end and arrange the environment to reinforce those types, leaving detrimental behaviors unreinforced.

Reflection

Many of Skinner's thoughts seem incompatible with the freedom which I have presupposed in the second chapter of this book. He denounces "autonomous man" as something which never really existed. But in doing so he seems, like Freud [53] to be rejecting the Victorian idea of man as enjoying an almost total freedom of choice, as being master of his own ship and able to change his destiny at will. As Freud pointed out that man is often driven by instincts when he thinks he is acting freely, so Skinner points out that man is often acting as his environment had conditioned him to act. In spite of himself, he seems to leave man a little room for choice. He is encouraging man to redesign his world. He wants man to choose that by which he will be conditioned. Perhaps the best interpretation of Skinner's thought is that man's freedom has a very narrow scope <u>as freedom</u>. But within that narrow scope man can choose among the various ways in which he will be reinforced. He has not the choice of being conditioned by his environment or not, but he has the ability to choose the things by which he will be conditioned.

How do Skinner's thoughts apply to the question of expressing my assent to a vocational attraction? It seems my choices of expression are limited, not only by my own personal talents and abilities, but by my past experiences. If one possible expression has been given a good deal of negative reinforcement I will be

---

[53] This point is made by Rollo May in <u>Love and Will</u> (New York: W.W. Norton, 1969), p. 205. Freud too expressed ambiguity about man's freedom. May quotes him as agreeing with a determinist view of man [pp. 180-181] and again [p. 195] as stating that the aim of therapy is to free the patient's ego to choose between two possible ways of acting.

strongly disinclined to choose it. I will be strongly disinclined to reject an expression that has been positively reinforced in my past. [54] The expression that I do eventually choose will itself become a conditioner of my future behavior. It will not only express my assent to the attraction but will affect my attraction. The attraction will change under the conditioning influence of the expression. Certain aspects of the attraction will be reinforced. Other aspects will be weakened or extinguished. Some new aspects may be added. Thus, the way in which I express myself will contribute to the development of my vocation.

That my environment (including, of course, the people in my world) shapes and influences my behavior is not difficult to see. Asher Lev's father might be a prime example for Skinner to use. He comes from a religious Jewish family with a history of active support for the welfare of their kinsmen. His own father was very active. He has an ability in political matters, is young and can take a great deal of hard work without tiring. He has a great reverence for the local Rabbi and considers him an almost infallible leader. There is a good deal of work to be done at the time and the Rabbi wants him to do it. How, under these circumstances, would one expect him to express his calling? It might almost appear that he has no choice. And maybe he doesn't. Maybe this is the only realistic expression available to him.

---

[54] Where I say "strongly disinclined" Skinner would probably say "incapable" since he admits of no other source of motivation except genetic endowment and conditioning.

Is he, then less free – or not free at all? Because his behavior can be predicted with a high degree of accuracy, is it therefore determined beforehand? If it is determined, it is determined by the man's promise of dedication, his decision "<u>that</u> I will..." The environment influences his "<u>how</u> I will..."

How would Skinner explain Asher Lev's vocation? He would have a hard time applying the conditioning and reinforcing model to Asher who successfully resisted just about everything in his environment. Skinner might resort to the "genetic endowment" of Asher – his artistic talent – as a determinant too strong to be overcome by conditioning. But that is no reason why it could not have been "influenced" or qualified by his environment. A better answer might be to say that the expression Asher gave to his talent had a strong positive reinforcing effect and allowed him to resist the negative reinforcement of his parents, especially his father.

This reinforcing effect of expression is important. Things become really real for me only when I express them in some way and especially when that expression is perceived by others. I do not feel the guilt of lying or stealing until someone else finds out about it. I do not have to face the absurdity of my suspicions until I express them aloud and see the look of bewilderment on the face of the other. Asher Lev had not only to paint but also to display his work in the "public arena." In external expression I not only share with others but I also separate myself in some way. I identify myself before them. I distinguish myself from the mass. I am now related to the others by communication, not fusion. And this exposes my fragility, my insecurity, my vulnerability as well as my uniqueness. I am, in the eyes of the others, identified with my expressions whether it be a painting, a speech, a job or a thesis.

We might call this the "reinforcing value" of the expression. I prefer to think of it as the "real-izing value", the value of making things real to me, of making myself real to me. It does not say "this is good" or this is "bad". The expression just says "Look, this is what you are really expressing – for good or ill!" Thus, if I am of good will, the expressions I use to give concreteness to my attitudes may have a "purifying" effect; they provide an opportunity to see where my attitudes are incomplete, unrealistic or not fully genuine. But neither the expression with its "realizing value," nor the feedback from my environment actually changes my attitude or expression. They provide indicators of the advisability of change. I decide to make the change. I do not choose a particular way of living because I have been conditioned to do so; I choose it in order to express my attitudes and reinforce them. [55] If my expression of my attitudes shows them to be what I had thought they were, it will have a reinforcing effect. I become more "real" to myself and to others

---

[55] This distinction between "because" motives and "in order to" motives is taken from Helmut R. Wagner, ed. Alfred Schutz on Phenomenology and Social Relations (Chicago: University of Chicago Press, 1970), pp. 126-129 and 180-183. Schutz points out that the distinction is often disregarded and all motivation is relegated to the "because" category. It might be objected that the "will-less" person described earlier acts only because of the influences at work on or in him. To drift with the tide of feelings involves a decision to do so. "Even if a man decides no longer to realize himself, he still realizes himself, albeit as a lazybone, a good for nothing a blockhead, and an idler...Man cannot do nothing, for doing nothing is also doing something." William A Luijpen, Existential Phenomenology (Pittsburgh: Duquesne University Press, 1969), p. 237.

in the expression. If, as is usually the case, there are elements in my attitude whose existence I deny, I may choose a form of expression that reinforces <u>them</u>. They may grow stronger with time and eventually take over my whole attitude. If, for example, I enter a monastery to escape from the prospect of intimacy with others, that fear may be reinforced under the guise of love of solitude and tranquility. I may be driven further from others. I will then lose the values of community life, human relations, <u>and</u> the possibility of any truly fruitful solitude. On the other hand, communal life may have the effect of weakening and eventually extinguishing my fear of others. It seems that either of these two processes can take place. Which of them actually occurs depends not on conditioning or natural selection but on the stance I take towards the two alternative possibilities.

The way in which I express my assent to a vocational attraction is important. It can tell me much about the original attraction. It can strengthen, purify and solidify the attraction or it can undermine and vitiate it. The processes of reinforcement and conditioning are powerful. But I am not totally at their disposal. In fact, they are at my disposal. But this presupposes freedom on my part. Thus it is necessary to place Skinner's thoughts in a broader context – that of man who is, to some extent, determined by his situation but who is radically free to take a stance toward his future, to make his own world.

<u>William A. Luijpen</u>
<u>The Free Subject and Facticity</u>

Skinner had viewed human action as a part of a process. A specific person is subjected to particular reinforcing agents in his environment and a given type of behavior results. Then the behavior itself is added to the list of conditioning agents. Not only individual elements, but the implicit structures of a situation and its relation to past situations are part of the environment. If we could account for all these influences, we could predict behavior accurately according to Skinner. Better yet, if we could control and arrange these influences beforehand we can control and arrange behavior.

William Luijpen [56] takes a different approach. He considers Freud's determinist views and Sartre's anti-determinist position. [57] He responds that "lived experience knows" that man is neither <u>wholly</u> determined nor <u>totally</u> free and responsible even for his passions. [p. 232] Luijpen is careful to insist that he is speaking of man's action as <u>human</u> action, that is: action in which "an objective evaluation of the motives concretely preceded the action..." [p. 235] If this was not

---

[56] The material in this section is taken from William A. Luijpen, <u>Existential Phenomenology</u> (Pittsburgh: Duquesne University Press, 1969). References to this work will be followed by the appropriate page numbers in brackets.

[57] Luijpen affirms the ambiguity in Freud's view of freedom which has already been pointed out. Joseph B. Simons, in "An Existential View of Vocational Development," <u>Personnel and Guidance Journal</u> (February, 1966), pp. 604-610, discusses Sartre's theory of vocation. Rather than explain vocational choice as a result of personality development, Sartre sees this choice as central to development. Career choice (which does not necessarily involve the experience of being called) is, for him, a crucial step either away from self-centered-ness toward altruistic love or in the opposite direction. He also emphasizes the importance of external expression. In Simons' words: "But only by revealing his true self to others will he, in turn, be able to see himself as he truly is." And "The sad fact remains that anyone who does not project himself before others as fully responsible can never discover the reality of others and, therefore, of himself." [Simons: pp. 604 and 606 respectively]

the case – as could happen when one is suddenly seized by a powerful passion or impulse – the act is not free and therefore not human.

Man's freedom is, however, limited. Man " 'finds' himself as 'already' merged with a particular body and as 'already' involved in a particular world." [p. 199] At any particular moment his "starting point" is already determined. The totality of the determinants is called his "facticity." All facticity includes potentialities. I can use my facticity in a variety of ways. Each action opens new possibilities.

When a man on the proper level of his manhood acts, the subject who he is reaches beyond the facticity of his existence toward the fulfillment of a possibility that is not yet filled. The newly established meaning then remains as a new facticity of his existence. There is, however, no facticity without potentiality: the newly established meaning opens the subject to another new possibility. [pp. 236-237]

Facticity limits, but it also allows. It closes some doors, but it opens others. I must start with who and what I am at the moment. I cannot change that. I cannot start from somewhere else. But I can plan what I will be, who I will be, what direction my life will take. It is not an <u>absolute</u> freedom, but it is a <u>radical</u> freedom; I am fundamentally responsible for what I make of my life.

Reflection

How shall we reconcile Skinner and Luijpen in the context of expressing my assent to a vocational attraction? I think it is largely a matter of emphasis. Possibly a crude example will help.

In a few weeks I shall have to travel from Louisville to Pittsburgh. Skinner would say (rightly) that I can't get there by will power. Luijpen would agree, but suggest that I can decide to go and take the necessary steps to arrange my getting there. I can go to Louisville, buy a ticket, get on the bus to Pittsburgh, stay on it when it stops at Cincinnati and Columbus and get off when it gets to Pittsburgh. I am in control of the trip – within limits. I can go no faster or slower than the bus. I cannot go by different route. I have "surrendered" myself to this vehicle and am allowing it to carry me along. It is doing the work. But if I hear the driver say "next stop: St. Louis" I will, hopefully, recognize that the bus is not taking me in the direction I want to go. I will get off, get another bus and retrace my steps. The mistake has been made and its results stand. I must start from wherever I am; I cannot just "erase" that part of the trip and start from Louisville again.

Something similar happens when I express my assent to a vocational attraction. A vocation will not develop just by will power. My whole being, my body, emotions, intellect, memory, will; everything must come to know, to experience the attraction and take part in the expression of assent. The way I express my assent, my decisions, attitudes and behavior, should reinforce the attraction and help it spread to areas that are not yet attracted. My expression is something of a vehicle carrying me along the way of vocational development. It is conditioning me. But it is not the inexorable process that Skinner makes it out to be. I am free to drop it when it has fulfilled its purpose or when I have found that it is leading me in a direction I do not want to go. When I have made a mistake in my choice of expression I have to undo the results or live with them. I cannot just "start from scratch" again.

Skinner plans his emphasis on the "process" nature of conditioning and reinforcement. The environment wields an influence. My actions depend on my genetic endowment and past experience. My behavior is controlled by external elements. Luijpen emphasizes my freedom to choose among the external elements that influence me, my ability to use them in the service of my own plans for my life. Luijpen does not deny partial determination and Skinner, at least implicitly, allows for freedom in choosing what kind of an environment I will be influenced by.

When I express my assent to my attraction by taking up monastic life, I am not just allowing my feelings to overflow into the external world. The expression is not just a by-product or "symptom." It is also an experimental proclamation. I am saying "This is me." The affirmation that it really is me or the assertion that it is not really me comes from the depths of my being. It does not come from the world as feedback. The world may reply that this behavior is not acceptable, not properly suited to my situation or not effective. But it is in my own heart that judgments passed on the authenticity of my expression. I may soon find out that monastic life is completely or largely artificial for me. Or I may find that it really "fits." It really expresses what is within me. But my behavior not only expresses, it also impresses. It confirms, strengthens and deepens the attitudes that have been externalized. If I am not attuned to my deepest feelings I may easily reinforce attitudes that are not genuine for me. If I am attuned I will learn much about myself, about my attraction and my approach to life.

We have seen something of how the subject's potentialities and limitations may affect the way he expresses his assent to a vocational attraction. We have also noted that the world in which the subject acts has some influence on his expressions, but the expression illumines the subject about himself and his attraction. This sets the stage for a new dimension of the attraction to open up, followed by a new level of assent and expression. Something remains to be said about the relationship between the interior and the exterior facets of that which is expressed.

III. RELATIONSHIP OF
SUBJECT AND OBJECT POLES

Emmanuel Mounier [58]
The Inner and Outer Lives

Mounier sums up all that I have been trying to say about attitudes and their expression when he says, "All the dimensions of the person are mutually sustaining and constitutive." [p. 44] Personal existence is held in tension between the tendency to get fixated on the objective and the movement toward introversion and narcissism. In regard to the latter tendency [59] he states that the subject

---

[58] The material in this section has been taken from Emmanuel Mounier, Personalism (London: Routledge & Kegan Paul, 1952). All references to this work will be followed by the appropriate page numbers in brackets.

[59] He has already pointed out the dangers of objectification, of placing my treasure in that which is outside myself. [pp. 39-40] Quoting Valery, he calls this being "shut up outside ourselves." [p. 43]

...must come out of his inwardness if he is to keep his soul alive. The flower of first love, says Kierkegaard, withers if love will not pass through the ordeal of faithfulness (of repetition) in the institution of marriage, which, after putting love to disarray, restores it to fuller bloom. [p. 43]

He speaks of there being a real "instinct" for exteriorization; man is "an inside in need of an outside." [p. 44] He concludes: "We must not, then, undervalue the external life: without it the inner life tends to insanity, as surely as the outer life becomes chaotic without interiorization." [p. 44]

Reflection

Words seem to fail when we try to express the relationship between the interior and the exterior. When Mounier says that man is an inside in need of an outside, he is immediately aware that this relates to the existentialist idea of a man necessarily "standing out" into a world. Man cannot be thought of as man without his world. The two are not identical, but neither has a true identity without the other. Plans, ideals, projects are only imaginary, they become real only by expression. External behavior is only meaningful, only really human behavior, if it is an extension of the thought and intention of the one who acts. The intention and the expression are two dimensions of the one human act and the dimensions are "mutually sustaining and constitutive." The tension between the two movements – toward exteriority and toward interiority – is not resolved by tempering one or the other element but by being open to both of them. Far less is it resolved by repressing one tendency and identifying myself totally with the other. [60] Both are essential though the emphasis may differ from one person to another or at different times in the life of any particular person.

"Concentrating in order to find oneself; then going forth to enrich and find oneself again; concentrating oneself again through dispossession; such is the systole and diastole of the personal life..." [p. 41]

While this oscillation takes place within the life direction I have chosen for myself, I must respect its own laws. I cannot plan a schedule of interiority and exteriority. An attitude of receptive volition is called for similar to that described by van Kaan and referred to on pages 64-65. Such an inability to "control" the movements in my life, though it may threaten my egotistical desire for security and stability, should have the effect of confirming in me a realization of my "creatureliness." Unlike John Denver, I will not have the slightest interest in becoming some kind of god. I will be only happy to become, more fully, a human being. And that "becoming" will have the character of a gift – it has been given to me. My past, the influences and reinforcers have been given to me. My genetic endowment was given to me. The present situation is given to me. The attraction

---

[60] The dynamics operating here are similar to those presented in Chapter one regarding Karen Horney's theory of the basic conflict. [pp. 49-51] In that case it was a question of a choice between moving "toward" people in relationship of dependence or moving "against" them aggressively. The healthy person chooses according to circumstances and is capable of moving "away from" others into solitude when necessary. Mounier is advocating a similar freedom with regard to emphasis on the interior and exterior dimensions of the human act.

I feel and the motivation to respond are given to me. The movement toward external expression is given to me.

With all these, my responsibility is also given to me. They are not automatic gifts. I can reject or resist them. They are gratuitously given to me but I am radically responsible for whether or not I <u>receive</u> them. Nor are they final and full-blown gifts. I am radically responsible for allowing them room for growth, for respecting their laws of development.

Yet they are still gifts, not loans. They belong to me. My vocation belongs to me. It is mine, but I must treat it responsibly. It also belongs to the whole world, to mankind. It is like raising a child. I have disposed myself for parenthood, accepted the child, nourished and protected him; he is <u>my</u> child. But he is not exclusively mine. I "owe" him to mankind, to the welfare of the human race. So with my vocations; it belongs to me, but also to others – to all.

There are a number of polarities that have been referred to in regard to the experience of being called. The attraction is influenced by elements within the subject and elements in the objective to which he is attracted. His assent must balance his managing will and his capacity for receptive willing. The interiority and exteriority of his expression sustain and authenticate one another. His vocation is a gift but also a great responsibility. It is his own but he owes it to the world.

Somehow man can unify all this into a single, simple, integral stance toward life. It is not the unity of a mathematical equation but the unity of a landscape with its contrasting colors, its movement and stillness, its sounds and its silence.

I cannot focus on each element at the same time. But I can be present to the whole which is more than just the sum of the parts. The contrasts do not cancel one another but contribute to the richness of the whole.

I can focus on one element at a time, however. And I can become so engrossed in that one that the whole of which it is a part is lost sight of. This can happen in human life as well. In the vocational experience I may put all my reliance on one movement and neglect its complement. This will, of course, cause problems. We have seen some of the problems that can arise in relation to the attraction in Karen Horney's theory of inner conflicts. We will now consider some of the ways in which difficulties can arise in expression of my assent.

IV. PROBLEMS IN

THE EXPRESSION

<u>Herman Melville</u> [61]
<u>The Monomaniac</u>

In his great novel, <u>Moby Dick</u>, Melville tells the tale of a man who seems to have run into problems with the expression of his assent to his attraction. He becomes obsessed with one particular aspect of his expression and with carrying it out successfully. He becomes taken up with material results to the extent that he risks, and loses, his life in a blind, stubborn drive to do the impossible.

The man is Ahab, captain of a whaling ship, who sets out to avenge the loss of his leg which resulted from his last clash with the great white whale, Moby Dick. His crew discovers too late that this is his sole interest in the trip but their protests melt before the wrath of his powerful personality. Upon encountering another whaling vessel, his one question is whether they have seen the white whale and his sole fear is that someone else may have killed it before him. [pp. 314, 349, 402, 433, 488, 530] He does not merely want the whale dead; he wants to do the killing. It is of little concern to him that some thirty other lives are involved in his mad rush to destruction.

But Ahab's pride is not totally blind to his limitations. As the carpenter carves a piece of bone to make him an artificial leg he mumbles, "Here I am, proud

---

[61] The material in this section is taken from Herman Melville, <u>Moby Dick</u> (New York: Random House, 1950). All references to this work will be followed by the appropriate page numbers in brackets.

105

as a Greek god, and yet standing debtor to this blockhead for a bone to stand on!" [p. 468] He recognizes the truth in the warning of Starbuck, the chief mate, "but let Ahab beware of Ahab; beware of thyself, old man." [p. 471] He sees, too, something of the foolishness of his past stubbornness. When his artificial leg is broken a second time he leans on Starbuck and says "Aye aye, Starbuck, 'tis sweet to lean sometimes, be the leaner who he will; and would old Ahab had leaned oftener than he has." [p. 551] But he quickly adds, in reference to his bodily handicap "Accursed fate! That the unconquerable captain in the soul should have such a craven mate." [pp. 551-552]

The true tragedy of Ahab lies in the fact the he is not just a monomaniac. As another captain had said of him, "stricken, blasted, if he be, Ahab has his humanities." [p. 81] Just a few days before his final encounter with the hated whale, Ahab seems to find himself for a moment as he stands at the ship's rail.

But the lovely aromas in that enchanted air did at last seem to dispel, for a moment, the cankerous thing in his soul. That glad, happy air, that winsome sky, did at last stroke and caress him; the step-mother world, so long cruel – forbidding – now threw affectionate arms round his stubborn neck, and did seem to joyously sob over him, as if over one, that however willful and erring, she could yet find it in her heart to save and to bless. From beneath his slouched hat Ahab dropped a tear into the sea; not did all the Pacific contain such wealth as that one wee drop. [p. 532]

He even shares something of the moment with Starbuck, reflecting on the hardship and loneliness of his life, how he sailed for Cape Horn the day after he married – having widowed his wife by marrying her --, how he has furiously pursued his prey for forty years "more demon than a man," [p. 533] and what an old fool he has been.

Close! Stand close to me, Starbuck; let me look into a human eye; it is better than to gaze into sea or sky; better than to gaze upon God. By the green land; by the bright hearthstone! This is magic glass, man; I see my wife and my child in thine eye. No, no; stay on board, onboard! –Lower not when I do; when branded Ahab gives chase to Moby Dick. That hazard shall not be thine. No,no! not with the far away home I see in that eye! [p. 534]

Starbuck enthusiastically seizes the opportunity to encourage the old man to turn back from his resolve but his pleas fall on deaf ears. Ahab turns his face away.

What is it, what nameless, inscrutable, unearthly thing is it; what cozening, hidden lord and master, and cruel remorseless emperor commands me; that against all natural lovings and longings. I so keep pushing, and crowding, and jamming, myself on all the time; recklessly making me ready to do what in my own proper, natural heart, I durst not so much as dare? [pp. 534-535]

Earlier they had met a ship whose captain, Boomer, had lost an arm in an attack on Moby Dick. He had learned his lesson with that one venture.

"He's welcome to the arm he has, since I can't help it...but not to another one. No more White Whales for me; I've lowered for him once and that has satisfied me...., he's best let alone;" [p. 439]

Ahab agrees but "What is best let alone, that accursed thing is not always what least allures. He's all a magnet!" [p. 439]

When finally encountered, the whale is chased for three days. The first two days he damages some of the small boats and one man is lost. On the third day he continues his relentless work though he never does any harm until he is attacked. In a last desperate attempt, Ahab bears down on the monster in one of the smaller boats howling, "Towards thee I roll, thou all-destroying but unconquering whale; to the last grapple with thee; from hell's heart I stab at thee; for hate's sake I spit my last breath at thee." [p. 564] The harpoon is hurled into the great whale, but running line catches Ahab around the neck and hurls him--voicelessly—into the sea. The boat sinks and the only man--Ishmael, in whose person Melville has told the story-- survives to report that "...the shroud of the sea rolled on as it rolled five thousand years ago." [p. 565]

Reflection

Most of us have had something of Ahab's experience. I want something and try to get it. My efforts fail and I try harder. Again I fail and I'm beginning to get annoyed. The thing I'm after is no longer desired as a possession, but is seen as an occasion of a challenge. I become bitter; I won't let myself be beaten, won't recognize or admit failure. I begin to despise whatever it is I'm after to the point where I want to get it in my power only to destroy it. There are moments (not to say days) when I felt that way about this book. Get it done, do it nicely and primly and properly so every one is satisfied, get it approved—then throw the thing into the nearest incinerator. There is, of course, another possible attitude. I might see the difficulties as labor pains which necessarily accompany bringing forth something that I will later be proud of and take joy in.

Captain Ahab is proud of his conquests at sea. He has grown wealthy in the whaling business. He is proud of his record. And now he meets a whale that defies his efforts. Understandably enough, he doesn't want to admit defeat. He cannot swallow his immense pride. He tries harder. But to put the necessary effort into his attempts he has to close the door of consciousness to a number of things. The object pole of his attraction becomes narrower and narrower. Killing Moby Dick is the primary, if not only, purpose of this voyage. It becomes an obsession. He is not able to concern himself with his own welfare or that of the crew. He gives no thought to what it may mean to his wife, to the owners of the ship; he must kill that whale at any cost. In trying to carry out his ambition he is confronted with a number of warnings. The reluctance of the crew, the other whalers who have been injured by the white whale, the loss of one of his men on the second day of the chase—he refuses to look at any of these omens for fear he might weaken in his resolve.

Ahab might have been justifiably considered as one who got into trouble as a result of the perversion of his original attraction. But he is also one who lost sight of the object of his attraction. He is taken up with the pursuit of one particular expression of his vocation to the exclusion of all others. That one expression loses all proportion. He ignores all the warnings that come his way telling him this is not a realistic objective. He is driven, obsessed, pushed on by some demon within him, he can think of nothing else. That one expression, killing Moby Dick has become his only value in life.

I have called whaling a vocation. Is that justified? Isn't it just a job, a career at best? I don't feel any obligation to defend every occupation as a vocation but something might be said for whaling. Vocation is a "nice" word. People with vocations are clean, well-dressed, educated people. We don't readily think of the unshaven, sweat-covered cursing whaler as the vocation type. Earlier [62] I mention the

---

[62] See page 81.

possibility of symbolic expression. It seems possible that the whaler may be struggling, in a symbolic way, with some of the same problems that the philosopher, the scientist and the psychologist are. These are men trying to come to grips with the truth about man and his relations with the world. They are struggling intellectually or experimentally to express, according to their various talents, the role of man and the nature of the elements against which these powers are pitted. Why cannot the whaler be seen as doing the same thing—according to his talents? He is struggling also with the great and deep mysteries of life, matching his powers against those of nature. The whaler is living out the struggle in a way that is in accord with his talents, physical strength, endurance and skill. He hasn't the philosopher's mind for intellectual probing or the scientist's patience and precision. Of course, the whaler never may think of his occupation in these terms. He might well resent the suggestion as an attempt to "justify" his occupation in terms of middle-class values. All the same, he may be living out the struggle[63] with more courage and deeper personal development than either the philosopher or

---

[63] When I speak of struggling with nature or matching one's powers against those of nature I don't mean to imply that nature is an enemy. That was Ahab's attitude – at least in part. John S. Dunne in Time and Myth (Garden City, NY: Doubleday, 1973), pp. 47-81, 110-111, sees Ahab as trying to destroy evil (symbolically). "It appears to be up to man to struggle against evil, to sail out against it like Ahab. Yet if man sails against the monster, if he attempts to set the world right, if he tries to destroy evil, Melville's story seems to say, he will only destroy himself." [pp. 51-52] In that framework it seems to me Ahab has already lost the struggle with evil, already been seduced by it and surrendered his whole being to it, when he allows his hatred and desire for revenge to become the guiding principle of his life. Even if he killed the whale he would have lost the battle – and that by an inglorious surrender.

scientist. Ahab's sensitivity, which only breaks through on a couple of occasions indicates that he was capable of greatness but lost sight of the relativity of certain values. As far as living out his vocation was concerned, killing the whale wasn't that important. But he became obsessed with this one particular aspect of the expression of his vocation and lost sight of the context in which it was to be seen. [64]

---

[64] It is interesting to compare Ahab to Don Quixote. In some ways Ahab's ideal seems to be summed up in Quixote's song "The Impossible Dream" from the play "Man of La Mancha." The words used here are from the record of the same name by Kapp Records Inc., New York.

      The song begins: "To dream the impossible dream, to fight the unbeatable foe, to bear with unbearable sorrow, to run where the brave dare not go..." But Ahab's aim had nothing of the glamour or romance as Quixote's dream or any other dream. It is more of a nightmare. He is filled with bitterness; one of Quixote's charms is his innocence. One wonders what would have happened to the demented knight if he had actually killed or seriously injured someone. It might have been enough to snap him out of his dream world. Quixote goes on to sing: " And I know if I'll only be true to this glorious quest, that my heart will be peaceful and calm when I'm laid to my rest." Ahab is not after glory. He never tries to justify his plan; he would probably not do a great deal of bragging if he succeeded. He is out to avenge a lost leg and, since the leg will not be restored, his bitterness will continue to prevent any possibility of his heart being peaceful or calm. He cannot win the leg back. The concluding words of Quixote's song are especially inapplicable to Ahab; "And the world will be better for this: that one man, scorned and covered with scars, still strove with his last ounce of courage to reach the unreachable star," Ahab accomplished nothing but his own destruction and that of his companions. His feeble effort to preserve something of the vision he has seen in Starbuck's eye by having the mate stay on ship fails. Quixote can be forgiven; he loved in a world of illusion and misread everything he saw. Ahab saw things as they were but rejected any values that didn't feed his vengeful pride.

It is not hard to see how Captain Ahab's vocation has become distorted by his narrowing down his response to one obsessive ambition. He lost the breadth of the original attraction, lost his concern with many essential values and betrayed his vocation. But it is difficult to say he has really lost his vocation yet. He is an old man nearly sixty and has a long life of whaling behind him. His obsession with killing the white whale is only a recent thing. But there does seem to be such a thing as a lost vocation. One can become well established in responding to his call and then, at some point, for some reason, find that the vocation has slipped away as mysteriously as it came.

Hermann Hesse
The Lost Vocation

In order to be able to lose a vocation I must first have one. I must have felt the initial attraction, responded to it with my assent and expressed that response in my life and behavior. This cycle of attraction, assent and expression then continues and grows and I commit my life – either explicitly or implicitly – to one particular state or course of action. This is not the end. The attraction grows deeper, the values involved become clearer and I become more free to respond to them. This response allows my potentialities as a person to develop and also teaches me my limitations. If all goes well, if I am faithful in my response and there is no indication that my way of expressing my assent is either out of touch with reality around me or contrary to my own personal abilities and needs, I may be said at some point to "have a vocation."

What happens, then, when a vocation is "lost?" Hermann Hesse, in a highly symbolic story [65] describes such an experience. The story is told in the person of "H.H. [p. 87] who, as a young man, had taken part in a mysterious journey through time and space [p. 26] with a group who belonged to "the League". These expeditions were always going on and there were many such groups. The members took a vow not to reveal the League's secret to unbelievers. One young man, under the influence of outsiders, loses faith in the journey and expresses the desire to leave this useless venture and return home. The leader absolves him from his vow – seeing he has forgotten the secret – and allows him to go. He leaves but repents and begins searching for the group in order to rejoin. One of the leaders says of him:

> We should be happy if he did find his way back to us, but we cannot aid him. He has made it very difficult for himself to have faith again. I fear that he would not see and recognize us even if we passed close by him; he has become blind. Repentence alone does not help. Grace cannot be bought with repentence; it cannot be bought at all. [p. 21]

Among the group, H.H. is especially attracted to a simple, cheerful servant named Leo who, he suspects, knows much more than those he is serving. One day in the middle of the dangerous gorge of Morbio Inferiore" [p. 37] Leo disappears and cannot be found. Several articles seem to have disappeared with him. Everyone in the group seems to have lost something that is indispensable to him. Later it is seen that some of these articles are still around and others are really not indispensable

---

[65] The material in this section is taken from Hermann Hesse, <u>The Journey to the East</u> (New York: Farrar, Straus and Giroux, 1956). All references to this book will be followed by the appropriate page numbers in brackets.

at all. But the morale of the group has suffered a severe blow:

> ....it was not only that I had lost faith in finding Leo again, but everything now seemed to become unreliable and doubtful; the value and meaning of everything was threatened; our comradeship, our faith, our vow, our Journey to the East, our whole life. [p. 40]

One absolutely essential document is gone. But soon there arises uncertainty as to whether it was brought along or was destroyed long ago. For a time H.H. is sure it was lost along with Leo and finds some security in that conviction, pessimistic though it is. But even that one certainty dissolves in the confusion and arguing. Many members feel the impending disastrous break-up of the group is at hand. It is.

Years later H.H. is trying to write about his experience. He thinks he is one of the few living members and wants to preserve the memory of the journey without betraying the League's secret. He finds it impossible to write his story.

He discovers that Leo, unchanged after ten years, is living in his own city. He is taken by Leo to the League's High Throne and finds that the journey is still going on all around him. He accuses himself before the president – Leo – of his crimes, his apostasy, his lack of faith in the League's continued existence and his thought of being its "historian." These are dismissed as mere "novitiate stupidities." [p. 100] But there are many more serious crimes, the worst being that he does not accuse himself of them but appears to be unaware of them. He must come to recognize and admit the depth of the breach that divides him from himself, his fellow man and nature.

Leo's disappearance had been a test and H.H. had failed. Only after ten years of wasted life had he come close enough to despair to seek the league again. He has tried to understand and vindicate human life, to fulfill the requirements of justice, virtue and understanding. [p. 106] He has failed and acknowledged his failure. He can now be reinstated in the league if he has sufficient faith, detachment, self-knowledge and if he is willing to depend on others and recognize his need of them.

In his section of the League's files, H.H. finds a wax or wood statue consisting of two joined figures. One, the larger, stronger, one resembles Leo. The other, weak and unstable, resembles himself. As he watches, he sees that the substance of the smaller figure is slowly, very slowly, flowing into the larger.

I perceived that my image was in the process of adding to and flowing into Leo's, nourishing and strengthening it. It seemed that, in time, all the substance from one image would flow into the other and only one would remain: Leo. He must grow, I must disappear. [p. 118]

This reminds him of a conversation he once had with Leo about the creations of poetry being more vivid and real than the poets themselves.

Reflection

Hesse's story is a symbolic description of the inward journey of self-knowledge. In its content, however, it pictures clearly some of the experience of losing a vocation or, better, discovering that a vocation has been lost. At the time the vocation is slipping away I do not recognize what is happening. I may know something is wrong and I look for particular problems. I magnify small difficulties or make up non-existent ones as did the people on the journey. I try to get one solid fact, however discouraging that one fact may be, to cling to: some one thing that I can be sure of. I hold it firmly in my grip while everything else fades slowly and inexorably away. Then I find that the thing I'm holding has no real meaning anymore, or a quite different meaning. It is like waking from a dream in which I have been clinging to a loved one to prevent separation only to find my arms wrapped around my pillow. The other world is gone and the connecting link has no significant meaning. Perhaps clinging to it was what woke me up and brought the dream-world to an end.

Once the vocation is lost, it is not easily rediscovered. "Grace" (the vocation is always experienced as a gift as was Asher Lev's talent) "cannot be bought with repentence; it cannot be bought at all" said one of the group's leaders. I may take corrective measures to rectify my self-concept, I may study and try to develop an appreciation of the values embodied in the vocation, I may explicate its meaning for myself, I may try to reinforce my desires by going through the exterior motions proper to that vocation. None of this can buy the gift for me. There is no do-it-yourself-kit for discovering or rediscovering a vocation. In either case it is a gift, or at least is experienced that way.

Self-concept, values, meaning, reinforcement, talent, will power, determination are like random notes on the musical scale without some melody to hold them together. The composer can put these notes together into a meaningful whole that expresses something deep within him. As he hears the tune over the years, its meaning will change for him as he himself changes. He and it grow together. But if he should lose the composition before it is published he will not be likely to sit down and make out the same piece several years later. He has changed; what he now expresses will be different. Or if he does not listen to the piece for a number of years it will probably be less meaningful to him when he does hear it again since he and it have not grown together. He is harking back to a past that has, to some extent, been lost. If his composition is really good, he will have as much appreciation of it as would another musician – and more since he has not changed completely. But it is not as completely "his" as it was originally or as it would be now if he had remained in contact with it. It is somewhat like returning home after several years of absence. It is not really "home" anymore, even if things are pretty much the same there.

Something similar happens with a lost vocation. The mysterious affinity, the deep, subtle intuition that this life is "for me" has evaporated. I may see others living the life I once led and hardly see or recognize the fact. I may even wonder what they see in such a life.

How does such a change take place? Does some deep intangible unifying element inside me just go "poof!", and I only feel the effects of this loss slowly as my external expressions of the vocation gradually lose their meaning? I think it might be somewhat the opposite at first.

Let me illustrate this. Two days before I left my monastery to go away to school I had a dream. I dreamed I was watching a group of men demolishing a small one-story building with sledgehammers and crowbars. The bricks had no mortar between them and the edges were rounded. Occasionally the hammering and prying would set the whole building to shaking and swaying back and forth. Someone

117

would holler a warning and those who could run would run. The men inside and on the roof stood still, terrified, and waited for the swaying to stop. When it did, they went back to work until the next time swaying began. After three or four such episodes, the building collapsed, killing several of the men. The onlookers commented: "How tragic! The building just collapsed on them without warning. They didn't have a chance!"

The dream's meaning for me was in the form of a question: "Is that what you have been doing? – have you just been holding your breath till each crisis blows over and never asking if maybe these little crises say something about the structure of your vocation? Now when you leave the monastery for the first time in twenty years will the structure of your vocation collapse around you? Will you find yourself standing on a pile of rubble wondering "Gee, how did that happen?" Vocations, like buildings, don't just collapse all at once. Weaknesses are there, signs are ignored and the weaknesses grow until the structure cannot support itself under normal stress.

If vocation can be said to develop from inside out – an inner attraction to which I give my assent and then express that assent in my exterior life – the loss of vocation may go in the opposite direction. Once a vocation is established (however that may be determined) I lose it by failing to give the inner attraction sufficient support in my daily life. Having expressed my assent by committing myself to some "state or course of action" I may forget that the attraction still needs some purification. Elements of the need for security, flight from guilt or whatever other false motives may have been involved are still present. They are weaknesses in the structure. If not checked, they will grow and eventually become the predominant motive behind the life I am living. Ahab should have asked himself a decade before his death "Is this what I really want to make of my life? Do I want to allow whaling to become such an obsession with me that it drives me out to sea the day after my marriage? Is it becoming the only value in my life?" The loss of his arm might have been seen as another warning that should have made him stop and think. But perhaps both warnings came too late. Maybe the "wrestling" with the powers of nature had already become an "assault" on the powers of nature, an attempt to overcome and destroy any power greater than himself. [66]

When a vocational attraction is first encountered, some effort and sacrifice may be needed but generally the process takes place fairly gracefully and spontaneously. I become habituated to the attraction and the ways in which I express my assent and we grow together hand in hand. It is so natural to me; it is as if it were always there just waiting to be found. It is taken for granted as "mine" just like my home was taken for granted as "mine".

---

[66] "Destroy" may seem too strong a word to use in this context. On the other hand, most of our conquests have something of the flavor of destruction about them. If I don't destroy the other physically I at least destroy him as threat, as challenge or as enemy. There is a different way of seeing things. Huston Smith in The Religions of Man (New York: Harper and Row, 1956), p. 209, gives an example. We commonly described the scaling of Mt. Everest as the "conquest" of the mountain. An Oriental writer says, "We would put the matter differently, we would speak of 'the befriending of Everest'." Wrestling with nature can be an attempt to "know it," "experience it" rather than to conquer or overcome it. It is the struggle, not the final score that really matters.

Trying to rediscover a lost vocation is quite different. In many cases it may be nearly impossible to do so. Repentence cannot buy it back; nothing can buy it back. The spontaneous affinity in the depths of my being is no longer there. My "innards" are aimed in some other direction now. My feelings, emotions, intuitions and interests do not fall into line behind my conscious desires quite so readily. As I seek consciously to rekindle the attraction, much in me may resist. My self-image has changed, my values have been rearranged in relation to one another, different meanings have come into my life, different behavior has been reinforced. It will be a very arduous task even to dispose myself for the resurgence of the "gift." Even then there is assurance that it will be given again. To serve a vocation, to nourish it with my substance, to become one with it as H.H. saw his image flowing into Leo's and nourishing it, is not something I can bring about by reason, decision and effort. Many things must simply "happen" and I must collaborate wholeheartedly in the "happening."

In considering the various elements that go into the composition of a vocational experience I have tried to focus on one aspect at a time. But vocational experience is not the sum of these aspects. There is always some mysterious, indefinable unifying principle that holds it all together. But this unifying principle is not the vocation either. The vocation is the whole works, the unified elements lived out concretely by a human person. It is like the human body. The body is not just the ensemble of organs, bones, muscles, etc. Nor is it the life principle. It is both, united in a dynamic oneness. Some organs can be damaged or removed and it is still a body. But at a certain point the material elements can no longer support life and it ceases to be a human body. It becomes a corpse. Who can say at what moment life has ceased? Who can say at what moment a vocation has come into being or been lost?

One final example will be given in hopes of avoiding the myopic view that usually results when elements of an organic whole are considered individually.

Francis Bitter
"Transference"

In his book on magnets, Francis Bitter tells a little about his childhood and how he came to be a physicist. [67] The children in his family used to play a game called "lost child". One of the children would pretend to be lost, destitute and deserted. The others would "adopt" him or her. The "new" member of the family would be taken around by the others and "introduced" to their friends, shown the city, shown how to use elevators and how to play various games. This whole game might go on for several days and be played several times a year.

In looking back on this childhood game, Bitter sees a possible connection between it and his future career as a physicist:

It seems to me now that this may well have been an appropriate exercise for a future scientist. Scientific investigations are started and discoveries are made as the result of a repeated review of well-known facts, attempts to rearrange them, to see them from a new point of view that will excite new interest and reveal new possibilities. And this is just what we were doing in our children's world.

---

[67] Francis Bitter, <u>Magnets: The Education of a Physicist</u> (Garden City, N.Y.: Doubleday Anchor Books, 1979), p. 20.

Reflection

In my subtitle I used the word "transference" to refer to Bitter's contribution. What I have in mind is the "transference" of a pattern of behavior, a pattern of thinking, or a unifying principle from one situation to a quite different situation. Bitter recognizes his game as an appropriate exercise. It may also be that he found the repeated review of facts, the rearranging them, the search for new points of view to be a personally fulfilling exercise. It allowed for the use of his talents, developed new abilities, and deepened his relationship with the world around him, making him feel more "at home" in that world. If that were the case, it is not surprising that he should, without being the least bit aware of it, be attracted to a career in which that same pattern of behavior will be appropriate.

While we reject B.F. Skinner's theoretical position that man is completely determined by his past conditioning, we readily admit that man doesn't "start from scratch" at each moment. Each new experience is understood largely in terms of past experience. I transcend that past experience by only a small increment at a time. [68]

---

[68] Harry Stack Sullivan, a psychoanalyst, states it is as axiomatic that we don't experience things that have no precedent – except very, very slowly. H.S. Sullivan, Collected Works, Vol II (N.Y.: W.W. Norton & Co., 1965), p. 69.
Alfred Schutz gives one reason why this may be so: "Only the already experienced is meaningful, not that which is being experienced. For meaning is merely an operation of intentionality, which, however, only becomes visible to the reflective glance. From the point of view of passing experience, the prediction of meaning is necessarily trivial, since meaning here can only be understood as the attentive gaze directed not at passing, but at already passed experiences." Helmut R. Wagner, ed. Alfred Schutz on Phenomenology and Social Relations (Chicago: The University of Chicago Press, 1970), pp. 63-64.

My cumulative past constitutes the present out of which my future will flow. But I am always present there overseeing the process, always taking a stand towards it. I am always, at least implicitly, accepting or rejecting, approving or disapproving, identifying with or dissociating myself from the spontaneous movements of my being. [69]

When I "transfer" a pattern of behavior from my past onto my present situation, some alterations are always called for. When such a "transference" is, in part, responsible for a vocational attraction, the needed alterations should become visible as I express my assent to the attraction. If attentive, I may notice that the commonly recognized expressions do not quite fit my attraction or my personality. Or I may see that the expression that comes most spontaneously to me does not relate harmoniously to the situation in which I find myself. The "transference" has given me a big boost in what may be the right general direction but I am responsible for working out a good many kinks and details.

I have put the word "transference" in inverted commas to avoid a premature identification of it with the concept of transference as found in psychoanalysis. Greenson defines transference, in the psychoanalytic sense, as follows:

---

[69] The psychologist Nathaniel Branden points out that thinking and feeling (or reason and emotion) are not to be seen as antagonistic to one another. They perform radically different functions which are not interchangeable. Either they function in harmony or both functions are sabotaged. Nathaniel Branden, The Disowned Self (Los Angeles: Nash Publishing, 1971), pp. 185-186.

Transference is the experience of feelings, drives, attitudes, fantasies, and defenses toward a person in the present which do not befit that person but are a repetition of reactions originating in regard to significant persons of early childhood, unconsciously displaced onto figures in the present. [70]

For Greenson, transference is always appropriate. What he seems to mean is that it is only <u>transference</u> in the psychoanalytic sense to the extent that is inappropriate, that it "does not befit that person." But such transference cannot <u>be</u> <u>wholly</u> inappropriate or it would not happen at all. There is <u>some</u> resemblance between the person to whom I am reacting now and the significant person in my past. It is when superficial aspect of the present person evokes a very strong and all-embracing reaction terms of the past that I am in real trouble. It will then be difficult to convert my reactions into consciously affirmed responses.

Something similar may happen in the "transference" aspect of my vocational attraction. If, in my case, I saw a monastic life in terms of my childhood experience of having to "lay low," to keep out of sight and be quiet in order to be able to live "safely" and without always getting blamed for something. I may be in for a few surprises. I may find that the pattern of behavior is not always appropriate. I will reflect on the situation: "Why isn't laying low appropriate now?" It was okay yesterday. Why do I want to lay low when it doesn't make sense?" Being honest with myself about these questions I will come to know myself and monastic life better.

---

[70] Ralph R. Greenson, The Technique and Practice of Psychoanalysis, Vol. I (International University Press, 1967), p.171. A thorough treatment of the concept of transference is given in this book on pp. 151-356.

I may correct my inappropriate reactions and become more responsive to the real situation. Or I may decide that I had misread the meaning of monastic life in terms of my own needs and conclude that I do not really have the <u>makings</u> of a monastic vocation. This is not to lose a vocation, it is to decide that my personality with its past and present elements do not provide the warmth and nourishment in which such an attraction can reasonably be expected to develop into a vocation.

<u>Conclusion and Transition</u>

In the first division, vocation has been treated as a phenomenon that may occur in the life of universal man. It was seen to develop through a cyclic process of attraction, assent and expression. The attraction and the expression were studied under the aspects of the subject-pole and the object-pole. The dynamic relation between these two poles was described, as well as some of the problems that can arise. The assent I give to the attraction was treated in a more linear fashion in terms of initial wishing, distorted willing, true willing and promise or commitment.

A final note pointed out how a person learns to respond to that which is new by applying patterns of behavior with which he is already familiar and then making adjustments. Man not only can, but must, reach forth to new experiences and new meanings. He must always search for more. Known reality is always in some way symbolic of an unknown reality and that new reality will be known in terms of its symbol.

This is true of the religious sphere. Man's knowledge of God first comes in terms of his knowledge of himself, nature and other men. But it is not limited to that.

It goes beyond these symbols while being based on them. The religious experience of man, his sense of being in the presence of the Holy, the Sacred, the Beyond, will have an influence of his vocational experience.

The influence of the religious dimension of man's life, bracketed in the first division of this book, will now be taken into account. The possibility of a unifying meaning prior to and beyond the visible world throws the object-pole of the experience into a new context and provides answers to the questions "Who is calling?" and "Who gives the gift?" Belief in such a unifying meaning also produces changes in the subject-pole of the experience relativizing his relationship with the material, visible world and endowing it with new meanings. It also reshapes his understanding of himself and his role in the world.

DIVISION II

UNIVERSAL RELIGIOUS MAN'S

EXPERIENCE OF BEING CALLED

INTRODUCTION

In the first division we considered the experience of being called as it might occur in the life of universal man. No provision was made for the possible implications of religious faith. The gap will be filled in the present division which will study the religious vocation of religious man. It will deal with religious vocation – vocation in which religious significance of the object-pole is the decisive element. Further, it will deal with the experience of religious man, that is, man insofar as he is already engaged in the service or worship of God or the supernatural.

The word "religious", when used as an adjective, is defined as "relating to or manifesting faithful devotion to an acknowledged ultimate reality or deity."[71] In this sense we can speak of a religious man or of religious beliefs. The introduction of belief in an ultimate reality or deity into the world of man is not just the addition of a new element which is then placed in juxtaposition to the rest. It is the addition of a new dimension which qualifies and transforms all other elements.

---

[71] <u>Webster's New Collegiate Dictionary</u> (Springfield, Mass.: G. & C. Merriam Co., 1975).

This is particularly evident in the attitude of primitive man for whom only "sacred" space - space that was associated with some manifestation of the divine - had any reality. All other space was "formless expanse." [72] A similar religious context made time meaningful. Sacred time was essentially different from profane temporal duration. There was a break in duration in which a primordial mythical time was made present. According to Eliade, primitive man passed from mere temporal duration into sacred time by means of ritual. Mere temporal duration was not, and could not be, made sacred. It could only be replaced by sacred time.

In the modern man's attitude things are somewhat different. He lives in a world of profane - non sacred - things. Only very few objects are considered to have sacred quality about them and they are usually man-made objects used in religious ritual. The sun, moon and stars, a tree or boulder may remind one of the divine beauty or immensity but they are not seen as sacred. They are not, for us, hierophanies - manifestations of the divine - let alone gods. Our concept of the divine is more removed from material connotations. God may be seen as a supreme

---

[72] Mircea Eliade, The Sacred and the Profane (New York: Harcourt, Brace and Company, 1959), p. 20. Eliade tells of an Australian tribe which possessed a sacred pole fashioned for them by a divine being. The pole was, for them, a cosmic axis and the area around it became "their world". In one instance the pole was broken "the entire clan were in consternation; they wondered about aimlessly for a time, and finally lay down on the ground together and waited for death to overtake them." [Eliade, p. 33] With the loss of their pole there was no more possibility of a meaningful world.

being, a personal divinity who created all that is. Another description might be "the Unknowable," which remains untouched by any human concept. Finally, no particular divinity may be specified. In some disciplines the concept of a divinity is replaced by an ultimate state of inner integration or union with all things.

This does not mean that a modern man is necessarily less religious than his primitive ancestors. It does indicate a different understanding of the object-pole of the religious experience. This difference is important for the question of vocation. How man conceives the objective referent of his religious belief will influence his understanding of the meaning of his own life and his role in the world. It will add new dimensions to the call he experiences and affect the way he expresses his response.

There are a number of points of view from which we could study religious vocation. First, we might consider the call of man from a state of non-belief to the acceptance of religious faith. The beginnings and development of religious faith will be discussed briefly but these are not the main focus of this division.

Another possible approach might be the study of the universal call to holiness. This approach would focus on the call to the believer to make his religious faith the center and foundation of his life, to grow in the love of God. Such a call is presupposed in this division but is not the main concern. A third possibility would be to study the call to a particular religion such a Buddhism or Judeism.

Finally, there is the call to a member of a particular religion to express his religious ideals in some specific way. It is this approach to religious vocation that will be taken in the present division. It is possible that one can express his religious ideals in any number of ways. We will be concerned with expressions that are themselves of a specifically religious nature. A man may live a deeply religious life and bring his religious ideals to expression in his marriage, his work, his relaxation and in all that he does. But these means of expression are not specifically religious in nature. Even caring for the sick and the poor need not be specifically religious actions though they may express a deep religious faith.

Two expressions that are specifically religious are preaching and ritual. These two actions make little sense apart from religious context.[73] Preaching is primarily expression by means of the spoken word, ritual is expression by action. For the sake of highlighting the religious element in this division we will look at some examples of religious vocation from the Old Testament, especially the prophets. A prophet such as Jeremiah is not an everyday occurrence, to say the least. In using him as an example, I do not mean to imply that religious vocation must be extraordinary. But in his life the religious dimension of the vocational experience stands out most clearly. Judges and Kings might also have been used but in their cases there seems often to be a strong admixture of military and political

---

[73] Some forms of ritual have been secularized over a period of time. Dancing might be an example. To the extent that it has been deprived of a religious context and content, it is questionable whether it should still be called a ritual.

motivation. The presence of these motives does not exclude the possibility of the religious vocation but makes it harder to demonstrate.

It is not presupposed in this division that all religious men and women are called to some particular state or course of action which specifically expresses their religious ideals. Nor is it to be thought that one who experiences such a call is necessarily more deeply religious or holier than one who does not. There can, however, be an attraction to express my religious ideals in some particular manner. It is with such attraction and its expression that this division is concerned.

In this division the specifically religious elements of vocational attraction and expression will be studied. The two chapters will be parallel to the first and third chapters of Division I. The second chapter of Division I dealt with the assent which a person gives to the vocational attraction he experiences. With the introduction of the religious dimension in the assent of the subject is still necessary for vocational development. This assent does not, however, seem to be essentially different from the human assent described in Division I. The quality of the assent may well be affected by the introduction of the religious dimension into the subject and object poles of the experience but the assent itself will not be explicitly treated.

CHAPTER IV

I AM ATTRACTED BY THE POSSIBILTY

OF REALIZING MY RELIGIOUS VALUES

When I experience myself in relation to God I am still very much the same person with the same potentialities and limitations. But I am involved in a new relationship. If it is truly a living relationship it places me in an entirely new frame of reference. My work, my friends, my joys and sorrows still have the meaning they had before. But a new meaning now grows out of the original meaning. All these things can be brought into the service of God. The situation might be compared with that of a young man who marries. His work and his friends do not really change. They fit into the new relationship. The friends are now also his wife's friends. His work is now her support as well as his. The new relationship infuses an added meaning into his whole world. In like manner, my relationship to God brings a new and deeper dimension to everything within my experience.

When I am attracted by the possibility of realizing my religious values I am most sensitive to this deeper meaning of the world. I am looking at the world with eyes that are open to its religious meanings. I have faith in those meanings and they are very important to me. The subject who is attracted brings his religious faith and outlook to the experience of being called.

132

As we saw in the first division, the attraction also has an objective – I am attracted to some state or course of action. I am attracted to it because it offers the opportunity of realizing my religious values. This attraction is an articulation and expansion of my attraction to God.

This chapter will deal with the attraction of religious man to a specifically religious vocation. It will consider the influence of the religious dimension on the subject of the experience and the ways in which this same dimension qualifies and transforms the objective state or course of action to which he is attracted.

I: THE SUBJECT-POLE

G.B. Montini [74]
Man's Religious Sense

Montini approaches the religious situation of modern man from the point of view of his pastoral experience rather than from any theoretical considerations. From this experience he concludes that modern man "is in the process of losing his religious sense." [p. 6]

Religious sense, Montini points out, is not a very precise term; it precedes human reasoning and refers to a natural religious movement in human nature itself. It is, Montini's words, "natural human aptitude to perceive that we have some

---

[74] The material in this section is taken from Giovanni Battista Montini, Man's Religious Sense (Westminister, MD.: The Newman Press, 1961). This booklet is a reprint of a pastoral letter written in 1957 to the diocese of Milan before Cardinal Montini was elected to the papacy and assumed the name of Paul VI. All references to the work will be followed by the appropriate page numbers in brackets.

relation to God." [p. 9] he speaks of perception, not imagination, since religious presupposes, for him, a real extramental referent. He rejects an "immanentist" explanation which would see religious sense as,

> ...something welling up from the subconscious, a sort of need for God that creates its own end and, becoming thus a conscious thing and combining with certain historical and sensible facts, finally emerges as religious faith. [p. 9]

It is through his religious sense that man first recognizes that he stands in a relationship with God. When that sense becomes active and aware of its own perceptions it is more aptly called religious feeling.

Karl Adam [75]
Religious Feeling

Adam begins where Montini leaves off. He states that the human mind has a natural disposition towards the experience of what is Holy so that "whenever it comes upon a genuine instance of holiness, it is permanently bound to it with absolute certainty." [p. 115] This feeling is quite different than that evoked by subjective values. It is the experience of something different, something radically new and outside my control. "The word 'mysterious' clearly expresses the content of this emotional experience." [p. 115]

---

[75] The material in this section is taken from Karl Adam, The Christ of Faith (New York: New American Library, 1962). All references to this work will be followed by the appropriate page numbers in brackets.

This "mystery" is not just something I do not understand; it is something which, in its essence, belongs to another realm. It is something I can never fully understand. Adam calls it a "mysterium tremendum – i.e., our first impression of it causes us to shrink away from it." [p. 115, italics in the original] The fear it instills is not fright or terror but awe and amazement at the ineffable.

This same power which instills fear into the heart of man also exerts a powerful attraction on him. He is both fearful and fascinated at the same time by that which he unerringly recognizes as genuinely holy.

> The human spirit is a priori possessed of the faculty of discerning the peculiarities of holiness wherever it is genuine and true – not when it occurs in distorted form, as in the appearance of ghosts, but when in fact it works upon us, repelling us and attracting us as the mysterium tremendum et fascinosum, thus establishing itself as a genuine manifestation of holiness. [p. 116, italics in the original]

Reflection

In my description of my vocational experiences there was no mention of the influence of the religious element. I spoke of the attempt to implement my concept of myself as one who was not interested in the status-seeking of middle class life, one who preferred a simple life of labor. But that idea of oneself was seen against an implicit background of creaturehood. However real the elements in the world around me might be, they did not contain, in themselves, the whole of their meaning. They had to be seen in relation to all else. The same was true of myself. If I am a creature I must be seen in relation to a creator and to all other created things and persons. A state or course of action that offers the opportunity to implement my concept of myself as a religious man will have a deeper, stronger power of attraction than one that does not offer such a chance. In the latter case, even if I could find adequate psychological and social fulfillment, there would always be the gnawing realization that something essential was being left out. There would be no <u>real</u> meaning to hold all the partial meanings together.

Adam's comments on the unerring capacity of man to perceive genuine holiness are reminiscent of von Hildebrand's treatment of the call of values. Man's perception in such matters cannot reduce to any fundamental laws of psychology or logic. It is the result of an innate capacity.

That vocational attraction is experienced as a "call" takes on a new meaning in the light of the "<u>tremendum</u>" aspect of religious experience. The attraction is experienced as having its source in the tremendous mystery which confronts me. I experience the attraction in terms of my interests and values, the possibilities available, and so on. But I also realize that these things cannot totally explain the attraction and, especially, the sense of obligation I feel to respond to it. It is not so much the task or life to which I feel attracted that I fear; it is the responsibility of answering to such immense power so unfathomable and beyond my control. Fortunately, at this stage I usually do not really understand all the implications. In my own experience something of the awe and wonder was evident in my attitude to the letter I received from the monastery. I stood holding the letter in my hand trying to realize that it had come from a monastery and had been written by a real live monk. It made the monastery more concrete for me but at the same time it linked me up more closely with the holiness embodied in it.

Something of the fascination seems also to have been present in my experience. From the time of my first contact with monastic life through the reading of a novel I was "hooked" on the idea. Even though I did little to follow up on the initial attraction the fascination remained and was easily aroused a few years later. A fascination that was based only on psychological needs would not have lain dormant so long.

Even the security and escape from guilt that I sought in monastic life may not have been altogether free from the influence of the religious dimension. Being human is a very insecure business. Our grasp on peace, happiness, even on life itself, is very tenuous. But the many little things that threaten my job, my comfort, my livelihood, my health and my life are not the most basic problem. They are only reflections of the vast, uncontrollable mystery against which my creatureliness stands out in all it vulnerability and frailty. My vague, implicit feelings of littleness and helplessness are "transferred" and brought into focus; they are contextualized in relation to a particular situation or event.[76]

---

[76] This is similar to Eliade's description of hierophanies – manifestations of the sacred. "By manifesting the sacred, any object becomes something else, yet it continues to remain itself for it continues to participate in its surrounding cosmic milieu. A sacred stone remains a stone; ..." [Eliade, p.12, italics in the original]

If it is realistic to look for a little dross in the purest of motives and intentions, it seems no less realistic to consider the possibility of a "silver lining" behind our least edifying attitudes and feelings.

Religious sense, religious feelings and religious faith are not static entities. They should, with time and effort, grow in strength and clarity. They should become the underlying, all-pervading meaning which gives our experiences, including the vocational experience, a meaningful place in life.

H.C. Rumke [77]
The Growth of Belief

Rumke, a Dutch psychotherapist, studies the question of growth of religious belief. His basic thesis is that unbelief is an interruption in development. [p. 13] The development of religious faith is seen to result from direct religious experience. [78] This experience consists of a series of structures or dispositions which follow one another. [79] In the first three stages I feel myself "meaningfully" linked

---

[77] The material in this section is taken from H.C. Rumke, The Psychology of Unbelief (New York: Sheed and Ward, 1962). All references to this work will be followed by the appropriate page numbers in brackets.

[78] Rumke adds a note of caution: "The principle that belief may arise from thought and will power is not denied. But I can only state that I have never observed it. What seems to be more evident is that 'thought' and 'will power' play an important part in transforming the experience and in giving to religion its place in life." [p. 17]

[79] Rumke lists the seven stages on page 17 as follows:
First stage: Feeling oneself meaningfully linked up with the whole of being.
Second Stage: The whole of being is felt as the primary cause of all being.

up with the whole of being" which is then felt as "primary cause of all being" and, finally, as the cause of my being. [p. 17] These three stages constitute the fundamental basis of religiousness according to Rumke. Belief really begins in the fourth stage in which it is recognized that the primary cause is God. Thus far Rumke has covered about the same ground as Montini and Adam.

In Rumke's fifth stage "the urge is felt for obedience to and responsibility for guilt towards God, the primary cause. God demands complete surrender." [p. 17] No explanation is given of "why" this happens. Such an explanation would be contrary to his acceptance of "religious instinct" or "intuition" [p. 12] and his conclusion that belief is "irreducible." [p. 20] He sees belief as "something which accompanies us in our development and maturity and... the various forms through which belief passes constitute development." [pp. 12-13]

Third stage: This primary cause is realized as cause of my being.
Fourth stage: The primary cause is God.
Fifth stage: The urge is felt for obedience to and responsibility for guilt towards God, the primary cause. God demands complete surrender.
Sixth stage: The approach to an attitude of surrender. The demand is considered urgent, but gives no clear sense of direction.
Seventh stage: This demand and surrender to it become fundamental rule of life.

Rumke takes strong exception to the Freudian and Post-Freudian psychologist who sees psychological factors as the source of religious feeling and belief.[80] Rumke does not deny that there are many cases in which "God" is merely the projection of a person's infantile need to be sheltered in loving protection. [pp. 42-44] But this is pseudo-religion and would fade away with a successful psychoanalysis.

> If to us God is a projection, we stand in front of this father-image in a childish attitude with childish demands and expectations. We may express this also as follows: the link which holds us to our father or mother, instead of promoting, truly hampers our belief.
> My experience in many cases of psychoanalysis has taught me that the road to belief is thrown wide open when all childish fixations have been abandoned. [p. 45]

Infantile needs are seen by Rumke as an obstacle to religious belief rather than its cause. He mentions the real possibility that a primary religious experience may be "clothed in the images of childhood." [p. 44] He feels a more acceptable solution to the question of the relationship between the God-image and the

---

[80] In spite of his reputation for being anti-religious, Freud seems to have maintained a healthy skepticism about the reliability of his conclusions concerning the question of religion. In answer to the suggestion of Romain Rolland that religion has its origin in an "oceanic feeling," a feeling of something limitless or boundless, Freud replies: "From my own experience I could not convince myself of the primary nature of such a feeling. But this gives me no right to deny that it does in fact occur in other people." Civilization and its Discontents (New York: W.W. Norton, 1961), pp. 11-12. Elsewhere he comments, "There are no grounds for fearing that psychoanalysis...., will be tempted to trace the origin of anything so complicated as religion to a single source. If psychoanalysis is compelled...to lay all the emphasis upon one particular source, that does not mean it is claiming either that that source is the only one or that it occupies first place among the numerous contributory factors." Totem and Taboo (New York: W.W. Norton, 1950), p. 100. He does, of course, still consider childhood experiences to be part of the source of religious feeling rather than an influence on religious feeling.

father-image reverses the approach of Freudian psychology. Rumke, quoting Binswanger, states:

> The bond which binds the child to the father is neither the example nor the starting-point of the God-father thought, but the reverse. The fact that the child is receptive to the child-father idea is the result of the typically ideal existence of the child-father idea born of our relation to God. [pp. 45-46]

The child's understanding of its father is based on an implicit intuition of God. As the concept of God becomes more explicit, it may become "clothed in the images of childhood." [p. 44] But it is not <u>composed</u> of the images of childhood. In Rumke's experience, the abandonment of childish fixations opens the door to the development and growth of genuine religious belief. The father image, then, may distort the idea of God or interfere with its growth, but the idea itself cannot be reduced to parent-child relations.

In Rumke's sixth stage the demand for obedience to God become stronger and more urgent though there is no clear sense of direction. Such surrender necessarily involves an experience of risk but "if we dare not take any risk, we run a greater risk from all sides by heading straight for complete sterility." [p. 74]

In the final stage demand and surrender become fundamental rules of life. One of the unavoidable characteristics of this stage is the demand of unlimited publicity. [p. 79] I must be willing to bear public witness to my religious beliefs. Religious faith cannot be a private chamber to which I retire for consolation or security.

Throughout his book, Rumke insists that genuine religious belief is an irreducible and normal aspect of growth and its <u>unbelief</u> that is to be explained by psychological abnormalities or refusal to undergo the maturing process.

Reflections

In a sense, Rumke seems to be telling me "Stop trying to figure out why people experience themselves as being called by God and try figuring out why they don't experience it!" In my own defense I would respond that I didn't really claim that I was going to "explain" the phenomenon of vocation fully. Rumke speaks of religious belief as being an irreducible aspect of growth.

Vocational experience, however, does not seem to be irreducible or a necessary aspect of growth. Some experience a vocational attraction, some do not. Vocational experience cannot be completely reduced to psychological and sociological factors. But it does seem possible to point out some such factors which do contribute to the constitution of the vocational experience.

Rumke mentions that the urgent demand for surrender to God that I experience gives no clear sense of direction. In the vocational experience the sense of direction is relatively clear; I am attracted to a particular state or course of action. If the concept of God may become clothed in the image of childhood it seems equally probable that the idea of serving God may become clothed in a garment of my talents, needs and potentialities. Since man is not a pure spirit, this would seem to me to be a fairly normal thing.

The original attraction is not the whole of vocation. I must give my assent to that attraction and express my assent in my decisions and actions. At times I may have to choose between serving God or finding satisfaction in fulfilling my own needs. For example, I may be shy by nature. When a situation requires that I express my religious beliefs publicly I might refrain from doing so in order to avoid the discomfort and embarrassment I would experience. Such failures are not uncommon. The important question then becomes: how do I respond to this infidelity? I may decide to lower my standards to a more comfortable level. Or I may "sweep my failure under the carpet," rationalizing it or simply distracting myself with other matters until the twinges of conscience die down.

There is, fortunately, another possibility. I may bring the decision into focus and ask myself: What does this say about my real desires? It seems to say that in this particular situation there was something more important to me than serving God. This particular situation may never occur again but that does not solve the problem. The problem is in my desires. My desires must be brought into order. They need not be "killed" but they must be disciplined – made disciples. How does this happen?

One way of viewing the matter is to see it the way Rumke sees the relationship between belief and a childish fixation. When the fixation is abandoned the road to belief is thrown wide open. If there is a genuinely religious core to my vocational attraction perhaps it only needs an "open road" in order to grow. I may only need to remove the obstacles. I must do at least that.

I mentioned that part of the attraction I felt for monastic life was probably due to the security it offered. But if the religious element in the vocation is to grow the desire for security and the fear of insecurity must fade out somehow. I must become indifferent, insofar as I can, to my security. The solution lies not in discovering a source of security but in accepting the inevitable insecurity which is so much a part of human existence. Only then am I free to follow my religious intuition when it inspires me in the direction of unfamiliar activities or new levels of self knowledge. Paul Ricoeur, in speaking of psychoanalysis as a reeducation of desire, says:

> Only desire that has accepted its own death can freely dispose of things... Only desire that has passed through what Freud calls resignation, i.e., the ability to endure the harshness of life...is capable of freely using things, people, and the benefits of civilization and culture.[81]

The death of parasitic desires is not an end in itself. They have to die that the one desire might live with increased vitality. But the one desire, the desire to surrender in obedience to the demands of God, is not for its own sake. It is not a matter of having "the right desire" in order to be "the perfect person." The objective towards which the desire is directed is the ultimate end. The God whom I am attracted to serve and who is felt to be doing the calling must be considered. The God who calls and the particular state or course of action to which I am called forms the object-pole of the religious experience of vocational attraction. In the following section the emphasis will be on the way in which the various religions understand God. The state or course of action to which I may feel called will be studied more extensively in the next chapter when we discuss vocational expression.

---

[81] Paul Ricoeur, The Conflict of Interpretations (Evanston, Ill.: Northwestern University Press, 1974), p. 194.

II. THE OBJECT-POLE

Huston Smith [82]
Concepts of God

When we speak of the differences among the various religions we usually have three differences in mind. First, we may be thinking of the concept of God and how it varies among the different faiths. Secondly, we may be interested in the history of God's dealings with men. Finally we might be thinking about the various ways in which man goes about serving or worshipping God. Logically, it would seem that the latter two questions would depend on the first. We decide who or what God is; then we can tell what historical events bear the mark of his influence and what we have to do to earn his favor and protection.

It would probably be more accurate to say the opposite: man has a religious experience in the context of some particular event or action and his concept of God arises from that experience. To the extent that this is true, there should be a good bit of common ground among the various concepts of God. A brief glance at some of these concepts will indicate that there are many common aspects.

Beginning with Hinduism, Huston Smith gives a brief outline of several of the leading religions. The following is only a very sketchy presentation of some of the key ideas which he points out in relation to the concept of God.

---

[82] The material in this section is taken from Huston Smith, The Religions of Man (New York: Harper and Row, 1958). All references to this work will be followed by the appropriate page numbers in brackets.

In discussing Hinduism, Smith gives little attention to the polytheistic aspect [83] with which it is so commonly associated. He quotes Shankara, an eighth century Hindu philosopher, who began a prayer with the address, "Oh Thou, before whom all words recoil." [p. 71] Human words shrink back from the attempt to communicate the being of the supreme reality. Neither the words nor the mind of man can adequately express it.

Man's mind has been evolved to facilitate his survival in this natural world. It is adapted to deal with finite objects. God, on the contrary, is infinite and of a completely different order from what our minds can grasp. To expect man to corner the infinite with his finite mind is like asking a dog to understand Einstein's equation with his nose. [pp. 71-72]

Nonetheless, man must try. "The name the Hindus give to the supreme reality is Brahman, from the root brih meaning 'to be great.'" [p. 72, italics in the original] Words can only aim man's thoughts in the right direction, they can never really bring him knowledge of Brahman. His three chief attributes are being, awareness and bliss. When applied to God these words mean something utterly different than what our human comprehension can grasp. Yet they point in the right direction. They are more applicable than their opposites. "Utter reality, utterly

[83] A more ample treatment of this aspect of Hinduism can be found in Robert S. Ellwood, Many Peoples, Many Faiths (Englewood Cliffs, N.J.: Prentice-Hall, Inc., 1976), pp. 91-99. John A. Hardon mentions the belief of the ordinary Hindu in three hundred and thirty three million male and female gods. John A. Hardon, Religions of the World (Westminister, MD.: Newman Press, 1963), p. 55. Part of the difficulty seems to lie as a multiplicity of individual gods or as aspects of one supreme divinity. Smith emphasizes the latter.

conscious, and utterly beyond all possibility of frustration, this is the basic Hindu view of God." [p. 72] Some schools of Hindu thought hold that God is personal, some that he is impersonal. Ramakrishna states that both schools are equally correct. That this statement happens to contain a logical contradiction is not really very important since God is beyond the laws of human logic.

The flexibility of Hinduism is even more evident in Gandhi's statement as quoted by Hardon:

> If I were to define the Hindu creed, wrote Mahatma Gandhi, I would simply say, a search after truth through non-violent means. A man may not believe in God and still call himself a Hindu. Hinduism is a relentless pursuit after the truth. Denial of God we have known, denial of truth we have not known. [Hardon, p. 41]

The question whether there must be a God or gods in order for there to be a religion comes up again in regard to Buddhism. Here we do not speak of serving or worshipping God, but of attaining Nirvana. Nirvana, meaning "to bow out" [84] or "to extinguish," refers to a state in which the "boundary of the finite self" is extinguished. [p. 125] This boundary is extinguished when man is released from the bonds of private desire.

---

[84] Smith's "bow out" may well be a typographical error for "blow out" which is the translation used by Ellwood. [Ellwood, p. 113] "To blow out" would also be parallel to, and synonymous with, "to extinguish." However, Smith states that the terms are not to be understood transitively but in the sense in which a fire ceases to draw or the fuel supply is exhausted. The fire is not extinguishes (by someone); it simply "goes out." Smart seems to express what Smith has in mind: "...the term 'nirvana,' which literally means 'cooling off' or 'going out.' As of a flame." Ninian Smart, <u>The Religious Experience of Mankind</u> (New York: Charles Scribner's Sons, 1968), p. 81. The apparently erroneous "bow out" may be closer to Smith's meaning than "blow out." The appetites and desires which enslave a man "bow out" of the picture.

Negativity Nirvana is the state in which the faggots of private desire have been completely consumed and everything that restricts the boundless life has died. Affirmatively it is that boundless life itself. [p. 125]

Is Nirvana God? Not if God is understood as "a personal being who created the universe by a deliberate act of will." [p. 126] Smith sees the possibility of considering Nirvana to be God in the sense of "Godhead." This appears to mean that most of the attributes that are proper to the concept of God can also be attributed to Nirvana. Quoting Edward Conze, Smith states that Nirvana is:

permanent, stable, imperishable, immovable, ageless, deathless, unborn, and unbecome...the real Truth and the supreme Reality;.....the Good, the supreme goal and the one and only consummation of our life, the eternal, hidden and incomprehensible Peace. [p. 127]

It is not explicitly stated that Nirvana existed prior to its being attained by any man. The implication of words like "ageless," "eternal," unborn" seems to indicate that it did.

Turning to Confucianism, Smith asks whether it is a religion or an ethical system. Confucianism is "a way of life woven around a people's ultimate concerns," and is based on a concern "to align man to the transhuman ground of his existence." [p. 188] The emphasis on sacrifice, augury and ancestor worship was abandoned in favor of emphasis on the obligations arising from the conditions of everyday life. But to abandon the emphasis on the transhuman is not to abandon belief in it. Confucius recognized a "cosmic demand" for the spread of righteousness and that the "will of Heaven" should be feared by a gentleman before all else.[85] [p. 191] He seems to have thought that we should concern ourselves with the world of which we have some knowledge and experience while admitting our limited knowledge of other worlds but not denying their existence.

Where Confucianism praises social responsibility and moral uprightness, Taoism "sings the glories of spontaneity and naturalness." [p. 214] The central concept of Taoism is the Tao, the way or path. The Tao can be understood in three senses. First, it is "ineffable and transcendent,...the ground of all existence." Second, it is "the way of the universe; the norm, the rhythm, the driving power in all nature, the ordering principle behind all life." [p. 199, italics in the original] Finally, there is a third understanding: Tao refers to "the way man should order his life to gear in with the way the universe operates." [p. 200, in italics in the original]

In the first sense the Tao seems to posses many of the attributes of divinity. It exceeds all thought and imagination. "If it were to reveal itself in all its sharpness, fullness, and glory, mortal man would not be able to bear the vision." [p. 199] Unlike Nirvana, the Tao is the source of all things.

---

[85] A number of ambiguities arise at this point which may result from variations in translation, different interpretations or progression of thought. Whether Confucius discussed the "will of Heaven," what the term meant, how it relates to "the Ways" is discussed briefly in Arthur Waley, trans., The Analects of Confucius (New York: Random House, 1938), pp. 30-33, 41-43. Smith may be oversimplifying for the sake of brevity. I certainly am.

The myriad creatures rise from it yet it claims no authority:
It gives them life yet claims no possession;
It benefits them yet exacts no gratitude;
It accomplishes its task yet lays claim to no merit.
It is because it lays claim to no merit
that its merit never deserts it. [86]

In spite of its being the source and benign custodian of all things, the Tao is not personalized. The "humility" of the Tao expressed in the above quotation makes it difficult for most of us to identify the Tao with God. We might, at best, say that it represents one aspect of our concept of God.

<u>Reflection</u>

What are we to make of all this? Can all the views be integrated into a single concept or must some of them be discarded as inaccurate? Some religious figures have said that it does not matter whether you believe in God or not, whether you believe in one God or many, or whether God is personal or impersonal. While there are, many elements in common among the religions, there are some striking differences. [87]

---

[86] D.C. Lau, trans., <u>Tao Te Ching</u> (Baltimore, MD.: Penguin Books, Inc., 1963), p. 58.

[87] Bernard Lonergan, in <u>Method in Theology</u> (New York: Herder and Herder, 1972), refers to the similarities among the major religions. Quoting Heiler, he points out seven common areas. Christianity, Judaism, Islam, Zoroastrianism, Mazdaism, Hinduism, Buddhism and Taoism agree "that there is a transcendent reality; that he is immanent in human hearts; that he is supreme beauty, truth, righteousness, goodness; that he is love, mercy, compassion; that the way to him is repentence, self-denial, prayer; that the way is love of one's neighbor, even of one's enemies; that the way is love of God so that bliss is conceived as knowledge of God, union with him, or dissolution into him." [Lonergan, p. 109] Lonergan simplifies matters somewhat by referring to God as "he" making God singular and personal.

It is not my intention to try to come up with a concept that will integrate all the similarities and resolve all the differences. It is more important to recognize that the concept I have of God is not God himself. My concept may point in the right general direction but it necessarily falls far short of the transcendent reality that God is. Whatever verbal or intellectual gymnastics I engage in, I never really come close to describing God as he is. He is always something more, something far beyond my ability to imagine or comprehend.

What does all this mean for the experience of being called? It is tempting to look back at the first division of this book and say "No, that is not it; vocation is 'something else.'" The influence of elements like self-concept, values, talent and acquired patterns of behavior all seem so secondary, so unimportant, so accidental. But that would not really be true. They are important. They are pointers in the direction of a greater importance. They do have meaning; their meaning is real but it is also an indication of a deeper meaning that cannot be put into words or concepts. Only if their meaning is real is it an indication of a deeper meaning. It is like a third understanding of the Tao: the <u>way</u> I should order my life that it may be attuned to the way the universe operates. This is not to impose an alien structure on my life. It is, rather, to live genuinely and spontaneously and to recognize in that living the reflection of the universal way of operation.

All this is not very encouraging to those of us who like to get things "crystal clear," to understand precisely what is going on. It gives me a certain sense of security to know where I stand. I feel that I can take care of myself. In regard to my vocation, for example, I can learn by various means about my self-concept, about why I like or dislike a particular kind of work or what meaning it has for me.

But with the introduction of the religious element a new principle if uncertainty is introduced. There are powers at work that are beyond my understanding and control. To some extent, my life is being mapped out in terms of meanings that are beyond me. They are not contrary to my meanings and values though they may appear contrary to <u>my understanding</u> of my values. For example: I enter a monastery in search of security or in order to escape from guilt. I am not aware of these motives at the time. I think I am entering the monastery to serve God in a simple, prayerful life. You might rightly say that I have good intentions but am lacking in self-knowledge. You might call the desire to serve God "surface reason" and the search for security "deeper motivation."

In reply to this accusation, it could be said that both desires are only reflections of a deeper need for a relationship with God. The need for security is not just a weakness resulting from difficulties in psychological development. It is also a token of man's basic dependence and vulnerability. The desire to serve God is not just a rationalization of a selfish motive. It is also an attempt to express a fundamental need that is much deeper than I probably realize at the time. This deeper need, growing out of my religious sense and religious feelings, should grow and develop and absorb into itself all surface motivations.

Such surface motivations are not to be seen as merely deceptions and obstacles. They are more like external stimuli that trigger resonance at a deep level. I feel the deep inner churnings but cannot identify them. I only know that they are real, they are genuine. With patience and fidelity, I can allow these inner feelings freedom to grow.

My religious experience, then, is a dialogue between two poles, both of which are somewhat mysterious to me. God, the object pole, is beyond my comprehension, my concepts, and my expectations. My own deepest needs and longings, the other pole, are also too subtle for me to understand fully. Yet I, in my conscious decisions, must act as something of a moderator in the dialogue to keep it going, to bring the two participants to unity. In this dialogue the two participants are not equals in any way. God always has the initiative; he guides me in the direction he wishes. I must follow. But the path is not often clear to me at the time I must act. I do what I think God is asking at the time. He may seem to be asking something that goes very much against my grain, something that I would not choose of myself and would definitely prefer to avoid. At such a time I must remember that his ways and his plans are far beyond my comprehension. Following his call seems to invariably bring with it suffering and anguish as well as peace and fulfillment.

Some of the most explicit personal accounts of being called to a particular religious state or course of action are found in the writings of the prophets of Israel. We will look to the prophetic vocation as an example of life to which one might be called. The use of this example of life is not intended to imply that all religious vocations must be of such an unusual or extraordinary nature. The prophets are a good example, however, since they clearly manifest that which is implicit in many less conspicuous callings. They lived to serve God whom they could not fully fathom, who did not always act in the way they might expect or desire. Yet he was their God and they were faithful to him regardless of the cost.

Robert Ellwood [88]
The Prophets of Yahweh

The religion of Israel stands out in striking contrast to the various faiths that were studied in the previous section. There is nothing of the liberal possibility of believing in God or not, of believing in one or many Gods, of seeing God as either personal or impersonal or both. Nor was the Israelite faith just another road to the one true God. Their God was the only God, he was a personal God; none of the other nations knew him.

Ellwood points out various explanations of why the Hebrews might have developed a monotheistic idea of God as supreme king of the universe. None of the explanations really proves adequate and Ellwood resorts to the Jews' own understanding:

---

[88] The material in this section is taken from Robert S. Ellwood, Many Peoples, Many Faiths (Englewood Cliffs, N.J.: Prentice-Hall, Inc., 1976). All references to this work will be followed by the appropriate page numbers in brackets. Quotations from scripture are from The New American Bible (New York: Catholic Book Publishing Co., 1970). This section presupposes a familiarity with the religion of Israel. For treatment of the history and beliefs of the Israelite people, see Ellwood, pp. 256-270 or Huston Smith, The Religions of Man, pp. 354-400.

The traditional Jewish interpretation was simply that God, for reasons of His own, Himself selected this people and made Himself known to them. This did not mean that He meant to make life smooth and easy for them; the call involved heavy responsibilities and frequent suffering. He established a covenant or agreement with them, that they would worship him, follow His law, and be faithful to Him; on His part God would preserve them throughout history,... [p. 258]

Over the course of the centuries religious faith takes on set forms of expression in concepts and rituals. There always remains, however, an element of unpredictability. Early in Hebrew history things were very unpredictable. Victory in war could not be assured beforehand in most cases. How could God's people be defeated? Eventually this was explained by the formula, "whenever Israel won, the Lord was pleased with them; when Israel lost, it was because there had been sin." [p. 262] This formula offered a certain amount of security for a time. A fixed, traditional form of worship and sacrifice also bought an element of stability, as did the existence of a massive and apparently permanent temple.

None of these things could ever wholly contain the heart of religion. There remains what Ellwood terms the "marketplace" or "prophet" approach to religion. [p. 8] There remains the person who has had an

inner confrontation with the divine, perhaps unwanted, full of dread, anxiety, wonder, and obligation, typified by a prophet alone meeting the awesome splendor of a God, accepting it, and following the God's hard will even if it leads to certain death. [p. 8]

The prophet Jeremiah is such a one. When the word of the Lord comes to him he protests, "Ah, Lord God!'...I know not how to speak; I am too young." [Jer. 1:6] Later he complains, "You duped me, O Lord, and I let myself be duped; you were too strong for me and you triumphed." [Jer. 20:7] He is tempted to escape his call

155

and the suffering and anguish it brings:

> I say to myself, I will not mention Him; I will speak in His name no more. But then it becomes like fire burning in my heart, imprisoned in my bones; I grow weary holding it in, I cannot endure it. [Jer. 20:9]

So Jeremiah goes about preaching the doom of what remains of his nation. The temple will be destroyed and the people will go into exile. He denounces their trust in the temple worship [Jer. 7:4] and sacrifices [Jer. 11:15] which cannot save them without a change of heart. The destruction and exile can apparently still be avoided with a change of heart and a sincere turning towards the Lord. This prophecy fits nicely into the formula, "serve God and you will win; sin and you will lose, at least until you repent."

There are other times when such simple formulas do not apply. King David repented of his adultery and murder but was told by Nathan the prophet that the child of his sin must die. He was told further that the sword should never depart from his house – that bloodshed would plague his descendants for ages to come. Later, David decides to take a census of his subjects against the advice of Joab the leader of his army. Without any indication of prophetic intervention, David sees the vanity of his act and repents. The Lord, through the prophet Gad, gives the king his choice of three severe afflictions. David picks what appears to be the least of the evils – three days of pestilence. When seventy thousand people had died the Lord regretted the disaster and brought it to an end. [II Sam. 24:1-17]

There are some strange elements here. That David should be punished even though he has repented is not too hard to accept. That the punishment should be so severe is surprising. That seventy thousand other people should be slain for David's sin is a bit scandalous if we claim God is just. That God should "regret" his action is, at least, strange. Most inexplicable is the introduction to the whole event: "The Lord's anger against Israel flared again and he incited David against the Israelites by prompting him to number Israel and Juda." [II Sam. 24:1] Thus it appears that the whole affair was God's idea in the first place!

Reflection

Our reason for looking at the prophets of Israel was to bring our thoughts about God down to earth a little, to see what we could learn from the experience of others. We have little difficulty accepting the fact that God should, for whatever reasons, choose one particular people as the object of his revelations. That he should reward his people with success when they are faithful to him and punish them when they sin fits nicely into our idea of what God should be like. We can rest relatively secure if that is the kind of God who is going to be calling us. It may be a little inconvenient at times but at least we know where we stand. We can "trust" such a God. But then comes the experience of Jeremiah. God asks something that we would rather not give. In theory we are willing to admit that he has a right to do that. In practice, we experience, as did Jeremiah, every imaginable resistance.

How do we explain such resistance? Usually with some platitude like "the spirit is willing but the flesh is weak" or "I'm only human." But the problem seems to be deeper than that.

However "refined" my concept of God may be, my religious experience is not the experience of a concept but of a reality. The God I experience cannot be depended upon to stay within the bounds of a concept. He will not always be experienced as being fair and just. He will not always seem to respect my limitations, my talents, my needs or my self-concept when he calls me to some state or course of action. His call to me may be such that it causes immense suffering to others. Why did the Lord incite David against the Israelites, prompting him to an act for which they would be punished?[89] This problem confronted the author of the book. This is the way he experienced the incident. Yet he loved and believed in the God who acted thus. His concept of God seems crude to us. It seems like the type of attitude that results in the derision of religious belief by unbelievers. Over the centuries our concept of God has become more "refined", less scandalous than that presented above. But there is a danger of limiting our experience within the bounds of a concept.

If I believe that God is all-powerful and all-loving how do I explain the volcano or earthquake that takes thousands of lives? Is it something that God "permits" without really wanting it? Then what causes it – surely not the will of man? Is it caused by powers of darkness, evil spirits, or chance? Then what has become of God's omnipotence? That man, with his free will can go against God's plan is not too

---

[89] The story of David's census is told differently in I Chronicles 21:1-17. In this version it is a "satan," an adversary or accuser, who rises against Israel and incites David into taking the census. A footnote comments that "the change in the term reflects the changed theological outlook of postexilic Israel, when evil could no longer be attributed directly to God."

hard to see. But how can nature go against his plan?

The alternative seems to be to continue to believe in God's almightiness and accept the possibility that he wills this suffering for reasons that we cannot comprehend. It isn't just that we do not <u>know</u> the reasons. It is that they are completely beyond our comprehension. No explanation would be sufficient. We would be like the dog trying to understand Einstein's equation with his nose.

Of course, we try. We gather data, establish premises, and draw conclusions. All well and good. But we must remember we are only sniffing at reality. We grasp only a trace of what is revealed to us and there is far more yet to come.

This is especially true in the matter of vocation. I have spoken of what I thought was going on in my own vocational experience – I saw it as "simply" a call from God. I spoke of some of the things that were "really" going on – the search for security and freedom from guilt and so on. But if it is a genuinely religious vocational experience there is a reality behind all these partial realities that gives them a unifying meaning. There is a deeper meaning that is beyond my comprehension. How do I cope with that which is so far beyond me and yet so close that it is the whole meaning of my life? Like the philosopher, I have to try to express it in words, to reduce it to meanings I can handle. Like the poet or artist, I may try to express the meaning of my life in terms of its aesthetic component. Like the whaler, I may live out the meaning symbolically in a way that is not as socially acceptable as most religious expression. [90]

---

[90] See page 110.

However limited my means of expression may be, it does not in any way limit that which I am trying to express. However apparently adequate my means of expression may be, it does not come near to realizing the whole meaning of my religious call. I am called to transcend my human abilities while retaining them, to transcend my limitations while remaining subject to them, to allow my humanity to be raised to unimaginable heights while continuing to embrace its lowliness, to accept a gift which may destroy many of the meanings that have made life tolerable for me. I cannot purchase this gift but I must pay for it for it will cost me all my energy, all my efforts; I will pay for it with all I am and have.

It is in living out my response to my call that I come to appreciate what is involved in it. It may be relatively easy for me to feel the attraction to religious dedication and make an explicit act of self-surrender. Living out that act for the rest of my life is a different matter. To get something of an idea of the difficulties I may encounter, we will look now at the expression of assent to a religious vocational experience.

CHAPTER V

I EXPRESS MY ASSENT TO

THE RELIGIOIUS ATTRACTION

Man, even religious man, is an embodied being. His body and its relationship to the world and to others must always be taken into account. As religious man, the relationship of his body, the world and others to God must also be considered. As his life has taken on a new meaning when he experiences the call of God, so also his world is seen in a different light. To say that God is "wholly other" than anything that I am familiar with remains true. But it is also true that I must see everything that I am familiar with in terms of this "Wholly Other." My response to God's call is a human response, my path to his is a human path, each step is a human step, each fall causes human bruises. The tremendous and fascinating divine mystery is experienced by a human person in a human world.

Again, it may be worth mentioning the relationship between my expression and the ideals that I am expressing. For the purpose of this book, we will be concerned only with the expression insofar as it is the primary way in which I live out my response to my vocational attraction, not just one of several ways. Further, we will be concerned with the situation in which the particular expression is chosen primarily in order to live out that response.

In this chapter we will consider the religious subject who expresses his response to a vocational experience and how his attitudes and aptitudes relate to the form of expression. Then the particular form his expression takes – the object-pole of the expression will be considered.

I.THE SUBJECT–POLE

Jeremiah
The Role of the Prophet

In the first division of this book we spoke of the role of talent in the expression of assent to a vocational attraction. Asher Lev was used as an example of one whose expression was strongly influenced by his artistic ability. [91] He would hardly have become a famous painter without some artistic talent. Contrary to much of what was said in the first division, a person may find himself in a role that goes quite strongly against his own inner grain, a role for which he seems to have very little aptitude, and a role in which, as a matter of fact, he fails to accomplish his obvious goals. Has he missed his vocation?

Jeremiah was such a man and from our vantage point we would not be likely to say that he missed his vocation. But how did it look to Jeremiah himself and to those who listened to him?

We have already seen some of the resistance Jeremiah felt when "the word of the Lord" came to him. He claimed that he was too young, that he did not know how to speak. But the Lord did not accept his excuses and set him "over nations

---

[91] See pages 75-79.

and over kingdoms, to root up and to tear down, to destroy and to demolish, to build and to plant." [Jer. 1:10] He is commanded by the Lord not to marry or have children in the Land of Judah as a warning to the people of the land that their future did not lie there. Faithfully the prophet followed the word of the Lord and proclaimed it publicly. His reward was a life of suffering, rejection and contradiction.

He suffered from ruthless enemies and weak friends. He suffered the hatred of his countrymen when the invading ruler offered him protection. [Jer. 40: 1-6] His prophecies were directly contradicted by the false prophet Hananiah and the Lord did not immediately give Jeremiah a reply. In the eyes of the onlookers he appeared to fail to have an answer. [Jer. 28: 1-11] Only later did the Lord foretell, through Jeremiah, the death of Hananiah.

As a final failure, Jeremiah pleaded with the people of Judah not to flee to Egypt to escape the Babylonian conquerors. His plea fell on deaf ears, the people fled and dragged him along with them. [Jer. 42: 7- 43: 7] In exile, the faithful prophet continued to speak the word of the Lord to his people until his death.

Reflection

It is easy for us today to look back at "the mighty prophet, Jeremiah" and take his sufferings lightly. He had the word of the Lord coming to him every time he turned around. He knew what was the right thing to do and knew that God was on his side and would not let him down. How do I know that? I have to "play it by ear;" I can never really be sure.

But does the above do justice to Jeremiah's experience? I do not think so. He has an initial experience that he was to speak the Lord's word to God's people. No contract was signed, no divine letters of recommendation were given, no identification card or credentials were presented which would prove to the people that he was a genuine prophet of the Lord. Only his faith in his own experience carried him on. God had spoken to him and he knew it. Jeremiah knew his message was "unreasonable." The Jewish people's history had been one of deliverance from their enemies by the power of God. They were his chosen people. Now this prophet was telling them to submit to foreign domination! He could not expect his message to be appealing. Jeremiah knew also that he was not overflowing with any particular "talent" for his job. Though he came from a priestly family, he was not quite twenty when he began his prophetic career. He was not as comfortable and confident of his ability as Asher Lev was in his. Asher stood alone but had his talent to back him up. Jeremiah stood alone but had the Lord to back him up. But that was not much comfort to him. The Lord could be pretty unpredictable. Where was he when Jeremiah was thrown into the cistern and left to sink into the mud? Where was his word when Hananiah contradicted Jeremiah? Where was he when Jeremiah was hauled off to Egypt? Nor could the prophet's vocation be explained in terms of an attempt to implement a self-concept. He was not a masochist but he kept doing things that only brought suffering and failure. Why?

The only answer seems to be faith. Jeremiah had faith. He believed in God. He trusted his experience of God. His faith was not just a private affair. He based his action on it. His prophecies can be explained in no other way. He trusted the

Lord who called him and risked all he had on the basis of that trust. He sacrificed the possibility of marriage and family as a sign [92] to the people. He accepted failure and persecution, contradiction and exile rather than remain silent. His faith in his experience of God's word told him he must proclaim it to the people. Everything else in his experience pointed in the opposite direction. Common sense, the advice of his elders, his own gifts and talents, his self-concept, the results of his efforts, his personal happiness; absolutely every purely human criterion tells Jeremiah that he is on the wrong track. But Jeremiah does not live by purely human criteria when he is hearing or proclaiming the word of the Lord. When he watches a potter working with his clay he sees the Lord forming his people. The human meaning is not absent from the situation but a deeper meaning is seen because the prophet, by reason of his faith, is disposed to see it. He still has a self-concept but the most important element in that concept is that of creatureliness, lowliness, total dependence on God.

---

[92] Carroll Stuhlmueller, in The Prophets and the Word of God (Notre Dame, Ind.: Fides Publishers, 1964), p. 115, states that Jeremiah's celibate life was undertaken "so that he could consecrate himself unreservedly to God's work." The text does not immediately give this impression. Different prophets were treated differently in the matter of marriage. Hosea was told by the word of the Lord to marry a faithless woman [Hos. 1:2, 3:1] as a sign of God's love for his faithless people. Ezechiel was told not to weep or mourn or shed tears when his wife, the delight of his eyes, was suddenly taken from him. This was to be a sign to the people that their temple, the delight of their eyes, and their sons and daughters, the delight of their hearts, would be taken from them. They should not weep or lament in that day but "you shall rot away because of your sins and groan one to another." [Ez. 24: 15-27] The prophets seemed to have no life of their own. They could not even take time out to cry over the loss of a loved one.

He still has values, but they are more fluid now; his understanding of them is subject to the word of the Lord as it may come to him at any moment in all its unpredictableness. And he must still display his "work" in the public arena. He must express himself to others.

> Life in this world puts heavy demands on him who wants to give himself entirely to the service of God, first of all the demand for publicity. A convincing religious attitude demands unlimited publicity. This demand cannot be avoided. It strikes many with a deep feeling of shame. Some maintain this is false shame. That may be so, occasionally. But there exists also a genuine religious shame which, like bodily shame, we must not renounce. [Rumke, p. 79]

The subject who expresses his consent to a religious attraction must become totally taken up into his new life. [93] No area of life remains exclusively his own. God may ask him to sacrifice his dearest possessions, to leave his homeland, to denounce his own people's actions, to cooperate with the enemy. The religious faith that the subject brings to his expression is not the source of its power. God is the source. But the subject must have faith in order to communicate the power of God by his expression. The person to whom he communicates God's word must also have faith in order to perceive and understand it as God's word.

Faith is also needed in a non-prophetic, more common expression of religious vocation. When I enter a monastery, for example, it is only by faith that

---

[93] In Hebrew, the verb "qara" (to call) has the basic semantic meaning "to give a name." In calling someone, God gives him a new name, a new essential destiny. Some very fundamental meaning of the person's life is changed (or, at least, made specific) in the context of his familiar everyday world. See Jean de Fraine, The Bible on Vocation and Election (De Pere, Wis.: St. Norbert Abbey Press, 1966), pp. 5-6.

166

I can know the value of the life I am living. Perfect external observance of the monastic duties, the reassurance of others, even worldwide reputation for holiness; none of these is any real assurance that my monastic life is being well lived. [94] But it is necessary to go a step further. Faith is necessary if monastic life is to even <u>have</u> any genuine religious value. Without faith a monastic life may be a good exercise in self-discipline, simplicity, frugality, regularity, and any number of other naturally good practices. But it will lack any real religious dimension. Faith is not the source of the sanctifying power of monastic life or any other life. God is the source. But only if I have faith can God's sanctifying power operate.

We have seen that a new and all-important element is present in the subject who expresses his assent to his religious attraction. That new element is religious faith which illuminates the whole of reality with a new meaning. This faith gives new meaning to the act of expression. What does this mean and what are the ramifications of this new meaning? To find out, we will look at the object-pole of the expression. How does the expression, the response to a vocational attraction, differ from the expression as studied in the first division?

---

[94] A good example of an apparently successful but inwardly vitiated monastic life can be found in Count Leo Tolstoy's <u>Father Sergius and Other Stories and Plays</u> (Freeport, N.Y.: Books for Libraries Press, 1940), pp. 33-112.

II. THE OBJECT-POLE

<u>Stuhlmueller</u> [95]
<u>The Word of the Lord</u>

The prophet speaks to the people. He does not proclaim his own word but the word of the Lord. It is not his own talent, ingenuity, experience, or virtue that is the source of this word. The word comes to him as a gift from the Lord. Only complete surrender to the Lord on the part of the prophet makes it possible for him to hear the Lord's word. The consequences of this surrender come home to him concretely when he proclaims the word. Why? What is the "word of the Lord" all about?

Stuhlmueller points out the difference between the Hebrew "dabar" and the Greek "logos" which are both usually translated as "word":

> <u>Dabar</u>, in its deepest etymological meaning, signified: "to push" or "to drive forward" according to Edmond Jacob and Thorlief Boman; "to go away with" in Gensenius' Hebrew Lexicon. The etymology of <u>logos</u> or <u>lego</u>, on the contrary, expressed the idea: to collect, to order, to arrange. [p. 24, italics in the original]

The word that was proclaimed by the Hebrew prophets was not just a verbal articulation of certain thoughts or truths. It is the "pushing," the "driving forward" of

---

[95] The material in this section is taken from <u>The Prophets and the Word of God</u>, pp. 19-62. All references to this work will be followed by the appropriate page numbers in brackets. In his scriptural quotations, Stuhlmueller uses the Confraternity of Christian Doctrine translation.

the power of God, present in the word, <u>bringing about</u> that which is spoken. [96] "God's word <u>is</u> God himself acting upon the listener." [p. 25, italics in the original] God's word is creative; it brings into being what it speaks. "No word, of course, contained so fully the life of God as the sacred name, Yahweh." [p. 33] Stuhlmueller see the name as expressing God's continuous presence and concern <u>"He who is always there with you."</u> [p. 33, italics in the original]

During each moment of man's life, God reveals Himself by love and care, and as man experiences the "word" of protection; he comes to know the mystery of God. It is a knowledge which is life, for it extends God's personal concern to every segment of man's being. [p. 34]

God was not only <u>at</u> man's side but also <u>on</u> his side. In this respect, abuses gradually crept in. God's word became, for man, a tool, a magic formula that was always at man's service. The God whose word it was found himself being ignored. "Instead of listening to <u>God</u> as He spoke, Israel forgot all about God and concentrated upon His promises." [p. 36, italics in the original] It was in these situations that God sent his prophets. They uttered his word and that word brought the punishment or the repentence by its power.

---

[96] This idea is more clearly expressed in some of the earlier texts such as Numbers 22: 1-6, 23: 11-12, 24: 10-14. In these texts Balaam is asked by Balak the Moabite to curse the Israelites "for I know that whatever you bless is blessed and whatever you curse is cursed." [Num. 22: 6] But the spirit of the Lord came upon Balaam and he blessed Israel in spite of the rewards offered by Balak. The implication is that the prophet is not just a "weatherman" predicting what will happen. Rather, what will happen is determined by what is said. The speaking of the word brings it about even, apparently, if the word is spoken as a result of bribery. Later reflection modified this crude understanding somewhat, but the idea of the effective power of the prophet's word, the "word of the Lord" remained.

"The prophets... would simply speak <u>the word of God</u> and then wait for its full effects to be felt." [p. 40, italics in the original] God was on man's side but would not be manipulated by man. So often in scripture the behavior of the Israelite was good solid common sense, good diplomacy, good military strategy. But it was not necessarily God's plan for them. "What man strove to acquire for himself, by himself, God was waiting to give. Israel, however, must accept it as <u>God's</u> creation." [p. 51, italics in the original] If Israel will accept her guilt and recognize her misery, then "in tender mercy God will then speak to the heart of His people... The word will be God himself, present to save and to make happy, creating a new wonder for his people." [p. 61] God's word not only affects external events but, above all, can create a bond of love between himself and man. Summarizing his thoughts on the prophetic word, Stuhlmueller says:

> The word of God, spoken by the prophets, was alive with God's power. It was and remains the presence of God. True to their ancient Near Eastern background, the prophets could not consider the word just a "thought" or "concept" of the intellect. It was thrust forward of all the powers of the one speaking. If the speaker was God, then it brought man into the dynamic, impelling presence of the Lord. [p. 61]

Reflection

The dynamics at work in the prophetic word brings to mind the dream I recounted in the first division. [97] The building I dreamt of was shot through with weaknesses. All warning of these weaknesses and the impending disaster were ignored by the workmen. They were seen only as temporary threats to be

---

[97] See pages 117-118.

dealt with, not as signs of an inevitable collapse. It was the shaking of the building – the warnings – that ultimately caused it to crumble. But the analogy limps badly. It would be more accurate to say that the weakness of the building caused both the shaking and the collapse. The weakness was already there. Or you could say that the hammering caused both the shaking and the collapse. Whatever way it is said, the whole process can be explained in terms of natural cause and effect. There is nothing mysterious about it – except, perhaps, the stupidity of the workmen.

But suppose I walk up to a perfectly solid building and say, "This building shall fall! Its beams shall sag, its walls will crack and crumble and the whole thing shall come down in a heap of rubble next Thursday!" And so it turns out. People would say I'm psychic or that I saw weaknesses that escaped others. They would insist that I said it because it was going to happen; they would never believe that it happened only because I had said it would. The human word does not have such power. And they are right.

But the word of the Lord does have such power. But then there is the problem of recognizing the word of the Lord. Jeremiah put a yoke around his neck and said that as he submitted to the wooden yoke so should the people submit to the King of Babylon. Hananiah broke the yoke and predicted that the Lord would break the power of the King of Babylon within two years. [Jer. 27:1- 28:4] Whom to believe? [98]

---

[98] This section deals with the expression of the prophet. Whether the prophecy is to be believed or not is the problem of the hearer, not the prophet. The prophet must answer for his own integrity, honesty and sincerity, not for the success he has in

Deuteronomy, 18:22 states that even though a prophet "speaks in the name of the Lord," if the prophecy is not fulfilled it was not the Lord who spoke the oracle. Jeremiah qualifies this criterion:

> From of old, the prophets who were before you and me prophesied war, woe, and pestilence against many lands and mighty kingdoms. But the prophet who prophesies peace is recognized as truly sent by the Lord only when his prophetic prediction is fulfilled. [Jer. 28:1-9]

This seems to indicate that the Lord sends his prophets to warn and rebuke, not to make promises of peace and prosperity. But then how can we explain, to take one of many examples, the fifty-fourth chapter of Isaiah which promises peace and prosperity in abundance?

Again, it seems we must fall back on faith. The hearers must, like the prophets, be men of faith. To discern the true word of the Lord they must be sincere, honest, and humbly aware that God's ways are not man's way.

As Jeremiah watched the potter working at his wheel [Jer. 18:1-10] he was disposed to see some message from the Lord expressed symbolically. He could "transfer" the actions of the potter working with clay to the patterns of God's dealings with his people. His faith disposed him to see a religious meaning. His eyes, imagination, intuition and intellect were all at work at the same time, but only faith allowed him to see the religious message, and see it as a word of the Lord to him. The hearer is likewise disposed by his faith to see in the prophet's words

---

convincing the people. He does not substitute a more effective word of his own when the word of the Lord fails to gain acceptance among the people. Still, the hearer is faced with the dilemma: whom to believe? The credibility of the oracle must be contained in the expression.

the word of the Lord. The word is alive with God's power and the hearer's faith allows God's power the freedom to work in him, to mold him as the potter molds clay.

We have looked at the prophetic vocation in some detail. Typically the vocation is expressed by the spoken word though there are many examples of prophetic actions as well. Another common expression of religious faith and feeling is ritual. Expression by prophecy is usually reserved to one with a particular vocation. Expression by ritual is more likely to be common to all people who embrace a particular religion. There are some cases, however, in which ritual is the main expression of one's vocation. Examples might be the priests of the various religious sects, the vestal virgins of ancient Rome or Buddhist monks.

In the following section, ritual will be studied in a general way. What is said will refer to religious ritual expression whether it is the specific expression of a unique personal vocation or not. In the reflection the findings will be applied to the situation in which religious ritual expression is also the primary vocational expression.[99]

Bouyer [100]
Ritual

A seemingly appropriate introduction to this section might be the old

---

[99] There are, of course, many other ways in which a person can express his assent to a religious vocational attraction. Some examples might be: caring for the poor or the sick or exercising political or military leadership as did the kings of Israel and Judah. The expressions will not be treated since they are not, in themselves, religious.

[100] The material in this section is taken from Louis Bouyer, Rite and Man (Notre Dame, Ind.: university of Notre Dame Press, 1963). All references to this work will be followed by the appropriate page numbers in brackets.

saying "Actions speak louder than words." In this way I could claim that passing from the word as expression to the act as expression is a progressive step. Unfortunately – or should I say fortunately? – The matter is not so simple.

Sacred words and sacred actions are, according to Bouyer, always found joined together. [p. 53] And in this conjunction a certain priority must always belong to the word.

A mere action, one without any real significance, one indeed in which the word does not enter as a determining factor, is by this very fact something subhuman and consequently religious. On the other hand, it is the word – and therefore humanity itself, which is realized through self-expression – that degenerates whenever it tends to suppress action. [p. 54]

There is a natural relationship between word and ritual action which must be preserved. The word does not give meaning to an otherwise meaningless act. Nor does the act give expression to an otherwise unexpressed word.

The ritual act has a natural meaning of its own. It has <u>its</u> <u>own</u> natural symbolism independently of any imposed meaning.

It is immediate, primordial creation of religiously minded men in which they have actively realized their effective connection with the divinity <u>before</u> they explain this connection to themselves. [p. 66, italics are not in the original]

Rites have always been thought of as the work of the gods, not the fabrications of man. They are not tools that man concocted so that he could participate in the life of the gods as revealed in myths. Rather, "the rites,...,antedate every detailed explanation of what is done in them." [p. 73] The myths are later attempts to <u>explain</u> the meaning of the rites as the work of the gods. These explanations only become necessary when man came to consider himself to be the rites' "principle agent, if not their author." [p. 73]

Two basic types of rites are distinguished. In the first, "a properly divine action is present so that the faithful may take part in it." [p. 67] Such might be a rite by which one participates in the creation act or the seasonal cycles. This type focuses on the "mysterium tremendum" which draws man out of himself. In the second type of ritual the emphasis is on the "mysterium fascinosum." Here the ordinary, mundane human acts of everyday life are present but are brought within "the sphere of the sacred." [p. 67] Such rites would concern eating, agriculture and so on.

Word and actions are not merely for the sake of expression of self. They are always communication with another. Bouyer does not hesitate to say that the "original word" of man is addressed to "the thou of religion, the divine Thou." [p. 56, italics in the original]

What actually is the religious relationship...? It is the basic relation of man to the world in its totality, but in this totality mysteriously apprehended as the unity, or rather the uniqueness, of the sacred, the completely Other. It seems then that the first words of a man are a cry toward God. [p. 56]

Reflection

With Bouyer, we once again approach the primordial. Man's religious sense, his aptitude to perceive that he has some relationship with God, and his perception of God as the "mysterium tremendum et fascinosum" were previously seen to be primary and irreducible experiences. [101] The growth of religious faith was also seen to be a normal part of human development. It is the interruption of growth that needs to be explained, not the growth of religious belief. [102]

---

[101] See pages 138-139.

[102] See page 142.

Our glance at the various concepts of God bought similar results. Whatever descriptions, concepts or attributes we might come up with. God was always "something else," always "wholly other" than what we could grasp. [103]

The prophetic word was similarly permeated with mystery. The prophet did not just make calculated predictions nor was he gifted with knowledge of the future. The word of the Lord was uttered through him, the Lord's all-powerful word which brings about that which it bespeaks. [104]

Now the ritual, as religious expression, is seen to be inundated with meanings that are "already there" before I begin to reflect on them. [105] I do not put the meanings there. I come to know the meanings through experiencing myself performing the rites. This knowledge is deep experiential knowledge, not just conceptual knowledge. I may try to conceptualize this knowledge and reduce it to a formula I can "handle." In doing so I may deprive the rite of its mystery and power, limiting its meaning to my intellectual formula. I no longer surrender myself to the rite letting it speak its primordial word in and through me. Rather, like false prophets, I may try to "use" the rite or the word for my own ends. [106] In that case the

---

[103] See pages 150-152.

[104] See pages 169-171.

[105] In this case it seems to speak of "the true meaning of a situation" as does Viktor Frankl [see p. 36 of this book]. That certain actions or situations have one particular meaning when seen from the point of view of religious symbolism is not to say that all situations have only one true meaning.

[106] Perhaps I do not even have to go this far in order to lose the word. The biblical story of Adam and Eve seems to indicate that a mere curiosity, the desire to

word or the rite will be able to exercise its creative power because it has been informed with my word, not the Lord's. The rites, as religious expression, are gifts from God and I must attune myself to the word they wish to utter in and through me.

When ritual expression is the primary way in which I express my assent to my vocational attraction, my attitude toward the rites is of immense importance. [107] If I surrender myself to them as to realities that surpass me I will be continually nourished and deepened by their power. I will see them as gifts given me by

---

know more than has been granted, is enough to cause the loss of what was already so naturally possessed. The original blessings can be regained only at the expense of long-sufferings. The regaining is itself a gift but the blessings are not held with the same spontaneity and innocence as they were originally. A good literary example of this movement can be found in Lucius Apuleius' The Golden Ass (New York: G.P. Putnam's Sons, 1915), pp 185-285. The beautiful young girl, Psyche, is placed in a rich palace, cared for by invisible servants and visited at night by an unseen lover, the god Amor or Cupid. Her jealous sisters tell her that her lover must be some kind of monster seeking to destroy her and in her curiosity to see her lover, Psyche burns him with some oil from her lamp. Amor leaves her and, after an attempted suicide, she sets out in search of him with the elements in the visible world as guides. After many trials and sufferings she is finally reunited with him. Psyche's problem also began with curiosity – wanting to know more about the joy than had been bestowed on her. It was not a search for joy but for knowledge. In so doing, she lost her innocent acceptance and possession of that joy and had to work and suffer to regain her happiness. The question seems to be whether it is possible to retain this innocent possession throughout life, or whether losing it and having to suffer and struggle to rediscover it is a necessary and unavoidable part of healthy human development.

[107] This does not mean that the attitude toward ritual is unimportant to religious man who does not have a specifically religious vocation. It is important in his case also. But a manipulative attitude towards ritual may not vitiate his whole life. His religious observance may be shallow or hollow. But he may, at the same time, be living a wholesome and fairly healthy life in his non-religious activities.

God. As I enter more deeply into their meaning I will come to know more fully the meaning of my own life and my relationship to God. I will be less inclined to try to run my own life my way and more open to the word of God in whatever way it may present itself to me.

If, on the other hand, I try to "use" and manipulate ritual expression to serve my own desires and needs I may develop a profoundly insincere stance toward myself and others as well as towards God. I may be going through the ritual motions without any real contact with their inner meaning. The rite may express my dependence on God while I am actually using it to try to manipulate him. Or it may express my dedication to helping others while I am actually dominating them or trying to do so. In these cases my whole life is basically warped. At just what point I actually <u>lose</u> my religious vocation is hard to say. In the examples just given I have certainly lost a large part of the spirit which should animate my life. I have lost touch with many of the values that are expressed in the rituals I perform. I have lost touch with my inner self, my community of fellow believers and with God. And in this state I continue to proclaim explicitly that my life is dedicated to God.

In religious vocation it is important that the expression correspond to the attraction that elicits it. But it is more important that my inner attitudes be in tune with the meanings that are already inherent in the expression. This is true of the examples of expression we have studied: prophetic word and ritual. It is also true of an expression that may not be, in itself, specifically religious such as caring for the poor or the sick. These ministries imply a genuine human care and concern which must be present if they are to be effective and fruitful expressions of my religious attraction.

Conclusion and Transition

In one sense this division has been a step backwards. After considering the experiences of being on the universal human level, we have had to go back and pick up a number of religious meanings that were already implicitly there but undeveloped. Nature does not precede religion. Religious meaning is there first but it must wait for nature to develop and give it support before it can come to fruition. It is something like what happens to a fruit tree. The fruit is not an after thought just because it comes last. It is the primary reason why we usually plant fruit trees in the first place. But a good bit of time is spent building a structure that can support and nourish the development of the fruit. Nobody asks why a particular fruit tree bears fruit. We might ask why a particular tree does not. The bearing of fruit is the natural outcome of development of the tree.

Religious belief, according to Rumke, follows the same pattern. Vocational growth and development also proceeds in a similar manner though it may not be so apparent. When I feel an attraction for some particular state or course of action my desire for it grows quite spontaneously and naturally. My interest increases, my assent becomes more explicit and I find myself comfortable in expressing that assent. Or, at least, I am less uncomfortable in the expression than I would be if I tried to resist the attraction. I do not feel there is something wrong with me because I feel this attraction. Only when the attraction meets with resistance will I recognize the presence of a problem.   Then I will have to make a choice between the attraction and some other value – my security or prestige, for example.

The expression of my vocation may vary over the course of my lifetime but each new expression grows out of what went before. Even if the new expression seems to be an "about face," it still grows out of the attraction and commitment of the person. If it does not, there has been an interruption or distortion in development.

Having taken this look at the implications of religious faith on the experience of being called, we will now consider one particular religion – Christianity. The link between human experience and religious experience should be even closer since humanity and divinity are seen to be united in the person of Jesus Christ.

DIVISION III

THE CHRISTIAN EXPERIENCE

OF BEING CALLED

INTRODUCTION

In Division II we have looked at the experience of the prophet Jeremiah. He "heard the word of the Lord." The word of the Lord "came to him." His hearing the word was an inner experience though it may have been connected with some external event such as watching the potter work at his clay. Another person standing beside him might have seen no connection nor any reason why the potter's work should be seen to have any religious significance for the prophet.

In the New Testament the call of the first disciples is described in more tangible, explicit terms. The man, Jesus of Nazareth, calls them to follow him. As the incident is narrated in the gospel, a bystander would have heard the words Jesus spoke. He could have testified: "Yes, Jesus called this man to follow him. I heard every word of it with my own ears." But what does the call mean? To the bystander it may have only meant, "Come on, let's go for a walk." To the disciple to whom the call was addressed it meant something quite different. Somehow he saw it as much more than an invitation to go for a walk. It was an invitation to a friendship, a friendship that implied a whole new meaning for the future. The invitation was not to religious belief or to any particular state or course of action as far as the disciple knew. He was called to enter into a personal relationship that would color and give meaning to every thought and action of his future life. The disciple may have been attracted by Christ's personal qualities, by the possibility of helping to free his country from Roman domination, by the chance of an exciting alternative to fishing or collecting taxes and by any number of other considerations. Eventually the attraction was simplified to the point where it consisted only of a personal love for Christ.

The disciples whose vocations are described in the gospels were not called from paganism to faith in God. They already believed in God. They were called to faith in Christ. This raises the question: what is so special about Christianity? Is it just one religious belief among others? Is Christianity implicit in the belief of universal religious man? What elements are specifically characteristic to the call to Christianity? The material in this division will work towards an answer to these questions.

The two chapters of this division will be concerned with the call to embrace Christianity and the call to grow as a Christian. As in the second division, the universal call to holiness is presupposed.[108] Some examples will be used to demonstrate the call to Christianity. The subjects in these examples will be men who already believe in God, that is, they already have religious faith. The vocation of

---

[108] See page 130.

such a person to embrace the Christian faith does not seem to be essentially different from the same calling as it might be experienced by a pagan. It might reasonably be argued that a pagan comes to believe in God as part of the preliminary attraction to Christianity. Such a question is avoided in this division which deals with what one is called to, not what he is called from.

In the previous two divisions, the chapters have been arranged according to the components of the experience of being called. In the first division a chapter was devoted to each of the three components: attraction, assent, and expression. In the second division, the elements of attraction and expression were explicitly studied. The assent was felt to be essentially the same as that described in Division I. The arrangement in this division will be different. The two chapters will deal with the call to embrace Christianity and the call to grow as a Christian. The elements of attraction, assent, and expression will be included in each chapter. The emphasis in this division will be on objective elements more than on the unique needs of the individual subject. We will look at what is common to all Christians as articulated within the Roman Catholic tradition. The objectivity of such elements as Baptism and Eucharist is not diminished by the fact that these elements may have a slightly different emphasis or nuance in the lives of various individuals because of their particular background or needs.

CHAPTER VI

I AM CALLED

TO EMBRACE CHRISTIANITY

When we look at a few examples of people who have been called to embrace Christianity, we see a great variety of experiences. Some who are called have previously been enemies of religion or enemies of Christianity. Some have been living good lives; others have been living lives of unrestrained vice. Some have been very wealthy; some have been very poor. These differences are in the subjects who experience the call. They are different types of persons and are called from different situations. But we do not have any particular difficulty in seeing that their experiences of being called are not essentially different.

There are cases, however, when there seems to be a considerable difference in the experience itself. The apostles, for example, saw Jesus standing there in front of them saying, "Follow me." Saul of Tarsus experienced his call amidst a barrage of extraordinary natural phenomena. For most persons who experience the call to Christianity there is nothing quite so sensational involved. They struggle, ponder, and decide the issue. It seems much like any other serious decision in their lives. Is it the same call? To find an answer to that question we will look, in this chapter, at the vocations of the apostles and of Paul. Their experience will be compared to that of a person today. Today a person being called to Christianity sees himself joining a worldwide organization with clearly delineated doctrines and disciplines. In order to see more clearly the common elements in the vocation to Christianity, whether in the present day or in the apostolic times, we will take a look at the rite of initiation, Baptism.

The Call of the Disciples

In the Gospels of Matthew and Mark we are told in very simple words of the call which Jesus addressed to the fisherman by the Sea of Galilee.[109] As Andrew and Simon were casting a net into the sea, Jesus called out to them, "Come after me and I will make you fishers of men." [Mt. 4: 19] The two responded by leaving their nets and immediately following him. Going on a little further he called out to James and John, who were mending their nets and they abandoned their father Zebedee, who was in the boat with the hired men, and went off in the company of Jesus. [Mk.1: 20]

Luke gives a slightly different version. The fishermen have toiled all night with no success. Jesus gets into Peter's boat and asks him to put out a little from the land. From the boat Jesus teaches the people on the shore. When he has finished he tells Peter to let down the nets for a catch. The nets are put down and such a load of

---

[109] Quotations from scripture are taken from <u>The New American Bible</u> (New York: Catholic Book Publishing Co., 1970).

185

fish is taken that Peter's boat, as well as that of his partners, can hardly hold the weight. Peter falls at Jesus' feet imploring him, "Leave me, Lord. I am a sinful man." [Lk. 5: 8] The others are equally astonished. Jesus tells them not to be afraid from now on they will be catching men. They take their boats to land and leave everything to follow him.[110]

Just how the disciples understood their calling is not laid out in detail in the gospels. There is some difficulty in separating their call to believe in Christ from their call to be apostles – to be sent out to preach faith in Christ. They seem to have had some difficulty in this matter themselves. Their occasional arguments about which of them was greatest seems to indicate a competition for first place in the apostolic hierarchy. Jesus responded to this feuding, not by establishing priorities of dignity among them, but by recalling them to the attitude of humility that is basic to their call to be his followers: "Anyone among you who aspires to greatness must serve the rest; whoever wants to rank first among you must serve the needs of all." [Mk. 10: 43-44] They had a somewhat selfish understanding of their role as apostles. When they see a man trying to cast out demons in Jesus' name they try to stop him

---

[110] A footnote in the New American Bible notes that this miraculous catch of fish is, in many ways similar to that recorded in the Gospel of John 21: 1 – 8. It is suggested that Luke is anticipating the mandate given by Jesus to Peter and the other disciples after the resurrection. The Jerusalem Bible (Garden City, N.Y.: Doubleday, 1966) states that Luke has placed the period of teaching the crowd and the catch of fish before the calling of the disciples in order to make their unhesitating response less surprising.

since he is not one of their company. [Mk. 9: 38-40, Lk. 9: 49-50] In regard to their role as apostles, they considered themselves to be an exclusive group.

Their vocation to believe in Christ was seen differently. They were to share that with all men. What did they believe about Jesus? Peter expressed his belief boldly enough: "You are the Messiah, ..., the Son of the Living God!" [Mt. 16: 16] Jesus attributes this faith to a revelation of his heavenly Father rather than to mere human testimony. But generally the disciple's belief in Christ has a large admixture of political overtones. Even after the resurrection, the disciples on the way to Emmaus are saying, "We were hoping that he was the one who would set Israel free." [Lk. 24: 21] And the Acts of the Apostles tells us that Jesus was asked by the disciples, "Lord, are you going to restore the rule to Israel now?" This question was put to him just before his ascension.

St. John's Gospel was written after many years of reflection on the life and work of Jesus. It is much more explicit than the synoptic gospels are regarding what one believes when he has faith in Christ. Here, however, we are concerned with the disciples' experience of being called. Their ultimate understanding of what that call really meant is, of course, central to their vocation. But it was not very clear in their original experience. For the time being we will mainly be concerned with their original experience. Its deepest meaning, which they only realized later, will be seen in our study of St. Paul's vocational experience.

Reflection

To one who has become accustomed to reading the gospels, the story of the call of the disciples may be somewhat taken for granted. It is easy to say that we would have done the same thing if we had been those fishermen. A bit of imaginative thought highlights what really happened.

Jesus was quite probably known to these young fishermen since he had been raised at Nazareth only a few miles from the Sea of Galilee. In Luke's account Jesus had already healed Peter's mother-in-law before calling the disciples. [Lk. 4: 30-39] Even so, the response of the disciples is not to be underestimated. They made their living by fishing. It was probably the only work they knew. They had been brought up by the sea among fishermen. And now they drop their nets at the summons of a young carpenter and follow him. Why? Because he invited them to do so. They knew he was a religious man and had leadership qualities. Perhaps he was the messiah, which might mean military or political abilities as well.

Whatever kind of leader he might turn out to be, it must have occurred to these fishermen that it was strange that he should call them. They were religious men but had not planned on becoming religious leaders. They were capable of fighting but had not followed the other insurgents who had tried to rise up against the Romans. They would have been little help in a political campaign. The disciples do not seem to have had a very clear idea what his calling them meant. When he spoke of his passion they did not understand. Jesus was patient, not expecting them to understand everything from the start. He did not ask them to leave their home town immediately, to change their lifestyle at once or even to leave their fishing trade permanently the first time he invited them to follow him. He asked them to respond as they could. At first he only asked some of their time. Later, when they were willing to give it, he asked more. Finally, they were to devote their entire lives to carrying on what he had begun.

The core of the disciple's attraction to Jesus seems to have been their love and loyalty towards him. And that was all he asked. If they kept their love and loyalty up, the rest would follow. When the time came to preach in his name, they would do it. They found him fascinating, and when some of their number left his company, they did not follow. John's version has them say, "Lord, to whom shall we go? You have the words of eternal life." [Jn. 6: 68] They had been getting along alright before Jesus stepped into their lives. Once they had met him, all was different. He had awakened their taste for a fuller spiritual life and their thirst could not be quenched by any substitutes, nor could it be ignored or forgotten. They were fascinated by him, but they also stood in awe at his power. He was not just another "nice guy." There was something of the "mysterium tremendum et fascinosum" about him.[111] Their love for him, and his expectations of them made them capable of things they never dreamed they could do. Talent, self-concept, training, social pressure, cultural background and conditioning do not begin to give an explanation. But personal love can only begin to explain it. It is an important element but it is not enough. What began as personal love became a love suffused with religious faith.

---

[111] See page 135.

Long after Jesus had passed from their sight they were still finding new meanings that had been implicit in their original fascination with him. They eventually came to see that all their values were incarnate in him. He embodied all that they desired or ever could desire. In embracing him, they possess all. But they also discovered new values. [112] Loving and responding to him opened up to them new vistas of value which they recognized and lived and tried to express in their preaching.

To see this aspect more clearly, we will look at the experience of St. Paul. Paul did not know Jesus as the other apostles did. But his personal experience of Christ was as real as theirs. The familiar story of the conversion of Saul of Tarsus on the road to Damascus is recounted three times in the Acts of the Apostles.[113] The three accounts are in agreement on all the essential points. Saul, a zealous Jew was persecuting the Christian Sect. He was on the way to Damascus to arrest some Christians there.

On the way a bright light flashed about him and he fell from his horse to the ground. A voice asked him, "Why do you persecute me?" "Who are you?" asked Saul. He was told in reply "I am Jesus, the one you are persecuting." Saul was told by the vision to go into Damascus where he would be told what to do.

---

[112] On pages 41-43 of this book we looked at Mounier's theory of personalism. He states that "Christian personalism goes the whole way and deduces all values from the unique appeal of one supreme Person." Emmanuel Mounier, Personalism (Notre Dame, Ind: University of Notre Dame Press, 1952) p. 68.

[113] The three passages are: Acts 9: 1-19, 22: 3-16, and 26: 2-18.

Blinded by the experience he did as he was told; his sight was restored and he was baptized. After a trip to Arabia, he returned to Damascus and was soon preaching that Jesus was the Son of God.

Amedee Brunot [114]
St. Paul's Vocation

There is no evidence of a gradual "coming around" to Christianity in the experience of Paul. His conversion and the experience of being called seem to have been instantaneous. As Brunot says, "If we are to understand St. Paul and his message, we must constantly return, as he does himself, to his first vision. It explains everything." [p. 27] On the basis of this vision Paul insists that he is to be considered an apostle: "Am I not an apostle? Have I not seen Jesus our Lord?" [I Cor. 9: 1]

The identity of Jesus, the whole meaning of his mission on earth, and the fact that Christ lives in all those who believe in him; these three great truths were made known to Paul. [pp. 29-30] From the time of his initial vision

Paul's whole life was to draw its inspiration from the depths of this experience, and the entire evolution of his thought was linked up, directly or indirectly, with this key point. [p. 31]

Paul does not boast of his position as an apostle, a preacher of the gospel; "I am under compulsion and have no choice. I am ruined if I do not preach it!" [I Cor. 9: 16]

---

[114] The material in this section is taken from Amedee Brunot, <u>Saint Paul and His Message</u> (New York: Hawthorne Books, 1959). All references to this work will be followed by the appropriate page number in brackets.

But it is of primary importance that the <u>true</u> gospel be preached. The vision on the road to Damascus is still so vivid in Paul's mind and the truth he learned from it is so certain that he even dares to say:

> For even if we, or an angel from heaven, should preach to you a gospel not in accord with the one we delivered to you, let a curse be upon him! I repeat what I have just said: if anyone preaches a gospel to you other than the one you received, let a curse be upon him! [Gal. 1: 8-9]

These are strong words! Paul was always aware of his own human weakness. But in the matter of God's revelation to him he was unshakable. He was saying, in effect, "If I ever deny the truth that I have given you, do not believe me. If another, even an angel, teaches you differently, do not believe him; in fact you should condemn him!" Such was the conviction that arose out of Paul's original experience.

Reflection

Those words of Paul show the strength of his belief in his original experience of Christ. No new experience could nullify his conviction. Paul is often considered an example of "instantaneous conversion." This may be a correct interpretation of what happened. There may, however, be another way of looking at his conversion. The energy with which he persecuted the Christians indicates that he feared the new sect. This could be explained as fear that the new teaching might be detrimental to Judaism. It seems also very possible that Paul was secretly attracted by the courage and zeal of the Christians and expressed his resistance to that attraction by persecuting them. Traumatic events have a way of distracting a person from his resistances. His defenses drop for a moment and that to which he is attracted appears before him clearly and he is confronted with his own attraction. This dynamic is often seen in the relationship between the sexes. A young couple may be resisting their attraction to one another and denying any such feeling. An emergency, an accident or a bad scare leaves them in each other's arms wondering why they had never noticed before how much they already love one another. Something similar may have happened to St. Paul.

This explanation is not intended to say that the conversion of Paul was merely a natural occurrence. It is intended to point out that St. Paul's experience may not have been essentially different from the experiences of many others. The important point is not so much the nature of the experience but how he responded to it. He took the event seriously. Perhaps his mysterious trip to Arabia [Gal. 1: 17] immediately after this experience was a flight into solitude where he could work through the meaning of the event and decide on his response. He put his faith in this one experience and based his whole future life on what he had learned through it.

There is no natural explanation for such fidelity. The emotional impact of the most traumatic experience fades with time. A negative experience – one of intense pain or terror– may leave me with some permanent phobia. But a positive experience – of joy or illumination – is not, in itself, enough to inspire my whole life to the extent that I will selflessly dedicate all my efforts to a given cause. Such an experience can, however, function as a cornerstone on which I can build. I reflect on the meaning of this experience and how to respond to it. I see in the experience meanings deeper than merely logical conclusions or emotional reactions.

As I respond to those meanings, I find in my experience of responding a newer, deeper knowledge of what the experience means. I allow the experience to bear fruit in my life. It is not just the experience that keeps me going, but my faith in what the experience revealed to me. To Paul, the experience revealed that Jesus is Lord that he is the fulfillment of the prophecies that he lives in all men.

All this is another way of saying that in vocational experience I feel an attraction, I give my assent to that attraction and I express my assent in my decisions and behavior. My assent and my expression give rise to deeper intuitions about the source of the attraction. The attraction takes on new appeal; again I give my assent to these new aspects of attraction and express my assent in concrete decisions and actions. The original attraction –even an attraction as unusual as that which St. Paul felt on the road to Damascus – is not the whole of the vocational experience. It is the beginning of the "gift" of vocation. But I must nourish that gift with fidelity and perseverance over a lifetime.

As far as the original attraction to Christianity is concerned, however, at least the first disciples and St. Paul could point to a concrete experience. Where does the potential Christian of today first experience the attraction to embrace Christianity?

<u>Romano Guardini</u> [115]
<u>The Church</u>

In studying the birth and growth of faith, Guardini looks to the Church as the principle and ground of faith as well as the atmosphere in which it is lived. This is not to say that the Church <u>gives</u> faith or that doctrinal instruction can awaken faith of its own power. "It is God who makes faith. It is He who awakens faith in the heart of the one whom He calls." [p. 104] He can do this without human agency if he so pleases, but that is usually not his way. Usually faith is awakened through the mediation of another believer.

Doctrinal instruction by itself is incapable of awakening faith in the hearer, only doctrine in which the teacher himself believes. It is when truth is loved and lived that it awakens faith. [p. 103]

For one who is born into a Christian family, the model for faith is usually embodied in the parents. Even so the person himself must make a choice.

At first, without knowing it, you have lived with them in their faith; then your own faith arose, became definite, and finally found the strength to stand upright. [p. 103]

In the body of the Church the individual believer finds himself nourished and supported but also confronted. The Church confronts him as "the repository of a sacred authority." [p. 108] It is the Church's role to teach, judge and command. The encounter between a vibrant, spontaneous faith and the precision and

---

[115] The material in this section is taken from Romano Guardini, <u>The Life of Faith</u> (New York; Paulist Press, 1963). All references to this work will be followed by the appropriate page numbers in brackets.

195

immovability of dogma may seem to present the possible danger of chilling or even killing the richness of life of the believer. Guardini sees a solution to this dilemma which preserves both elements.

> Upon encountering dogma, a spontaneous and living faith may also become involved in a crisis: we must resign ourselves to this as something inevitable. But if faith always emerges victorious if it assimilates dogma, it then acquires a spirit of decision and awareness of responsibility and of destiny which are simply irreplaceable. It need not lose its vibrant energy. It has only to gain by the seriousness and pain of discussion. [p. 114]

Dogma is the atmosphere in which faith develops character. At certain times dogma may function as a warning in the life of the believer, but more often it will be "a guide on the road toward a higher liberty." [p. 114]

Reflection

In light of this section from Guardini, it may seem that faith has become more "humanized," a little more down to earth. There are no miracles involved, nobody being knocked off his horse by a thunderbolt. It is simply a matter of seeing what those around me are doing and, if I find it attractive, following their example. So it may appear.

The call to embrace Christianity is not merely the call to membership in a social or cultural body. The attractiveness of such a social body may be what rouses my initial interest. But if I am really being called to Christianity, there are deeper elements involved. Like the disciples and St. Paul, I am being called to a relationship with Christ. In the case of the disciples, the attraction of Jesus was originally mixed with the desire to help liberate their country, to make a name for themselves and to find something a little more interesting than fishing. The man who is attracted to Christianity today may be looking for a religion with a strong tradition or an adequate doctrinal framework. Like the disciples, he must go beyond these initial motivations or, rather, he must let the true Christian motivation permeate them and dissolve their grip on him.

The time will come for the Christian when he may find little experience of security in the doctrinal framework. The long tradition may no longer seem to support him. What is he to do? In the initiation rite of Baptism he symbolically underwent death and rose to new life. He gave up his grip on self-centered and worldly desires, renounced the pomps of this world and committed himself to a new life dedicated to following Christ in faith and love. Now the time has come to incarnate that symbolic act in daily life, to let go of the little security blankets, the false hopes and the idealized self-image. It is time to face some of the fears that have been avoided along the way. The basic choice is between serving Christ or serving himself. His whole life will be a series of such choices. With each choice he does the best he can. He is not perfect. His motives are not perfect. His understanding of his motives is not perfect. He makes mistakes; he makes wrong choices; he is tempted to despair when he sees how blind or foolish he has been. But he goes on. However long he may have been baptized, he is always engaged in becoming a true Christian; he has never fully arrived.

The person working his way towards embracing Christianity also experiences a certain ambiguity. He, too, would like to be able to make crisp clear-cut decisions. But that is not the way life is. He recognizes his attraction to Christianity. He tries to get information, to ponder his attraction, to talk to others who have made the step. All this is good. But the decision to embrace Christianity must always be an act of faith taken in a certain degree of darkness. He is always faced with the attraction and with obstacles. Nobody can make the decision for him; he has to stand alone and decide, "Shall I or shall I not make the leap?" What makes the difference? What is the determining factor that tips the balance one way or the other?

To try to answer that question would be dangerous. Sociological, psychological or rational explanations can always be brought forth. They are not irrelevant, but they are not enough. They might explain why a person attaches himself to a particular group – those who make up the Church – but to associate oneself to the group is not necessarily the same thing as to embrace Christianity.

Christianity can be embraced only in an act of faith. That faith may be weak and fragile. It may be covered over with fear, diluted with selfishness and distorted with misconceptions. But it is there. It must be nourished and given room to grow and expand. Risks must be taken on behalf of this faith even when its presence can hardly be felt. To do so is itself an act of faith. We find ourselves continually returning to the heart of the mystery when we try to explain faith. It is a gift which must be accepted without being fully understood. We can only accept it, give it our assent and try to express it faithfully in everyday life. This is what the disciples and St. Paul had to do.

Christianity is an incarnational religion. It is centered around mysteries that cannot be explicitly expressed in conceptual terms but are expressed symbolically. We will now look at the initiation rite, Baptism, to see what its symbolism tells us about the Christianity to which we are called.

Jean Danielou [116]
Baptism

In studying the liturgy, Jean Danielou gives special consideration to the interpretations of the early Fathers of the Church and to types found in the Old Testament. For our purposes, we will look only at the interpretations the Fathers give to the initiation rites.

The baptismal ceremonies actually began, in the early Church, at the beginning of Lent, when the catechumens were enrolled and the quality of their lives was examined. This was followed by daily exorcisms and catechesis leading up to the renunciation of Satan and adherence to Christ.

After these preparations, the baptismal rite begins at the Easter night ceremony. The initiate's clothing is first removed, symbolizing the removal of the old man as well as stripping away the same of the sinful Adam which had brought about the need for clothes in Eden. This is a reference to Genesis 3:7. The disrobing also signifies the restoration of the primeval innocence of man who stands before God in a spirit of filial trust.

---

[116] The Material in this section is taken from Jean Danielou, The Bible and the Liturgy (Notre Dame, Ind.: University of Notre Dame Press, 1956). All references to this work will be followed by the appropriate page numbers in brackets.

While stripped, the initiate is anointed with oil. This anointing, like the anointing of athletes, is to strengthen the initiate for his future struggles with the powers of darkness. This is a reference not only to the struggles of everyday life in the world but especially to his struggle and conquest which is about to follow in the baptismal immersion itself.

The actual Baptism consists of both immersion and emersion.[117] The initiate is symbolically plunged into a purifying death and raised up, a new creature by the power of the Holy Spirit.

The immersion symbolizes the purification of the initiate from sin. It is a cleansing, a bath. But it is also a death; we are baptized into the death of Christ and buried with him. "We have been planted together with him in the likeness of His death." [p. 45] Christ underwent the reality of death; we imitate his death symbolically but receive the reality of salvation.

> Baptism is an "antitype" of the Passion and the Resurrection, that is to say, it is at the same time like and unlike the original... In the death and Passion of Christ, there are two aspects which must be distinguished: the historical fact is only imitated: the sacramental rite symbolizes it, represents it. But the content of saving grace allows us a true participation (koinonia) [italics in the original]: The two aspects of the sacrament are thus defined perfectly: it is an efficacious symbol of the Passion and the Resurrection, representing them corporeally and actualizing them spiritually. [p. 45]

---

[117] Danielou explains the importance of immersion at greater length than that of emersion. Another treatment of Baptism which may help the reader to a fuller understanding of the symbolism can be found in Alexander Schmemann, Of Water and the Spirit (Crestwood, N.Y.: St. Vladimir's Seminary Press, 1974), pp. 37 –70. Also Danielou is speaking mainly of adult baptism. Schmemann treats the question of infant baptism briefly on pages 67-69.

Thus the waters of Baptism are not only the tomb in which the sinful man is buried but also the womb from which the new creature emerges. The new Christian is conformed to Christ's death, not for the sake of death, but that he may share in Christ's resurrection.

After the triple immersion, the initiate is clothed in white. "These white robes are given to replace the old garments taken off before Baptism which were figures of the 'old man'." [p. 49] The white robes symbolize the new man robed in innocence and incorruptibility in place of sin. He has recovered the robe of light and grace which Adam had before the fall. A final rite, which Danielou discusses at some length, is the sphragis or imposition of the sign of the cross on the forehead of the initiate. This sign or seal identifies the new Christian and has many overtones of meaning, including a relationship to the circumcision of the Old Covenant.

The sphragis [italics in the original] of Baptism, then, signifies a contract of God with the baptized person whereby God grants him irrevocably a right to the blessings of grace. The baptized may withdraw himself from taking advantage of this right, but he cannot cause the right itself to be revoked. [p. 68]

This variety of rites manifests the spiritual riches of Baptism: the death of the old sinful man, resurrection to a new life of innocence and incorruptibility, and the seal of God's future help and protection.

Reflection

In studying the call of the first disciples and of St. Paul, the striking feature was the personal nature of the call. The disciples were called by Jesus as he walked by the seashore. St Paul saw him in a vision and heard his voice. In studying the

201

role of the Church, we did not see this personal element with the same clarity. At least that is the way it might seem. Jesus was not seen in the flesh or in a vision. No audible voice was heard but that of men like ourselves. "No, we do not see Christ, but we know him by faith." This expression implies that faith is an alternate way of knowing Christ. Actually, it is the only way of really knowing him. Many people knew the young carpenter from Nazareth. They knew him as a man whose name, Jesus, means savior. But they did not know that in his name was their salvation. They knew he existed, but they did not believe in him. They did not have faith. Knowing Christ during his earthly life was of little avail without faith in him. Not to have known him thus is no great disadvantage to one who has faith.

How does Christian faith differ from the faith of universal religious belief which we studied in the previous division? Another way to state the question would be: What is so special about Christianity? It is just another articulation of the same basic experience that we find in other religions?

As noted above, it is not especially important if one did not know Christ as man during his earthly life in Palestine. This is not, of course, to say that that earthly life was not important. All that is peculiar to Christianity had its origin in that earthly life. Of special interest here is Christ's passion, death and resurrection. In this mystery the redemption of mankind was definitively accomplished. But man must accept that redemption; it is not forced upon him. He does not accept redemption by conforming to a set of precepts but by accepting a whole new life as his own. He surrenders his old sinful life and undertakes to allow Christ's life to be lived in him. It is not as though Christ's life on earth was cut short and he is allowed to <u>continue</u> it in the Christian. It is rather that the same life – with its love for God and man, its fidelity to the Father's will, and its passage through death to new life – is <u>lived</u> <u>anew</u> in the person of the Christian.

In Baptism I am introduced into the Christ-life symbolically by immersion and emersion. I have been granted, in this sign, the Paschal Mystery. If I die with Christ, I shall rise with him to new life. Only that in me which dies will also rise. Only if my harshness dies can his gentleness come to life in me. Only if my selfishness dies can his generosity blossom in my life. Only if my ambition dies can his humility pervade my life. But this is not some kind of a "deal" in which I look over the goods to be obtained and decide whether or not to pay the price. Rather, I give myself and trust in God's promise. I submit to death and let him take care of the new life for it is really a <u>new</u> life, a life of which I do not really have any previous experience. I do not know what it is like to be gentle with Christ's gentleness. I do know that my harshness has seemed to be necessary for survival at times. But Christ's call says, "Give it up; drop it." No ten days' free trial; no "satisfaction guaranteed or your harshness back." I do not have to know what is going to replace it. I have only to believe, to trust that, when I accept death, Christ will come to life in me. I cannot manipulate the process so as to retain my life and have his also. I let my desires, my longings; my needs die and trustingly accept what he gives in their place. All this, again, takes place with faith as the only guide. The question is not why this death-life dynamic works or how it works or what are the terms. The question is: Do I believe enough to surrender myself to it? The new life comes to me as a gift – not an unexpected or unhoped for gift – but a gift of his choosing, not mine.

In Baptism I am incorporated into the mystery of Christ's death and resurrection. This is what the Christian is called to: a movement through death to new life. Such a movement is implicit in other religions. In Buddhism, the death of desires makes possible the manifestations of Nirvana. In most ethical or moral systems, peace and happiness come to life when I allow my selfishness to die. There is a similarity. But there are differences too. Nirvana, peace and happiness are natural results of particular kinds of behavior. Buddha may have been the first to discover Nirvana but, if he had not done so, somebody else would have. He did not institute it though he may have been the first to experience it. If Christ had not undergone death and resurrection, nobody else would have. Participation in the Paschal Mystery is not something within the reach of human power; it is a free, unmerited gift of God to man.

Another way in which Christianity differs from other religions is in the matter of relationship with God. God remains the Wholly Other, the One who totally transcends man. But he also becomes, in Christ, a man among other men who walked the earth. We know relatively little about the details of his earthly life. This is not particularly important. What is important is that he was truly man. He experienced humanity just as we do. According to scholastic theology we may not say that Christ was a human person; he was a divine person who took on a human nature. But according to ordinary everyday experience, he was all that a human person could be. While God remains the Wholly Other, he is also available to us in an intimate relation of friendship. He can be found not only in the gospel narratives but in the depths of our own hearts and in the people around us.

Perhaps the simplest way to sum up the call to Christianity is to say that it is a call to discover Christ in all things and to rediscover all in him. Like all simple summaries, this sounds – and can easily be – platitudinous. But to the believer it is an oversimplified and inadequate description of an indescribable experience of intimate love, trust and surrender.

With Baptism, the new Christian has been incorporated into Christ's death and resurrection. He has felt the attraction to Christianity, given his assent, and expressed the assent symbolically in the sacrament of initiation. Christ has come to birth in his life. Now Christ must grow in him. Every fiber of the Christian's being must undergo the Paschal experience of death and resurrection to new life. Every fiber must come to an intimate experiential knowledge of the love and mercy of Christ. Baptism is the introduction into the new life. We will look now at the way the Christian grows into a deeper intimacy and identity with Jesus.

CHAPTER VII

I AM CALLED TO GROW

AS A CHRISTIAN

In Baptism the new Christian has expressed his assent to his attraction to Christianity. In one sense the attraction can be considered to cover the period from first interest to the decision in favor of Baptism. The assent could be considered predominant during instructions and preparation. Baptism and the subsequent Christian life would correspond to the expression of assent. This linear model is valid. For my purposes, however, I have preferred to use a cyclic paradigm. The vocational experience takes place in a series of attraction, assent, and expression cycles with each new attraction growing out of past cycles. The more I grow in my vocation, the more each new attraction is a call to my whole being and the more whole-hearted is my response to it.

In Christianity the attraction to ever deeper surrender to Christ's call should grow throughout life. This chapter will be concerned with some of the elements in Christian life that are closely connected with that growth. In the second division we saw two expressions of the vocation of universal religious man: word and ritual. In chapter six we saw the words of Jesus as an invitation to the first disciples and

Baptism as a ritual of initiation into Christian life. In this chapter we will again study word and ritual. Reading the word of God in scripture will be considered as a means of growing to deeper union with Christ. The Eucharist will then be considered as the ritual expressing unity among Christians and their participation in the sacrifice of Christ. This will be followed by an examination of the attitude of identification with Christ and what it means for him to live in the Christian. Finally, there will be a section on grace, the gift of God which makes all Christian life possible.

Adrian van Kaam [118]
Formative Scripture Reading

Reading the Bible has long been recognized as a means of growing into a deeper relationship with God. The efficacy of such reading depends on the manner in which it is done. In speaking of formative scriptural reading, Adrian van Kaam has in mind reading that is done for the sake of such personal spiritual growth. He distinguishes formative reading from informational reading. Information reading is the type of reading that most of us are familiar with. We read to learn facts: How are the peace talks going? Did they settle the strike? Who won the ball game? We do informational reading about scripture also. This reading keeps us informed "about the doctrinal, theological and exegetical aspects of the sacred text." [p. 125]

---

[118] The material in this section is taken from Adrian van Kaam, The Woman at the Well (Danville, N.J.: Dimension Books, 1976). All references to this work will be followed by the appropriate page numbers in brackets.

Such knowledge protects us against making erroneous interpretations or accepting those of others.

Formative reading, on the other hand, "is meant to enlighten our unique inner formation in Christ." [p. 126] This reading is done slowly, in a relaxed manner with emphasis on the quality of reading rather than on the amount of information taken in. The text is approached as if it were written for me alone and is allowed to reveal whatever messages the Holy Spirit may wish to convey to me at the present moment. Sensitivity to such messages will grow slowly with fidelity to the practice of formative reading.

A main virtue to foster during this reading is docility which could be described as an inner availability to any word of the scriptures the Spirit may use to awaken us. Docility implies a serene receptivity that quiets our aggressive mind – a prayerful openness to the mystery that may hide itself in the sacred text; it is an attitude of childlike wonder ready to be surprised by unexpected manifestations of the Divine. [pp. 136-137]

The reader remains free to stop at any moment to reflect on any word or passage that happens to strike him. He may come across a text which evokes a resonance in his life. He should stay with it awhile and allow it to have its full effect on him. He may ask himself how this text fits in with his daily living or in what way it sheds light on his spiritual growth. If no resonance occurs, the reader patiently waits for the Spirit's own good time. He remains faithful to his formative reading, trusting that God will enlighten him when the time comes.

At times a text may arouse a strong resistance in the reader.

We should prayerfully reflect on what in us might possibly give rise to such negative feelings. Does a text weary us because it indicts attachments the Spirit wants us to overcome? Do we feel offended because the text questions some merely human aspirations we have totalized in our lives, idolizing them beyond any directiveness God may give us? If we have to admit this is the case, we should implore him to gradually lift us beyond such attachments, ambitions and idols. [p. 140]

Formative scripture reading makes the word of God come alive for the Christian. The scriptures are no longer just another religious book, albeit a special one. They become an intimate companion in our spiritual journey towards intimacy with Christ.

This is the kind of reading that can enlighten us in darkness, deepen our dwelling in God's presence, fortify our fidelity to the life call, prompt our commitment to the divine transformation of the world, orient our whole life to intimacy with the Eternal Love that carries us. Briefly, it is the kind of reading that illumines and nourishes the life of self-formation in Christ through the Holy Spirit. [p.129]

This type of reading is not without its dangers. The messages received from scripture may be distorted by any number of irrational feelings and desires. "Therefore, we must check out the meanings and directives gathered in our reading." [p. 141] The more enthusiasm the inspiration seems to arouse, the more it may be necessary to check it out. There are a number of criteria which should be used in testing the validity of an inspiration derived from formative reading. The inspiration must be in tune with Church doctrine and compatible with reason and common sense. It should be such that it would be judged advisable for me in the minds of wise, sensible and spiritually experienced Christians. At least it must be such that it would not be positively rejected by them. It must bear some valid relation to the actual scripture text. The inspiration must tie in with my graced form of life as known from past graced experiences and not be subject to reasonable objections from the community or family of which I am a member. Finally, the effect of the inspiration on my inner life is important. Does living the new insight bring peace and equanimity and facilitate prayer? All these matters have to be considered in checking out an inspiration. But the checking out should come after the inspirational reading and not interfere with the reading itself.

The reader can submit himself to the discipline of formative scripture reading but he cannot force results. Inspiration is a gift from God and must be received as such.

The human attempt to read scripture with docility and equanimity is a sign of our promise to cooperate with his grace of formative reading once it touches our lives. The human attempt is necessary yet it may tempt us to forget that its outcome is only provisional, a shadow of what is to come, that is, the divine enlightenment of our soul that is a pure gift of the Spirit communicated to us in and through the scripture text. [p. 151]

Reflection

In the Old Testament the prophets of Yahweh proclaimed the word of the Lord, usually to large groups of people. In the New Testament Jesus addressed his word of invitation to the apostles. They, in turn, proclaimed his word to all who would listen. In reading scripture, I, too, am confronted with the word of the Lord. It is a word addressed to all men but also a word addressed to each man. In formative scripture reading I look for the particular messages that are meant for me. It is not like looking up a passage in a book. When I do that I know what I am looking for, I find it and I know I have found it. In formative reading I may never know what passage may strike me or what its message will be. I am not certain for some time whether or not the inspiration is valid for me. I must be sensitive to inspirations as they come and faithful to them once they have been validated.

Sensitivity and fidelity seem to be major factors in growing as a Christian. We like to have a nice clear message that is unmistakable and then have it renewed periodically. That is not God's way. He speaks softly, loud enough to force that attention. True, the prophets sometimes thundered at the top of their voices and were heard by everyone in the neighborhood. Often the prophet's voice was heard but the word of the Lord was not. Sometimes the word of the Lord was heard – or seemed to have been heard. The listener was struck with compunction and fell on his knees begging for mercy. This lasted for a couple of days and then faded away. Why? We do not readily accept lack of fidelity as an answer. "So I get an inspiration – one inspiration; I hear what sounds like a word of God – one little experience of apparent enlightenment; am I supposed to turn my whole life around on the basis of that? If it is really a message from God it will come again!" This is usually the way we justify our procrastination.

It is not immediately apparent to us how similar this attitude is to that of the Jews in the Old Testament. The psalmist laments:

They kept not the covenant with God; according to his law they would not walk; and they forgot his deeds, the wonders he had shown them. [Psalm 78:10-11]

Even recent favors are forgotten or not taken seriously.

And they tempted God in their hearts by demanding the food they craved. Yes, they spoke against God, saying, "Can God spread a table in the desert? For when he struck the rock, waters gushed forth, and the streams overflowed: Can he also give bread and provide meat for his people?" [Psalm 78: 18-20]

In the New Testament we see Jesus feeding the multitude with a small amount of bread and fish. [Jn. 6: 1-15] The people are amazed and want to make him King. But the very next day they are asking what sign he will work so that they can put their faith in him. [Jn. 6: 30] In the Gospel of Luke we see Zechariah conversing with an angel – presumably a fairly extraordinary event, even in the life of a Jewish priest. To the angel's message Zechariah replies, "How am I to know this?" [Lk. 1: 18] One wonders what kind of a sign might have convinced him.

In contrast to all these examples, there is the case of Mary who also receives a message from an angel. She responds: "How can this be since I do not know man?" [Lk. 1: 34][119] The angel does not object to this request for an explanation. Mary was sensitive to the one message; she did not need more and did not ask for more. The angel's greeting had troubled her and she had wondered what it meant. [Lk. 1:29] Later – about twelve years later – we see that after finding Jesus in the temple, Mary "kept all these things in memory." [Lk. 2: 51]

---

[119] In a footnote, <u>The New American Bible</u> paraphrases Mary's question, as meaning "How is she to know that the child she is now to conceive will be the Son of the Most High?" This seems unfaithful to the text. Mary asks how it will be done, not how <u>she can know</u> that it will be done.

She preserved the experiences intact, pondering them and trying to enter more deeply into their meanings. She was faithful to them. They were not valid only for a time. A conversation with an angel – whatever that expression might mean – is an unusual occurrence. But the novelty of such things wears off quickly. A few weeks later one could easily ask: Did it really happen? Was it just my imagination? Did I exaggerate its importance?

The messages I may receive in formative scripture reading will probably not be as explicit as those which came to Zechariah and Mary. But they are God's word to me and I am responsible for protecting and nourishing that word. If I fail to do so, the word may be repeated to me at a later time, but it may not. My failure to respond to one inspiration may dull my sensitivity to the next one.

Growth as a Christian is a very modest business. It consists of responding to the invitation of God as it appears in the small things of every day life. If I do not hear his word in the small and ordinary, I will not be likely to hear it in the spectacular. If I cannot hear him speaking in scripture, I will probably not hear him speaking if an angel appears to me or if I get knocked off my horse by a bolt of lightning. At best, I will experience a temporary spurt of enthusiasm which will soon cool off.

The word of the Lord may come to me not only in scripture reading but also in many of the activities of daily life.[120] The Lord speaks not only in word but in ritual. In the Eucharist we see many indications of the direction growth as a Christian is to take.

Jean Danielou [121]
The Eucharist

In studying the Eucharistic rites, Jean Danielou considers them in the context of the Easter Vigil ceremony in the early Church in which Baptism, Confirmation and the Eucharist, in combination, formed the introduction of the new member into the Church. He does not discuss the fore-Mass and reading – what we would call the Mass of the Catechumens – since this part was replaced by the procession of the newly-baptized into the Church. His study is principally concerned with the three principle parts of the Eucharist, the preparation or Offertory, the great prayer of thanksgiving pronounced over the gifts, and the distribution of communion to the faithful.

As is his custom Danielou goes to the early writers of the church to seek their interpretation of the meanings of these rites;

---

[120] This section has dealt only with formative <u>scripture</u> reading. Formative reading can be done with other spiritual literature as well. Three books by Susan Annette Muto will be found useful in general spiritual reading: <u>Approaching the Sacred</u> (Denville, N.J.: Dimension Books, 1973), <u>Steps Along the Way</u> (Denville, N.J.: Dimension Books, 1975), and <u>A Practical Guide to Spiritual Reading</u> (Denville, N.J.: Dimension Books, 1976).

[121] The material in this section is taken from Jean Danielou, <u>The Bible and the Liturgy</u> (Notre Dame, Ind.: University of Notre Dame Press, 1956). All references to this work will be followed by the appropriate page numbers in brackets.

If we go to the principle Eucharistic catecheses, we find that two chief themes constantly recur in explaining the primary significance of the sacrament: the Mass is a sacramental representation of the sacrifice of the Cross, the Mass is a sacramental participation in the heavenly liturgy. These two essential themes run through the whole Eucharistic liturgy. [p. 128]

That the Mass is the sacramental representation of the sacrifice of the Cross is familiar to most Christians. The idea of participation in the heavenly liturgy is less common today.[122] In the Eucharistic catecheses, however, it seems to have held a fairly prominent position. The deacons who prepared the offerings on the altars were figures of the angels. The newly baptized, entering the church in procession, are seen to be entering the heavenly sanctuary according to St. Gregory Nazianzen:

In Gregory's vision, the paschal night opens out into eternity. The baptized have already entered into it. The boundaries between the earthly world and the heavenly have been done away with. The baptized already mingle with the angels. They are about to take part in the liturgy of heaven. [p. 130]

The center of the heavenly liturgy is the priestly action of Christ in his Passion and Resurrection. The sacrifice of Christ subsists in three modes; in its execution at a certain time and place in history, in its eternal celebration in heaven, and in its sacramental representation on earth. Communion of the faithful is seen

---

[122] The idea of the Christian life as a life that is associated with the angelic life and participation in it is discussed by Jean Leclercq in The Life of Perfection (Collegeville, Minn.: The Liturgical Press, 1960), pp. 15-42. Leclercq is speaking specifically about vowed religious life, especially monastic life. However, he states that "Basically, the religious life is nothing but a way of living the Christian life in the Church." [p. vi] Thus it seems he would apply his comments to Christians in general.

215

to be a sharing in the "bread of angels" [p. 139] and a foretaste of the eternal banquet.

More familiar to most of us is the idea of the Eucharist as a sacramental representation of the Sacrifice of the Cross. "Christ is the altar, the offering and the priest." [p. 130] As the offering, bread and wine become, by the consecration, the Body and Blood of Christ.

But what is rendered present on the altar is not only the Body and Blood of Christ, it is His sacrifice itself, that is to say, the mystery of His Passion, His Resurrection and His Ascension, of which the Eucharist is the anamnesis [italics in the original], the efficacious commemoration: ... [p. 136]

This efficacious commemoration not only recalls the sacrifice of the Cross; it also makes it present. It "is not a new sacrifice, but the one sacrifice of Christ rendered present." [p. 137] It is the same sacrifice that is offered daily, "not one today and another tomorrow." [p. 137]

The kiss of peace, which formerly followed the offering of the gifts, again emphasizes unity, this time a unity among the participants at the Eucharist. The kiss signifies the union of souls. It is a sort of public profession of the charity that exists among the various members of the one Body:

All of us, many as we are, we form one body because we partake of the same Bread. We must, then, before approaching the sacred Mysteries, carry out the rule of giving the peace by which we signify our union and our charity toward one another. [p. 133]

In communion the Christian receives spiritual nourishment by his participation in the sacrifice, the Death and Resurrection, of Christ. "Indeed the mystery of the Passion and Resurrection is rendered present only in order to apply its effects to us." [p. 139]

Quoting Theodore of Mopsuestia, Danielou states: "In participating in the mystery, we commemorate in figure His Passion, by which we shall obtain the possession of the good things to come and the forgiveness of sins." [p. 140]

Reflection

In Baptism, we saw the new Christian incorporated into the passion, death and resurrection of Christ. He was stamped with the sign of the cross and granted a right to the blessing of grace. Baptism is only a beginning. The best way for the Christian to grow in his faith is to stay close to the Paschal Mystery into which he has been introduced. This has been made possible in a special way by the Eucharist. The new Christian is not introduced into the faith and then left to his own devices.

In the Eucharist I am called to renew participation in the death and resurrection of Christ. I am called not just as an individual but as a member of a community. The call is an invitation to grow more in conformity with the life of Christ, to allow the old man of sin to die daily so that the life of Christ may come to greater fullness. But it is also a call to grow in love for the others in the community. Christ is not only found in the sacrament but also in all his members. Loving them is not just "practice;" I am not just exercising my loving faculty on them so as to be better able to love Christ. In loving them I do love him, for he lives in them just as he lives in me.

The Eucharist is not just an "opportunity" to enter again into the Paschal Mystery. It is an invitation to do so. That is its meaning. [123] The Eucharist not

---

[123] Following his chapter on the Eucharistic rites, Danielou studies a number of Old Testament figures of the Eucharist as well as several figures of the whole initiation process. See The Bible and the Liturgy, pp. 142-207.

only provides an invitation; it also provides a means. The Paschal Mystery is made present and available to the Christian. He is invited to participate in it. He renews his commitment, he is given spiritual food for his daily efforts to further Christianize his life, and he receives a foretaste of the good things to come.

This last element, the foretaste of things to come, brings us to the second essential theme which Danielou mentions, the celebration of the heavenly liturgy. How am I to participate in this theme? I can study all the symbolism involved, consult experts, meditate on the subject, but what if it does not move me? What if it leaves me cold? I can appreciate the representation of the sacrifice of the Cross and my participation in its fruits. I can see – at least by faith and sometimes by intuition – Christ living in others and struggling to get a stronger foothold in my own life. I can feel the truth of that; it means something to me. But this heavenly liturgy idea; it may not move me at all. I can say, "Yes, I believe that the angels and saints in heaven are praising God along with us." I believe it, but it is somewhat dead faith, mere intellectual assent. And yet, according to Danielou, it is an essential theme of the Eucharist; the sacrament is <u>calling</u> me to share in the heavenly liturgy. In a sense I can <u>hear</u> the call but I do not <u>feel</u> it. It seems to have no motivating power. If it were a call to some particular action, like giving the kiss of peace when I did not feel

I had any peace or love to share, I could go ahead and do it. But in the case of the celestial aspect of the Eucharist, it is a call to appreciate and experience a dimension of the sacrament that has no appeal for me. What am I to do?

I might attack Danielou as archaic. I might defend my position as more enlightened and realistic, not so triumphalistic and abstract. I might denounce those who "think they feel everything the Fathers said just because they can repeat it verbatim."

All these solutions would seem to be aimed at convincing someone – probably myself – that I have already grown to the fullness of Christianity. That would be very unchristian conviction. I cannot grow as a Christian if I think I have already arrived. I must always remain a beginner. I must always be willing to accept the fact that there is plenty of room for progress. When I see some element of Christianity that I cannot appreciate I should see it as an area in which I am being called to grow. But how?

Perhaps the answer can best be found in the part of the Mass that I do appreciate. This is an opportunity to participate in the Paschal Mystery. The appreciation of the heavenly liturgy aspect of the Eucharist is not something I can bring about by myself. If it is to be a truly Christian attitude, it must be a gift. I must accept it as such. But I must also dispose myself for it. How? The Resurrection is always preceded by a death. What is it that has to die in me? Maybe it is the concept I have of myself as a full-grown Christian who has a full appreciation of all the Church's teaching, a mature appreciation of all the aspects of the sacraments, and so on.

I resist when a situation comes along that indicates the contrary. When I hear that participation in the heavenly liturgy is an essential element of the Eucharist, I may try to deny its significance, or I may try to muster up, by my own ingenuity, an enthusiastic appreciation of it. Neither solution attacks the real problem. Both ways try to maintain my status as full-grown Christian.

That self-concept must die. I must let go of it. And I must let go of it without seeing what will replace it. I have to accept the fact that I am not yet fully Christian and be open to further growth without being certain what direction that growth will take. I must trust that the new life that comes awake in me will be God's gift. That new life, those new attitudes, will have to be checked out as the inspirations received in formative scriptural reading had to be checked out.[124] Sometimes I may have to wait a long time and not have anything to show for my patience. But faith tells me that if I die with Christ, I shall also rise with him to a new life. I died and rose with him in Baptism. I renew this conformity to his death and resurrection in the Eucharist. I must also try to live it out in my daily life. Each attraction to further growth is also an attraction to a partial death. I give my assent to that death and express my assent by trying to abandon the inadequate attitude or behavior, simply giving it up without replacing it with anything except faith and hope that God will supply.

---

[124] See pages 209-210.

What will God give in place of the old man? The new life is always a gift and always something of a surprise. But something can be said about it in general. For a description of the person living a more full Christian life we will turn to a small book by Paul de Jaegher, S.J.

Paul de Jaegher [125]
Identification with Christ

In growing to a closer union with God, the Christian generally passes through two stages: intimacy with Christ and identification with him [p. 11] In the stage of intimacy, the Christian feels Christ to be living within him as in a tabernacle. He is always there as a companion and intimate friend. At this stage one might say, "I live and Christ lives within me." Christ is a guest, a friend, a helper and support, a close companion. This presence contributes greatly to the richness of the Christian life, making the personal relationship with Jesus a central element in everyday life.

With time and fidelity, however, this intimacy gradually deepens and changes into identification. Now the Christian no longer experiences Christ as merely present within him, but also as acting within him.

---

[125] The material in this section is taken from Paul de Jaegher, One With Jesus (Westminster, Md.: The Newman Press, 1952). All references to the book will be paraphrased, in most cases, rather than quoted directly. This will be done in order to avoid a terminology which is no longer current. For example, de Jaegher speaks of the person as "the soul" and uses feminine pronouns. I will ordinarily replace this with "the Christian" and use masculine pronouns. Whether paraphrased or quoted directly, all references will be followed by the appropriate page numbers in brackets.

Jesus continues to live, to love, to suffer, to pray to his Father in and through the Christian. De Jaegher makes an important clarification:

> Let it be well understood, or we run the risk of considerably minimizing the sublime ideal just mentioned, that there is no question of offering oneself to Christ that he may descend to our own level and live <u>our</u> life within us: we must offer ourselves to Christ that he may live <u>his</u> own life in us. [pp. 13-14, italics in the original]

In the stage of intimacy, I may be asking Christ to unite himself to me and act within me so that I may live my life in a more pure and holy manner, be more faithful to prayer and the practice of virtue.

Identification is different from this. In the stage of identification, the Christian is no longer concerned with his own purity and holiness, his own prayer and virtues. Now Christ is asked to live, not only in, but through the Christian. It is not a new life he is to begin which, however holy, would be circumscribed by the limits of a puny creature. [p. 14] It is Christ's own life that is to be continued in the Christian. The interests, views, love and desires of Christ are to come alive in the heart of the Christian; gradually, Jesus is substituted for self. It can then be truly said, "The life I live now is not my own; Christ is living in me." [Gal.2:20]

This transition does not take place overnight. Nor is it usually accomplished once and for all. Often the person finds himself slipping back into self-centered ways. He seeks to establish his own ego, to make himself the center of his world. But the consciousness of Christ dwelling within reveals every attempt of his natural and selfish life to regain its former ascendancy. He will have a clear intuition of whatever is not Jesus and could not be Jesus in him. [pp. 23-24]

De Jaegher concludes his book with a series of suggested resolutions. [126]

One of them seems especially suited to liberate a person from the narrow world in which he tends to confine himself:

> I should also like my spiritual life to be full of wide and manifold interests. Instead of concentrating on myself, as if I were the center of the world, I shall adopt the wide views and vast interests of Jesus who lives in me. The whole world will thus be mine and the millions of souls that belong to Jesus will also belong to me. My prayers, joys, sufferings, work for souls, everything will be enlarged and ennobled. [p. 49]

This suggestion leaves the Christian wide open to whatever God may ask of him. But de Jaegher does not claim that the way of identification he has described is for all. It should not be forced on one who has no attraction to it but should be made known to all who can profit from it. The implication is that most Christians should find it useful at some time in their lives since it is based on the doctrine of sanctifying grace and is very characteristic of St. Paul's teaching.

---

[126] Several of these resolutions seem as appropriate to de Jaegher's "intimacy" stage as to his "identification" stage. He does not intend to imply that the "intimacy" stage is selfish or self-centered. In a footnote on page 15, he states: "We believe that there is no better and more indispensable disposition for a life of identification with Christ than the precious acquisition of a true devotion to Jesus, the guest of the heart. As a matter of fact, in practice, souls pass usually through the stage of life of loving intimacy with Jesus present in the soul, before even thinking of a life of identification with him." He goes on to say that the two are "two successive degrees in a life of perfect union with Christ." [p. 15]

<u>Reflection</u>

My first contact with de Jaegher's book came after hearing of two people whose lives, independently of one another, had been completely changed by it. They were on the verge of giving up their religious faith when they came, by chance, upon the book and read it.

We have been speaking about the Paschal Mystery, about death and the gift of new life. We have spoken about the symbolic incorporation into the mystery in Baptism and its representation in the Eucharist. Mention has also been made of implementing this mystery in my everyday life by dying to my own desires and letting Christ bring me a new life. De Jaegher seems to carry things to their logical conclusion: In a sense, I seem to even give up my self, my subjectivity, since another lives my life, lives in and through me. This is not actually so; I remain the subject of my actions but they are all performed in the spirit of another. Still, such a movement seems to be the ultimate in death and new life.

The surprising thing, then, is that this high ideal should be so effective in attracting those who are on the verge of abandoning even the <u>lowest</u> of religious ideals, on the verge of abandoning religion altogether. A similar case is mentioned by Thomas Merton.[127] A young married woman, apparently baptized and brought up as a Catholic, sees no logical reason for the existence of God. Arguments

---

[127] This story is told in <u>Contemplation in a World of Action</u> (Garden City, N.Y.: Image Books, 1973), p. 395.

and proofs make no impression on her. Then one day some priest tells her: "Look, God wants your heart, not your mind: God loves you!" Suddenly the whole problem dissolved. She sensed who God is, how much she needed him, how he loved her and was calling her to love him in return. It was all clear to her in a flash. How does this sort of thing work?

It is easy to say that God gives his grace where he wills. But in these cases maybe there are some laws that deal with resistance that can be clarified. We seem to gravitate toward complexity. We build a little wall of defenses around our religious faith to protect it against attacks of any kind: temptation, criticism, argument, and so on. Pretty soon we are spending all our energy defending the defenses and the faith itself is not getting much attention. It struggles to make itself heard in daily life but we are too busy with "more important things." The faith is still there, but it cannot find articulation and expression except in abstract, theoretical formulae that do not really move me. Then, with a few brief words, somebody hits the nail on the head. In a flash, without any reasoning processes, it is clear that this is the real heart of the matter; this is what I really want. So it seems to have happened in the above examples. What the persons in question were really looking for was a personal relationship with Christ, a relationship of love.

At this point another problem arises. There seems to be a limit to how much can be said explicitly about this relationship. Very quickly things start getting sticky and sentimental. Is this just a cultural hang-up? Is the topic simply too personal to be expressed in any but the briefest and simplest terms? Probably the latter. At any rate, this personal love for God in Christ seems to be at the heart of Christian faith. No intellectual assent to a body of truths, no elaborate and airtight theological system, no profoundly symbolic sacramental order will remain alive without it.

This personal love for Christ is always a response to his invitation, to his initiative. The love itself is not just human love; it is a gift also. To try to get an idea of what this means we will consider, briefly, the concept of grace. It is on the concept of sanctifying grace and the abiding presence of God in the soul that de Jaegher has based his thoughts on identification with Christ.

Cornelius Ernst [128]
Grace

In trying to establish a perspective for a theology of grace, Cornelius Ernst gives a survey of the word charis (grace) in the New Testament. He tries to show that it is not used to indicate one gift among several that God gives to man. Rather, it "qualifies the whole of God's self-communication as a gift beyond all telling." [p. 29] It indicates a wholly new mode of relationship between God and his creatures.

Ernst then goes on to a survey of the understanding of grace in the Christian tradition. He points out a shift in meaning from grace as God's mercy

[128] The material in this section is taken from Cornelius Ernst, The Theology of Grace, Theology Today Series, No.17 (Notre Dame, Ind.: Fides Publishers, 1974). All references to this work will be followed by the appropriate page numbers in brackets.

itself to grace as the created gift which his active mercy brings about. [pp. 12, 53] The Reformation brought both Catholic and Protestant theology to a limited view of revelation in which the emphasis is on "what happens to man, and indeed the individual man, not what God does in his self-manifestation." [p. 60]

Ernst feels that today a new approach is possible. He distinguishes an "unchanging relationship between God and man" from a "changing understanding of this relationship." Recognizing the validity of both elements, Ernst sees two ways of approaching the study of the relation between God and man. One way would formulate a doctrine of God and man first and then view the relationship in the light of these preconceived terms. The other way consists in trying to speak out of the awareness of the union as we already sense it today in our own experience. Ernst chooses the latter method.

For Christians there can be no question but that the center of our awareness of the union of God and man is Jesus Christ. Consequently the center of any theology of grace must also be Jesus Christ. [p. 69]

It is primarily in our experience of Christ in faith that we are to understand the union of God and man. Meeting Christ in faith is a "new kind of understanding and a new kind of meaning," [p. 69] which modifies and extends the range of understanding and meaning we had before.[129] It is within the enlarged world of meaning found in the experience of Christ in faith that Ernst locates grace.

---

[129] Ernst suggests the term "meaning" as a contemporary replacement for the term "being" of earlier Western philosophical traditions. Like "being," "meaning" transcends the distinction between subjective and objective and has the same kind of universality and obviousness. He calls meaning "that praxis, that process and activity, by which the world to which man belongs becomes the world which belongs to man." [p. 68]

One element in the process of meaning is the emergence of the question "Why?" "Destiny" is Ernst's term to designate "the sense and the direction of the process of human meaning." [p. 70]

Christianity gives a unique answer to the question, "Why?" Human destiny is determinate and is disclosed in the destiny of Jesus. His is predestination, a fulfillment of God's purpose, in which we share by our union with him in faith. The destiny of the Christian lies in the hymn of praise which survives when all other meanings fail and one is reduced to despair:

> Struggle against it as we may, we have to be lifted up with Jesus into the transcendence of his Cross in a common destiny with him. This is the final expression of the love of the Father and the love with which Jesus loved and loves his own: it must be the living and luminous center of any theology of grace, a love in and beyond death. [p. 70]

The content of this destiny or calling is transformation. If meaning is a process and praxis, then the new dimension of meaning discovered in faith in Christ may result in a transformation as real as, or more real than, any transformation that man effects in the world. Grace must also be real if it is primarily understood to be "the novelty introduced into our lives in our experience of Jesus Christ." [p. 70] "Real" has been understood in the past to mean that which objectively exists, a thing whose existence can be demonstrated empirically. Ernst suggest a different understanding:

We should take as our primary instance of the real what has already been proposed as the primary instance of meaning: the "genetic moment" in which man is transformed as he transforms his world. By analogy, we may say that budding is more illuminatingly the moment of the real than the flower or the soil out of which it grows: the genetic moment is the prime moment of the real, the moment of truth. [p. 74]

The genetic moment is not just insight; it is a mystery. "It is dawn, discovery, spring, new birth, coming to the light, awakening, transcendence, liberation, ecstasy, bridal consent, gift, ..." [p. 74]

The transcendent newness which is unfolded in the life of one to whom Christ has been communicated as Gift is Ernst's understanding of the primary sense in which the word "grace" might be used. This novelty will manifest itself in many ways in nature, the sacraments, forgiveness, freedom, and so on. Ernst considers some of these and, without claiming to have arrived at a clear and concise definition of grace, concludes his study:

> If we are to discover the mode of human existence as God's gift, we have to learn to "let go," so as to receive all as gift; allow the breath of the Spirit to aerate our heart's blood, to liberate us into the freshness and fertility of newly-germinating life. We have to be roused from our dreams of reality, and waken to the reality in the dreams. "Behold, I make all things new." [pp. 93-94]

Reflection

A reader with a scholastic background will probably not be very satisfied with Ernst's presentation since it does not go into detail. He does not delineate actual grace, prevenient grace, efficient grace, and so on. He is only trying to establish a perspective for a theology of grace.

What he has said ties in well with much that we have said about vocation, and especially the Christian vocation. Vocation is always experienced in some way as a gift. It is experienced as the emergence of a new meaning out of a world that is familiar. This new meaning, or world of meaning, comes mysteriously in a genetic moment, a moment of recognition and realization. It is important, of course, to preserve the content of this moment, not to just take for granted that there are plenty more where that one came from. It is safer to assume that any future breakthrough will depend on my attitude towards this one. St. Paul's conversion and the three cases mentioned on pages 224 and 225 of this book might be viewed as typical instances of genetic moments. Such a graced experience is not unusual, but the operations of grace are going on all the time in less conspicuous ways. The formative scripture reading of which Adrian van Kaam spoke depends on such graced moments for its efficacy. [130] But these moments may be more like weak sparks than bolts of lightning. In growing as a Christian I must learn to be attuned to the slightest tremor of such movements, to preserve them, reflect on them and respond to them. They do not always involve a pleasant experience. In fact, grace is always related to the Cross according to Ernst. It is always a participation in the dying and rising of Christ if it is really a graced experience. I give up, or am stripped of, my dependence on the previous meanings which have held things together for me and a totally new realm of meaning irrupts into my life. I may struggle hard to keep that with which I am familiar. Or I may recognize its inadequacy, want to give it up but be unable to do so. I cannot avoid the death aspect of the Pascal Mystery. And perhaps the hardest thing about death is not knowing what will come after, losing everything I am familiar with, everything I depend upon, and not knowing what if anything, will

---

[130] See pages 207-210.

follow. The only way I can undergo the death-new life movement is in a spirit of trust and hope. I must trust in the efficacy and power of Christ's death and resurrection and hope for its fruit in my own life and the lives of others. Each genetic moment will bring a temporary springtime with it and something of the experience that "this is it; now everything's going to be alright." That experience will seem to fade, but actually it is only a matter of some of the sensible novelty having worn off. The new understanding, the new meaning has become part of my world. Without ceasing to be a gift, it is, in every sense of the word, <u>mine</u>. What Shunryu Suzuki says of Zen meditation might be said of the Christian's daily dying to his limited human desires:

> If you continue this simple practice every day you will obtain a wonderful power. Before you attain it, it is something wonderful, but after you obtain it, it is nothing special. It is just you yourself, nothing special.[131]

In the case of the Christian, however, it is not <u>just</u> you yourself. It <u>is</u> something special, but not special as a goal that has been attained. The new powers, the new meanings, become the context in which I am to surrender my life to Christ in the hope of a new genetic moment of graced transcendence.

---

[131] Shunryu Suzuki, <u>Zen Mind, Beginner's Mind</u> (New York: Weatherhill, 1973), p. 47.

CONCLUSION AND TRANSITION

In this division we have studied the call to embrace Christianity and the call to grow as a Christian. Much emphasis was put on the incorporation of the Christian into the Paschal Mystery of Christ. Redemption has already been achieved and the Christian enters into that achievement. It is not a redemption that he attains by his own efforts; it is a gift. Growth as a Christian is also a gift, a whole network of gifts.

In many ways, the death and new life that is at the heart of Christianity is prefigured in other religions as well as in the natural order itself. Outside Christianity, however, it is not apparent that the new life is anything more than the natural outcome of death. It is necessary to note, however, that Christianity is not confined to those who have been baptized officially and belong to some particular Christian sect. It must include all who have undergone the genetic moment, the grace experience of death and resurrection to life in Christ. Though many such persons may never have heard of the Christian Church as an institution, who can say that Christ does not live in them – especially when it is sometimes fairly obvious? It seems, though, that it would be to their advantage to be able to understand their inner life in an explicit doctrinal and sacramental framework.

Within explicit Christianity, there are many concrete ways in which a person can foster and express the Christ life within him. One of these is the vowed religious life as it is found within the Roman Catholic tradition.

DIVISION IV

THE CALL TO

THE VOWED RELIGIOUS LIFE

INTRODUCTION

In the first division we studied man, on the universal human level, experiencing a call to some state or course of action. In the second division we looked at religious man being called to a life in which he could express his religious values. The third division did not follow this same pattern. It did not deal with Christian man being called to a particular way of life. It dealt with the call to embrace Christianity and the call to grow as a Christian. This division will be concerned with the call of a Christian to a particular state of life in which he may express his Christian values, namely the vowed religious life.

We have seen a number of elements which participate in the constitution of a vocational experience. On the human level, this experience was seen to be influenced by the talents and self-concept of the individual, his previous conditioning and the meanings and values that he found in his world. The vocational experience began with an initial attraction to which the person gave his assent. He then expressed this assent in his decisions and behavior. This gave rise to a new attraction and the procedure was repeated.

Gradually, after a considerable period of time had passed, it was possible to say with a certain amount of assurance that this person had a vocation to do such and such. I have used the term "vocation" in a fairly limited sense, not in the general sense of "job" or "career." In my use of the word I have referred to a situation in which a person is attracted to a particular state or course of action <u>primarily</u> in order to thus realize his ideals and express his values. At the same time, he realizes his ideals and expresses his values <u>primarily</u> by embracing this particular state or pursuing this particular course of action. Thus I would not say that a teacher has a vocation to enhance the intellectual growth of mankind if he becomes a teacher primarily in order to make money. Nor would the term apply if teaching were only a secondary way of realizing his values.[132]

The introduction of the religious dimension of man and the world in Division II brought new elements into play in the experience of vocation. Man's religious sense – a primary recognition that he has a relationship with God – and his sense of God as the "Wholly Other" introduced new horizons of values and a deeper sense of obligation.

In Division III the Christian vocation was studied. In the case of the first disciples and St. Paul, the term "call" took on a more explicit meaning. It was quite clear that someone called and it was clear that that someone was Jesus of Nazareth.

---

[132] This use of the term is explained more fully on pages 14-16.

Even so, a lifetime of dedication was needed before the full meaning of the call was understood. Today Christ's human voice is no longer heard but the Church continues his invitation. Men are invited, through the Church, to incorporation into the Paschal Mystery in Baptism, the sacrament of initiation. Like the first disciples, the Christian of today is called to a life of friendship with Christ. The call presupposes continual growth in intimacy and love. This is affected through grace to which the Christian disposes himself by formative scripture reading, the sacraments and a number of other means. Growing in grace, he deepens his personal relationship with Christ until he can say with St. Paul, that it is no longer he who lives but Christ who lives in him.

In this division we will study the Christian life as expressed in a particular concrete state of life. In a religious context, the most common use of the word "vocation" is in reference to the call to the vowed religious state or to the priesthood.[133] Less frequently it is used in reference to the married state.

---

[133] Joseph J. Sikora, in <u>Calling: A Reappraisal of Religious Life</u> (New York: Herder and Herder, 1968), pp. 9-28, raises the question of whether or not "vocation" is a viable concept. He cites four generic vocations: the priesthood, married life, the religious life, and the single life consecrated to God. The question of viability is raised in regard to the religious life in the light of four objections: that sanctity can and should be found in other forms of life, that religious life often impedes apostolic activity, that religious life often appears to impede spiritual growth and that it prevents maturity and full human growth in many. Sikora affirms the value of religious life but asserts the need for re-evaluation of its operation in the modern world. Richard Butler, in <u>Religious Vocation: An Unnecessary Mystery</u> (Chicago: Henry Regnery Co., 1961), contends that the term "vocation" should only be used in reference to the call to the priesthood. The call to religious life should be considered an invitation from God that is extended to <u>all</u> Christians but which does not contain the same sense of "necessity or obligation"

This division will be concerned with the call to the vowed religious life. The Christian who is called to the vowed religious life embraces that state primarily in order to express and incarnate his religious values. The living of the religious life is the primary way in which he expresses these values. Within religious life there are many different articulations. Generally, there is the distinction between active and contemplative orders. Among the active or participative orders there are a variety of apostolates such as teaching, nursing and caring for orphans. Among contemplative orders there are those that emphasize communal life (coenobitic) and those that place more emphasis on solitude (eremitic). Within each order and each community there is a certain amount of difference among the ways in which individuals express their vocations. Each subject brings his own particular needs, abilities, talents and limitations to the vocational experience. Out of the interplay between the subject's aspirations and the objective possibilities and demands of the situation there arises an attraction.

There can be no simple (or even complex) formula by means of which it can be predicted what state of life will be most suited to a particular person. The unknowable areas of the human temperament and character are too vast; the originality of human freedom is to unpredictable, and the workings of divine grace

---

to respond. p. 156. Butler seems to feel that one who experiences himself as called to the priesthood is under obligation to respond but one who feels called to religious life is not. This may fit his understanding of the word "vocation" and its usage in Cannon Law, but it does not seem clear that his interpretation is backed up by experience.

are too mysterious to allow such a formula. We can only point to some of the elements that seem to be involved in the vocational experience.

The subject who experiences himself as being called brings certain permanent and transient characteristics, certain abilities and limitations, certain needs and desires. In the case of the Christian being called to the vowed religious life, all these elements are influenced by the power of grace. But the attraction is also affected by the object-pole of the experience: the life to which the subject is attracted. In this case, he is attracted to a celibate life in which he will live in poverty and obedience. Such a life is primarily designed to foster his spiritual growth in love and dedication.

This division will contain only one chapter which will be divided into two sections, one dealing with the subject-pole of the vocation to religious life, the other with the object-pole. We will consider only the call to enter the religious state. The call to grow as a religious will be treated in the fifth division.

CHAPTER VIII

I AM CALLED

TO THE VOWED RELIGIOUS LIFE

I. THE SUBJECT-POLE

Adrian van Kaam [134]
Life Call, Life Form, Profession

In Adrian van Kaam's personality theory the deepest level of man's being is his spiritual dimension. Man is basically a unique emergent self. As spirit, man is always tending to express and incarnate his spiritual identity in various modes of presence and projects. His unique spiritual identity is not a detailed blueprint which is to be expressed in a preordained way. It is, rather, a general orientation, never fully known, in which a particular person's emergence may most fully take place. This unique emergent self with its particular identity is both a gift and a call from God.

God first loved me into being as a new emergent self, unique on this earth. He lovingly continues to call me to that uniqueness he meant for me from eternity. I must answer this call to be myself by commitment and consecration, by a life that offers to God a wholehearted "yes." [p. 138]

---

[134] The material in this section is taken from Adrian van Kaam, In Search of Spiritual Identity (Denville, N.J.: Dimension Books, 1975). All references to this work will be followed by the appropriate page numbers in brackets.

This "yes," or assent, to the call to be myself must be lived out in a variety of modes. Some modes are more fundamental and lasting; others are temporary and passing. There is, in each person, a fundamental, underlying call which is gradually unfolded to his understanding as he perceives and incarnates aspects of it. Modes of expression that are congenial with this fundamental underlying call, insofar as it is known, should be retained; those that are uncongenial with it should be dropped. This fundamental, underlying call is termed "life call" by van Kaam:

> Life call refers to the mystery of all-embracing divine call; a call that covers the unique being of my whole life in all its aspects; a call that enables me to surpass as spirit self each finite temporal and concrete situation in which I find myself here and now; a call that articulates itself during my life in many specific calls. [p. 146]

Life call is not the same as the permanent life situation in which it is expressed. Such a permanent life situation is called a "life form." Van Kaam recognizes three fundamental life forms; "the married life, the celibate life in priesthood or religious community, and the celibate life in the world." [p. 153] Life call and life form are not identical but are so closely related that "I cannot spiritualize myself if I don't see and live my life form as an expression of my life call." [pp. 153-154]

Besides expressing life call in a particular life form, each person usually expresses it also in a profession or job. A job or profession is often referred to as a "vocation" and there is a certain truth in this. But it is not a vocation in the same fundamental sense as in a life form. In the Catholic tradition, the word "vocation" is generally used to refer to the category which van Kaam designates as "life form."

Thus van Kaam distinguishes three levels of calling: fundamental life call, life form and profession or job. Each of these levels is expressed in a particular "style." Corresponding to the life call is a fundamental life style, a way of being in the world, a way of reacting and responding that allows me to adapt to my environment and to express the self that I am. "The life style is fundamental precisely in that it touches upon all modes of my inner and outer behavior. It is the primary vehicle of incarnation." [p. 153] This life style is relatively permanent. Early in life a person begins to develop a life style. At first this style is not usually congenial to healthy personal development; "it is a style of unconscious anxious and defensive reactions to the environment." [p. 156] This seems to be necessary for the child since he does not yet have any means of coping with the vast world in which he finds himself. "Even religion can be understood and used as a defense against the anxiety of the spirit." [p. 158]

Gradually, by a process of purification, this uncongenial life style must be changed to a style that will be a more suitable expression of the person's true spiritual identity. "The whole spiritual life is a story of dying to the old style of life and being reborn with Christ to a new one in tune with our eternal calling." [p. 159]

As there is a fundamental life style, there is also a vocational style, a way of reacting and responding that expresses my commitment to my life form. The vocational style is flexible and can change according to circumstances but should remain in harmony with the chosen life form and a congenial fundamental life style. Finally, there is a professional style. Within any given profession there are

240

a variety of styles that can be successfully adopted. No one individual, however, will find all of them equally compatible with his temperament and character. Thus a quiet, slightly passive person who undertook the legal profession might be better working in research than trying to become a prosecuting attorney.

In the harmoniously spiritual person, we find an integration of the fundamental, vocational and professional styles. For example, a person like Thomas Aquinas seems to have expressed beautifully in his writing, teaching, and interacting with others the style of his spiritual identity and holiness, of his vocation as a priest and friar, and his profession as a scholar and university professor. [p. 155]

A person may not always be able to find ways of expressing himself that are in accord with his taste. He may have to settle for a job that is not worthy of his talents in order to support his family. Such situations cannot always be avoided. Still, he must approach the situation with the realization that the support of his family is a more fundamental obligation than the fulfilling of his talents or ambitions. He should strive to integrate all the elements in his life into a style of living that is compatible with his deepest identity insofar as he knows it.

The more my spiritual life becomes incarnated and integrated the more I will reach a unity of life style that expresses personally, vocationally, and professionally the person I have been called to be from eternity. [p. 171]

Reflection

Van Kaam's term "life call" includes all the elements that we have previously considered as aspects of the subject-pole of the experience of being called. But it is not just a concept that expresses their sum. It is a concept that expresses the meaning and purpose of a particular person's whole life. It might be compared to the "seed of destiny" of which I spoke in the introduction to this book.[135] It would probably be misleading to try to carry this comparison too far. My life call is not something that grows; it is already complete. My knowledge and understanding of it is what grows. This seems to correspond to experiences and justify the use of the term "eternal vocation." There are two ways in which eternal could be interpreted in this context; it could mean I am called <u>for</u> all eternity or it could mean I am called <u>from</u> all eternity. In regard to religious vocation the latter meaning is the common one. Jeremiah expressed his experience of a vocation that was there before he existed:

> The word of the LORD came to me thus: Before I formed you in the womb I knew you, before you were born I dedicated you, a prophet to the nations I appointed you. [Jer. 1: 4-5]

St. Paul experienced his vocation in a similar way:

> But the time came when he who had set me apart before I was born and called me by his favor chose to reveal his son to me, that I might spread among the Gentiles the good tidings concerning him. [Gal. 1: 15]

The vocational experience is often so profound an experience that it seems to have been preordained. Even the old whaler, Captain Ahab, felt that his fateful pursuit of Moby Dick had been eternally decreed.

---

[135] See page 1.

This whole act's immutably decreed. "Twas rehearsed by thee and me a billion years before this ocean rolled. Fool! I am the Fates" lieutenant; I act under orders.[136]

The person feels that what he is called to is bound up with the fundamental meaning of his whole life. But it is hard to see how his experience can tell him what was being done long before he was around to experience anything. I may say that my experience tells me that my vocation is the whole meaning of my life but my experience cannot reach back into eternity. In a religious context I may conclude from theological considerations that my call is eternal. In van Kaam's terminology, it seems to be the life call, rather than the life form (to which he applies the term "vocation"), that is eternal. Perhaps it is better to avoid the term "eternal vocation" altogether, at least in the sense of having been called from all eternity. While such a term may increase the security of one who has found his vocation, it might easily increase the anxiety of those still searching. The disadvantages of the term "eternal vocation" do not prove that there is no truth in it. But it is much easier to see how the experience of vocation has ramifications for all eternity.

In van Kaam's terminology, Jeremiah's life call might be described as a call to warn his people against infidelity to the Lord. Paul could be said to have been called to preach the good news of God to those who had not yet heard it and protect its integrity in those who already believed. Both men chose to live a celibate life

---

[136] Herman Melville, Moby Dick (New York: Random House, 1950), p. 552, The story of Captain Ahab's pursuit of the whale was told on pages 105-108.

form in the world, Jeremiah as a priest and prophet, Paul as a missionary. In these two examples, life call, life form and profession seem to be integrated. Their life form of celibacy was in the service of their life call and profession. Their professions were the primary way in which they expressed their life call and were chosen primarily in order to express those life calls.

In some examples, however, there may be a discrepancy between van Kaam's terminology and that which I have been using. He presents Abraham Lincoln as an example. Lincoln's life call appears to have been "to live an exemplary life of effective concern for equality of justice among men." [p. 151] His life form was marriage and his professions were those of "lawyer, politician, statesman and president." [p. 152] His life call and profession seem to have been in harmony with one another. To translate van Kaam's terminology into my own: Lincoln expressed his values and ideals <u>primarily</u> through his professions, and chose those professions <u>primarily</u> in order to express his values and ideals. The same cannot be said of the relationship between his ideals and his marriage. It took some effort to keep his marriage from interfering with the professional expression of his life call. [137]

---

[137] That Lincoln's marriage sometimes threatened to interfere with his profession does not necessarily prove that the marriage was a mistake or that it was not compatible with his life call. In many ways his wife contributed to his profession while proving an obstacle in other ways. Some of the contributions are mentioned by Carl Sandburg, <u>Abraham Lincoln: The Prairie Years</u>, Vol. I, (New York: Harcourt, Brace and Co., 1926). p. 431. It may also be possible that Lincoln's profession did not provide opportunities for some aspects of his life call. These opportunities may have been provided by his marriage.

In the introduction to this book I gave a brief account of my own vocational experience. It was a call to the vowed religious life, specifically a monastic life. What kind of life call would be likely to find its expression in a contemplative monastery? Obviously the monk gives up many things. Like other religious he gives up marriage and family, some degree of material possessions and the freedom to control his own life. But he also gives up the positive practical contribution he might make to the culture, the opportunity to minister to the needs of others, to alleviate their sufferings and to spread the good news of Christ to them. None of these things are incompatible with loving God. What value is realized in the life of the monk that can justify all the goods that he sacrifices?

To say that the monk's prayers are contributing more to these worthy causes than any practical efforts may be true. But I think a deeper answer is demanded. Somehow it seems that, if monastic life is to be justified, the monk must suffer his share of the things all men suffer. If he is freed from some of the inconveniences of others, he is also without some of their distractions. It seems to me that most of the pain and suffering in the world consists in a concrete instance of man's experience of his own fundamental frailty, insecurity and dependence. I work hard to establish a successful business and suddenly it collapses and I am left with nothing. I devote myself to my wife and family and they are snatched from me in a fire or auto accident. I work hard to develop my athletic ability and find myself bedridden and paralyzed for life. I place my love or trust in another and find myself scorned or betrayed. In each of these cases I have tried to establish myself in the world and the foundation has collapsed beneath me confronting me painfully with my mortality, my inadequacy, my dependence and insecurity – with all the frailty of the human condition. My efforts were not attempts to secure my life in a shell of illusions; they were legitimate and praise worthy efforts to incarnate human values. But success in such efforts can distract me from my human condition which I will eventually have to face in one way or another.

The monk tries to go to the heart of things, to avoid this danger of distraction, to face the human condition and experience it fully. But this is only meaningful and possible in the context of God's love. Outside that context it would be an exercise in pessimism or masochism and would lead to despair. But in the light of God's love it ought to lead to a peace and humility that allows the monk to surrender his life to God without fear or hesitation. Since he is clinging to nothing, he has nothing to lose. This is not a clever way of avoiding the pain of loss by not having anything. It is rather a voluntary acceptance of the pain of loss. Such a sacrifice presupposes an appreciation of what is given up. It also presupposes that what is given up is given up for a purpose. The monk gives up natural and human supports so he can be free to depend on God alone. To put it another way: he dies so that Christ may come to life in him. He immerses himself in the Paschal Mystery in the faith that this is where the meaning of his life lies and no other course of action on his part could be more valuable or profitable to himself and the rest of mankind. He cannot and need not justify it rationally. It only makes "sense" from the point of view of faith in the Paschal Mystery. It is the way in which some people

choose, and are chosen, to live out this mystery. Others choose, and are chosen to

live it out in other ways. It is not a matter of comparing monastic life with other

forms of religious life.

> In speaking of the loftiness of the monastic ideal and of the excellence of this particular way of life, we nowhere mean to give the impression that the monastic Orders are by their very nature superior to other religious institutes for, after all, the chief dignity of the monk lies in the fact that he has abandoned competition and the quest for human glory and is content to be the last of all. [138]

While it cannot be predicted who will or should choose what vocation, there

are various sociological and psychological factors that are relevant and can be

studied in order to determine their influence on the vocational experience. For an

understanding of these we will turn to the works of Luigi Rulla.

Luigi Rulla [139]
Self-Transcendent Consistency

In his two major works, Rulla presents a fairly elaborate theory of religious

---

[138] Thomas Merton, The Silent Life (New York, Farrar, Straus and Cudahy, 1957), p. xiii.

[139] The material in this section is taken from the writings of Luigi Rulla. His basic theory of vocation is presented in Depth Psychology and Vocation (Rome: Gregorian University Press, 1971). A later book, Entering and Leaving Vocation: Intrapsychic Dynamics (Rome: Gregorian University Press, 1976), written with Joyce Ridick and Franco Imolda, presents results of a considerable amount of research based on the theory. A brief article by Roger Champoux, "New Perspectives in Religious Formation," Supplement to Doctrine and Life, LXX (July – August, 1977), pp. 203 – 224, outlines some of the more important thoughts presented in Rulla's two books.

vocation. Much of what he says has been mentioned in one context or another throughout this book so it will only be necessary to point out some of his main ideas here.

Rulla emphasizes the idea of self-transcendence. He sees two components in the person embarking on a vocation.[140] There is the ideal self which consists of my ideals – what kind of person I would like to be (self-ideals) – and my understanding of the ideals of the institution which I am entering (institutional ideals). In addition to the ideal self, there is the actual self which consists of my conscious self-concept, characteristics that can be discerned by psychological tests (latent self), and my self as a social being (social self).

Consciously proclaimed ideals may be either in the form of values or attitudes. Values are enduring ideals or goals to be attained (terminal values) or modes of conduct (instrumental values). Attitudes are more specific and temporary dispositions which may serve values, but they may also stem from needs of the individual and interfere with growth in his religious vocation.

For wholesome vocational development there should be a consistency among the various elements. Inconsistencies can be conscious as when a person recognizes the gap between his ideal self and his actual self. But they can often be subconscious. An example of such a case might be the person who values community life highly. This attitude may stem from and serve a need to depend on

---

[140] Rulla uses the term vocation in a slightly different sense than I have been using it throughout this book. For him it means entrance into, and life in, the priesthood or a religious order. I have been using it in the sense of the experience of being called to such a life.

others rather than stemming from and serving Christian charity. The significance of inconsistencies varies greatly depending on how central they are to vocational commitment. The subconscious inconsistencies have a particularly negative effect, especially when they represent the dominant motivation of the person. In the process of living the religious life, a person may overcome some of these inconsistencies so that his motivation for persevering is different from his real motivation for entering. Those inconsistencies that are not worked through may actually be supportive of perseverance but detrimental to apostolic effectiveness. One of the fundamental requirements of successful vocational growth is the ability of the subject to internalize the values presented to him by his new vocation. He must internalize them because of their intrinsic value, not because of personal needs they may fulfill, and because they are in harmony with his own consistent ideals.

Thus Rulla identifies this theory as one of self-transcendent consistency. The self-transcendence is accomplished and supported by a consistent self and fosters self-fulfillment, effectiveness and perseverance.

Reflection

The first thing that comes to mind in reading Rulla's theory is the difference between his approach and that of Donald Super.[141] In Super's view, the choice of a particular vocation (by which he meant a job or career) was an attempt on the part of

---

[141] Super's theory was treated on pages 22 – 25.

the subject to implement an already formed self-concept. Rulla takes a more progressive approach. He sees vocation (specifically religious vocation) as an attempt to realize an ideal self, to become the person I think I <u>should be</u>, rather than an attempt to express the person I think I <u>am</u>.

Another interesting distinction Rulla makes is that between perseverance in vocation and apostolic effectiveness. If the search for security is one of my reasons for entering a monastery I may find the security I am looking for. I may find it to the extent that I would never dream of leaving the monastery. But the person bent on establishing his security seems to never be secure enough. At first I may feel secure enough just by being in the monastery. Before long, however, I will find things within monastic life that begin to threaten me. This situation or that person will be more than I can handle and again I will retreat into a "safe" zone. Perhaps I am asked to assume some position of responsibility. I may become panicky and refuse or, if I do consent, I may be so afraid of failure that I am unable to really give the job my full attention. Thus, as Rulla states, my effectiveness is impaired. In this example the inconsistency lies in thinking I have embraced monastic life through a desire to fulfill a higher, spiritual responsibility, while the real motive is a fear of the ordinary responsibilities of daily human life. This aberration reminds us of the statement of Emmanuel Mounier regarding transcendence: "A reality that transcends another is not one that is separated from and floating above it, but a reality that is superior in the quality of its being." [142] I cannot develop a spiritual sense of responsibility

---

[142] Emanuel Mounier, <u>Personalism</u> (Notre Dame, Ind.: University of Notre Dame Press, 1952), p. 65.

independently of an ordinary human sense of responsibility. This is not to say that I have to have a fully developed human sense of responsibility first. The two may develop simultaneously but I cannot flee from the demands of human responsibility and expect to grow spiritually. I cannot fight tooth and nail to preserve every vestige of my own fragile little ego life and still enter into the Paschal Mystery of death and resurrection with Christ.

The presence of such inconsistencies does not necessarily indicate the absence of a vocation however. Many times they can be worked through if I am willing to be honest with myself. If part of my motivation for entering religious life was a search for security, I may occasionally find that security threatened. I must not react immediately but must distance myself from the situation and see it in the context of my whole life. Do I want my life to be available for the service of God or do I want to live securely? The crucial question will have to be faced as squarely as I can face it even though all the elements may not be as clear to me as I would like them to be. I should take a little time to make the decision, if that is possible, and reflect on the choice later when I can see things a little more clearly. Growth does not consist in never making wrong choices but it does require the honest admission of those choices. Growth in the religious vocation will be the topic to be considered in Division V so we will not pursue the topic further here. The important point is to recognize that one begins where he is, with his assets and liabilities. They are part of the ground out of which the vocational experience must grow.

We have considered some of the aspects of the subject-pole of the experience of being called to the vowed religious life. We will now turn to the object-pole, the vowed religious life itself. The three vows of poverty, obedience and chastity will be considered as particular expressions of the Christian life.

II. THE OBJECT POLE

Barbara Albrecht [143]
Evangelical Poverty

Albrecht, in seeking to point out the contemplative foundation of vowed poverty, begins by considering four kinds of poverty. First there is material poverty – not destitution – but a poverty that causes some pain and inconvenience. It is not the most important level of poverty but it must be practiced because Christ practiced it and because any spiritual poverty would otherwise be a sham.

A second kind of poverty is experienced in sickness, loneliness, anxiety, boredom and despair. These may be found in the midst of an abundance of material goods.

The third kind of poverty consists in having the heart of a poor man, a child who depends on God for everything. He receives everything as a gift from God, uses things freely and with gratitude, gives them away when others need them more than he does.

Finally, there is evangelical poverty. This presupposes a personal call to

---

[143] The material in this section is based on "Evangelical Poverty" by Barbara Albrecht which appeared in Review for Religious, XXXIV, No. 6 (November, 1977), pp. 918-923.

follow Jesus out of love. It involves freely giving up the management of one's whole life. Such surrender goes beyond having the heart of a poor man but it must include the spirit of poverty, trust and gratitude. It is more than giving up things; it is giving up oneself wholly. The evangelical counsel of poverty creates a new relationship of obedience in following Christ more closely out of love and in response to his call.

Albrecht then proceeds to trace the <u>origin</u>, the <u>standard</u>, and the <u>aim</u> of evangelical poverty. She sees the origin in the gospel message of God's self-emptying love. The Father makes himself poor for our sakes by giving up his own Son for our salvation. He does this voluntarily not for the sake of poverty or for some profit to himself, but for the sake of others; he does it out of love. The Son, too, becomes poor. He becomes a servant not only of God but of men. He accepts rejection and failure, suffering and death at their hands. He does not call upon the twelve legions of angels to help him. It is through poverty, not riches and power, that he saves man. Like the Father, the Son does not take on poverty for his own sake or for the sake of poverty itself. He becomes poor in order to bring the world to faith. Thus evangelical poverty originates in heaven, freely chosen by the Father and the Son, in order to enrich mankind.

What, then, is the standard by which we are to measure our poverty? The standard, according to Albrecht, is Christ. He is the master and exemplar. But since the servant cannot be greater than the master, our dedication to poverty can never compare with his. Measured against him as a standard, our essential poverty, our real lack of love and generosity, our total weakness and dependence, become disconcertingly obvious. It is this poverty that Christ came to heal, to replace with his riches. He became poor, not for the sake of poverty, but to make us rich.

Finally, Albrecht considers the aim or goal of evangelical poverty. The goal
is, as has already been indicated, the overcoming or transforming of our poverty.
Poverty is undertaken for the sake of enrichment; it is to turn the poor into heirs of
the kingdom and give them a share of God's joy.

The religious must translate Christ's poverty into an authentic expression in
today's world. Interior detachment is necessary but it must be expressed in a
practical way by living material poverty and renouncing some goods on behalf of the
poor. This presupposes a genuinely healthy appreciation of these goods. Besides
material goods, there is the problem of power. Power is a means at the disposal of
the wealthy but not of the poor. The Church cannot totally give up all the means at
its disposal. But such means must remain at the service of the poor – all who are
called to the kingdom of God. There can be no triumphalism, false security or
privileged status for the Church. The Church must be poor and at the service of the
poor in order to enrich them with the wealth of Christ's victory.

Reflection

In Albrecht's thoughts on poverty we see, once again, the centrality of
Paschal Mystery. We become poor with Christ in order that he may enrich us. We die
in order that he may come to life within us. If we were to speak in Rulla's
terminology, she would probably classify poverty as an "instrumental value" – a mode
of conduct designed to help in the attainment of some end or terminal value.
No doubt evangelical poverty serves this function. There is, however, the

possibility of taking too functional a view of poverty as if it were <u>only</u> a means to a greater end.

I think there is another way of looking at evangelical poverty. It can be seen as an instrumental means of attaining union with God but it is also an indication that such union has already been achieved. To be poor for Christ's sake is to already be united to him. I may not feel the union but it exists. I may feel I have given up all and am waiting to be filled with Christ, to be united to him. But in faith and in act I am already in union with him. I am already living a life of identification with Christ; it is he who is living in me. It is <u>his</u> poverty in which I am sharing. Such union may not be a pleasant experience but nobody ever said Christianity was supposed to be totally pleasurable. God cannot be known by the feelings or by reasoning powers but only by faith. Christ, living in me by faith, is already the fullness of the riches of God. It is the experience of that fullness that is not yet complete. Christ lives in me but I have not allowed him to permeate my whole being. And the reason he cannot live in me totally is that I am not yet completely poor; I still want some other things besides him. I am enriched with Christ to the extent that I share in the poverty he lived while he was on earth.

Only a poverty that springs from such a personal relationship can avoid excesses or artificiality. My use of material goods will be ordered to this relationship. I will not seek material things for the sake of the comfort, convenience or prestige that they offer me nor will I avoid ownership in order to <u>appear</u> poor. My attitude toward poverty will flow spontaneously in response to my relationship with God. I will be ready to give up anything or possess anything that furthers and deepens that relationship. Whatever possessions I may have in the service of others, I will always remain fundamentally poor and divested of everything because all that I have is held in the service of others. It may have to be given up at any moment if the service of others should so dictate.

There is a third way of viewing evangelical poverty. It is a means to an end and a participation in that end. But voluntary poverty can also be seen as a response to a value. This attitude is expressed in the Book of Ruth when Ruth refuses to leave her mother-in-law, Naomi:

Do not ask me to abandon or forsake you! For wherever you go I will go, wherever you lodge I will lodge, your people shall be my people, and your God my God. Wherever you die I will die, and there be buried. May the LORD do so and so to me, and more besides, if aught but death separates me from you! [144]

The religious acts in a similar manner. Having come into contact with the Lord, he desires to give up everything to follow him. He does not just give up everything. He also follows Christ. He desires to be free of other attachments which might set up a conflict of interest. The following of Christ consists in imitating his poverty but also in imitating his dedication to doing his Father's will. The religious shares in this aspect of Christ's life also. This aspect can be most clearly seen as analogous to the vow of obedience.

---

[144] Ruth 1: 16-17. This quotation is taken from the <u>New American Bible.</u>

Thomas Merton [145]
Religious Obedience

In seeking to articulate the place of obedience in religious life, Merton refers to the distinction between reform and renewal. Vatican II called for the latter, not the former. Reform is proper to the situation in which the formal structures of a society or institute are collapsing or in danger of collapse. In that case it is necessary to clarify existing rules or make new ones and enforce them by tightening up the discipline.

Renewal is something deeper, more living and more total than reform. Reform was proper to the needs of the Church at the time of the Council of Trent, when the whole structure of religious life had collapsed even though there was still a great deal of vitality among religious. Today the structure and the organization are firm and intact; what is lacking is a deep and fruitful understanding of the real meaning of religious life. [p. 136]

What is needed today, according to Merton, is not an appeal to the will of religious to be more faithful to the existing structures, but an explanation of the true meaning of obedience and a deeper understanding of its value. Especially in America, religious tend to look for quick, easy, efficient solutions to problems. In the question of obedience it is a renewed attitude that is needed.

The obedience of the vowed religious is not the obedience of a child to its parent or of a citizen to government. It is not primarily ordered to the smooth and efficient functioning of the institute. This last concept may have <u>some</u>

---

[145] The material in this section is taken from Thomas Merton, <u>Contemplation in a World of Action</u> (Garden City, New York: Image Books, 1973). All references to this work will be followed by the appropriate page numbers in brackets.

justification in modern active religious orders, but can easily lead to abuse. Merton

is primarily interested in obedience in a monastic context and in that situation such a

concept has no justification at all.

> How is monastic obedience to be understood?

> Monastic obedience is seen by the monk as a way to imitate the obedience and love of Christ his Master. Since Jesus "emptied himself taking the form of a servant" [Phi. 2: 7], the monk will seek also to empty himself of his own will and to become a servant, above all because this is Christ's "new commandment." [p. 136]

Religious obedience must be understood in a setting of love and discipleship. The

disciple tries to have the attitude of Christ, the Master, who served not only his

Father but also his followers. He wishes to serve in humility and love. The superior,

as well as the religious, is involved in this service.

> The work of obedience implies a loyal collaboration between superior and subject, in which both [italics in the original] strive, each according to his function, to understand and carry out the will of God. It is not that the superior arbitrarily makes his own will the will of God by issuing a command, but that he objectively and in the fear of God seeks the divine will, and in doing so, does not neglect to consider first of all the spiritual good of his subjects. [p. 141]

> The superior and the subject each brings his own proper service and

responsibility to each situation. The subject does not abdicate his responsibility for

his actions and the superior does not ignore the spiritual welfare of his subject. Each

tries to serve God in the framework of the mutual relationship between them. Each

respects the rights and duties of the other and tries to cooperate with him. To view

obedience only from the point of view of sacrificing oneself in "blind obedience" to

an impersonal institution does not usually meet the needs of modern religious.

Religious life is certainly a sacrifice but it is more. It is a way of returning to God in and with Christ. Much of the sacrificial nature of religious life is realized through the practice of obedience. But this must be complemented by an approach in which "the obedience of love rooted in faith becomes at once a sign and a principle of living unity in Christ, and a way of "returning to the Father" in and with the loving obedience of Christ." [p. 139] This obedience aims at a concrete and personal union of love in Christ.

A deeper understanding of this aspect of obedience need not lead to any change in structures or constitutions of religious orders. But it can restore authentic meanings to already existing structures. These meanings should be clear not only to those who live within the particular structures, but to all who observe such persons. The meaning of religious life cannot be allowed to remain abstract. "Everything must converge on the central living mystery of unity in Christ and illuminate it – or rather spread the illumination which it receives from it." [p. 144]

Reflection

In Merton's treatment, we see that obedience, like poverty, is Christ-centered. It is not an end in itself nor is it an abandonment of personal responsibility. Rather it is a way of exercising responsibility. It could be thought of as another aspect of poverty: I give up even my own desires and plans. Perhaps a better way is to view both poverty and obedience as two articulations of dedication.

Dedication, in the vowed religious life, does not only determine what things one will do; it also determines what things one will not do.

In the first part of Charles de Foucauld's "Prayer of Abandonment" we see a more or less typical expression of submission to God's will.

I abandon myself into your hands; do with me what you will. Whatever you may do, I thank you: I am ready for all, I accept all. Let only your will be done in me, and in all your creatures. [146]

At our first reading of this prayer the "only" in "Let only your will be done in me," may not stand out as particularly significant. The next line amplifies the meaning of the "only:" "I wish no more than this, O Lord." It is one thing to be willing to accept whatever God sends. I can probably safely do that. But in this prayer I am saying far more than I realized at first. I am saying that I want God's will to be done in me – and that is all I want. I do not want anything else besides that will. I want no life of my own, but only his life. I am saying that I want all my own personal interest to die out and only leave room in my life for Christ's interests. Another way of saying it would be: I want his interest to be my only interest. Again, it is a matter of my dying and his coming to life in me. He increases and I decrease; I no longer live but Christ lives in me.

Obedience is not abandoning responsibility any more than Jesus abandoned his own responsibility by doing his Father's will. Religious obedience is the accepting and living out the responsibility that has been assumed in Baptism and renewed in the Eucharist. It indicates what the subject is called to when

---

[146] Edward Farrel, <u>Surprised by the Spirit</u> (Denville, N.J.: Dimension Books, 1973), p. 126.

he experiences an attraction to the religious life. Religious vocation is a call to give myself completely to Christ to allow him to live his life in me, to have no life of my own that is not at his disposal. In this context, Rulla's theory of vocation as a call to transcendence, to go beyond what I am to what I should be, seems far superior to Super's idea of implementing an already formed self-concept. One step further might be taken. Eventually the religious will have to come to see his vocation not as a call to live up to <u>his</u> ideals but to cooperate fully in Christ's plan for him. He must be careful not to try to articulate his own ideals too concretely in advance or he may be in danger of serving a fine theoretical ideal at the expense of a living personal relationship to Christ.

The centrality of the personal relationship brings us to the third vow, the vow of chastity.

<u>Joseph Sikora</u> [147]
<u>Chastity and Interpersonal Communion</u>

Sikora begins his treatment of chastity by asking if the shift in the understanding of marriage does not have some implications for our understanding of vowed chastity. Formerly the primary end of marriage was considered to be procreation. While this is still generally held by theologians to be valid, there is much more emphasis on the role of personal love and communion. "Interpersonal

---

[147] The material in this section is taken from Joseph Sikora, <u>Calling: A Reappraisal of Religious Life</u> (New York: Herder and Herder, appropriate page numbers in brackets).

communion is one of the primary values of human life, and human sexual love is ordinarily the primary and fullest mode of this interpersonal communion." [p. 128] It is also true that the two sexes are complementary and need each other for full growth and maturity. Since we come to know the meaning of love of God through understanding love for others, does not vowed chastity weaken the person's ability for any affective relation with God or man?

In spite of these arguments, Sikora feels that the theory of religious chastity is sound, that it should and does lead to detachment and love for God and for others. He begins his response with a distinction borrowed from Maritain between the two kinds of love: <u>amour d' amite'</u> (ordinary friendship) <u>amour de folie</u> (love unto folly).

In ordinary friendship there is a mutual sharing and communion. But each person does not give himself <u>entirely</u> to the other. Each has other friends as well. He may share all he has but not all that he <u>is</u>. A similar relationship may exist between man and God. A man may have "a personal affective regard for, communion with, and commitment to God that does in fact go beyond what he might have for any human friends." [p. 135] This merely means he is living a moral life and would sacrifice other friends or interests rather than offend God. The relationship of friendship with God is not, however, entirely parallel to human friendship. Graced supernatural friendship with God calls for deeper participation by man in God's life; he cannot be one friend among others. He must eventually become one's <u>All</u>.

The second kind of love – love unto folly – goes far beyond ordinary friendship. It involves not only a sharing of goods but a complete giving

262

of oneself. It is foolishness if looked at solely from the point of view of reason. There may still be other friendships at the same time, but they cannot be of the same kind as this one.

This is love of the other as one's All, and a person can have only one All, in whom he is totally absorbed and to whom he is totally given in all that he is and has. Such a love means complete communion of spirit and complete openness to communication and all actual giving. [p. 137]

This kind of love – love unto folly – can unfold either in the natural or the supernatural order. In the natural order it is manifested in marriage where it is incarnated, symbolized and raised to its highest intensity in the sexual act as well as in the spiritual domain of affective communion. It is only possible to have such a relationship with <u>one</u> person at a time. In successful marriage is found the most completely other-centered love that is possible within the natural order. [148] These characteristics remain when such a love is elevated by grace but a new impetus towards communion with God is added to it.

Love unto folly can unfold in the supernatural order also in making God one's All. [149] Again it is clear that one can only have one All at a time

---

[148] Sikora states that the metaphysical structure of natural human love requires that even such an unselfish love of the other is still love of the other as another self and thus somehow as a good-for-the-self.

[149] In this case, according to Sikora, the love is <u>not</u> for God as another self. The focal point of the love is altogether outside the self; it is love for God as the transcendent and infinite Good.

so that a relationship of this kind with God and another person simultaneously would
be impossible. Such love for God is not found in its pure state in this life but is
always mingled with a greater or lesser degree of natural love with its shortcomings
and limitations. All the same, it tends towards purity and wholeheartedness. It is
incompatible with a simultaneous love on the level of human sexual union.
Moreover, such human love cannot be the basis on which one achieves an "adequate
reflex articulation" [p. 140] – a mode of expression – of his love for God.

Passive contemplation, without the possibility of adequate active
articulation, must begin here; this is a way of renunciation of means and a way of
darkness for the spirit – in which it must be led by the Spirit rather than find its own
way. Every articulation in terms of earlier experience is now simply insufficient to
express what is now felt, and no acts are in any way adequate to testify to the true
intensity of this love. [pp. 140-144]

The only human relationship which is excluded from a "love unto folly"
relationship with God is a similar relationship with another person. This does not
say that married persons cannot love God with such a total love. But, if they do,
Sikora feels that it will necessarily lessen the martial union to the point where it can
not be considered as a mutual "love unto folly" relationship for each other. Such a
relationship is proper to a successful marriage but it is not possible to have the same
kind of relationship simultaneously with a spouse and with God.

Thus, the voluntary renunciation of marriage is a preparation, at least in a
negative sense, for a higher mode of love for God. But it can also point toward and
call for the striving for such a love. There will still be other interpersonal human
relations and these are necessary and helpful. True, they pose some dangers but

these should be tolerated in view of the greater good that is sought. It would be a distorted religious ideal that would cripple human love. Besides orienting the person to the love of God, religious chastity is a sign of the eschatological kingdom already present through grace. It bears witness to the power of grace, allows a clearer, more detached vision of material and spiritual reality and frees the religious for his specifically religious apostolate.

Reflection

Like poverty and obedience, religious chastity is a giving up of something good for the sake of something else. In order to be able to fruitfully give up marriage in a spirit of true Christian sacrifice, one must first have a healthy appreciation of what is being sacrificed. He must realize its value. Entering religious life should not be a way of escaping the responsibilities of human relationships. It is, rather, a call to a total commitment to an interpersonal relationship which presupposes an adequate ability to relate to others.

I suspect that many readers will resent Sikora's insistence that a successful marriage will be limited as a "love unto folly" relationship if one or both of the partners enjoys a total love for God. His argument is logical enough. But there is a danger in thinking that what is logical is necessarily true. The workings of grace are not subject to the dictates of human reasoning. If Christian charity is Christ loving in me, who am I to say what he can and cannot do? However, Sikora's main point is that vowed chastity is ordered to the development of a deep personal love for God. This again emphasizes the central objective of the vocational experience. It is a call to follow Christ, to love him, to surrender all to him.

Like obedience, vowed chastity can be seen as a means to an end. It can also be seen as a response to the experience of God's love. As in human love, I experience the generous love of another for me and respond by loving in return. The love that the other gives me draws out my own capacity to love. The love of the other allows me to love, invites me to love and obliges me to love.

Vowed chastity, or celibacy, seems to be more appropriately explained by appealing to the reasons of the heart rather than to those of the intellect. To try to justify celibacy on the grounds that it leaves one free for apostolic work is a nice practical argument. But in giving up marriage I am giving up a great human love experience. Am I replacing it with something equally valuable, equally human, equally deep? I am if I replace it with a love experience that is as great or greater. It seems a human being has an obligation to develop his capacity to love. For many, marriage is the only realistic way this can be done. For some, marriage is out of the question for one reason or another. For others, there is the experience of an invitation to love that does not include marriage. It is not unlike the man with several lady friends who might make good marriage partners for him. If he falls in love with one of them, the attraction of the others decreases. He need not necessarily reject them as friends. But he no longer sees them as persons to whom he might commit his whole life. He does not <u>need</u> them in the same way he did before. He has given his assent to one attraction and the lure of the alternatives dies away. This is not the result of a reasoning process by which he decides that he can only have a total love relationship with one person at a time. It is simply that he

266

gives his assent to one particular attraction rather than to the others. This provides the nourishment for that attraction and it grows stronger.

The person called to the vowed religious life makes a similar choice. It might be argued that there is a big difference between choosing marriage with one girl rather than another and choosing religious life rather than marriage. The real need, however, is not that I fulfill my need to love and be loved in a particular way or state of life. The important thing is that I fulfill that need <u>somehow</u>. If I can fulfill that need in religious life my attraction to marriage will be considerably lessened. If I enter into a successful marriage, whatever attraction I may have felt for the religious life will probably fade before long. I have a need to love and respond to love. It is important that I choose <u>a</u> way to meet those needs. As my love grows, it will be generalized and broadened to take in others without interfering with the unique love to which I have committed myself.

The call to the religious life is a call to love. It is the call to give oneself wholly in love. It is an invitation to love Christ and let him love in me, to share his love with others and to love them with his love.

Conclusion and Transition

In this division we have studied the experience of being called to the vowed religious life. In the subject who undergoes the vocational experience we have seen a fundamental life orientation or life call which guides and directs his vocational preference. We saw also that this call is an invitation to a transcendence founded on a progressively integrated personality. In the object-pole of the experience we have seen the three vows of poverty, obedience and chastity as ways in which the religious expresses his response to God's call. Each of these vows is a facet of the living out of the Paschal Mystery.

As in all the vocational experiences we have studied in the previous division, religious vocation does not come to an end when the subject enters a religious order. He continues to experience the call to grow more deeply and fully in the life he has embraced.

In the fifth and final division, we will study some of the elements that are conducive to such growth.

DIVISION V

THE CALL TO GROW

AS A VOWED RELIGIOUS

INTRODUCTION

Thus far we have studied the vocational experience as it may occur on several levels. First we saw the experience of vocation on the natural human level. Next we took into account the implications of religious faith and the possibility of a vocation that is specifically religious, though pre-Christian. Following that, the call to embrace Christianity and to grow as a Christian was considered. Finally, one particular form of vocation within the Christian life that of the vowed religious, was studied. In each instance it has been seen that the vocational experience rises out of an interaction between a particular subject and the possibilities of some state or course of action to which he might commit himself. The subject experiences an attraction to that particular way of life in which he sees the possibility of realizing his ideals. He gives his assent to this attraction and fosters it, at least implicitly. He then attempts to express his assent in some concrete way in his daily life. In doing so, he finds elements in himself, which resist the new way of life, and some adaptation has to be made. Vocation has been viewed as an experience which continues throughout life.

This division will deal with the ongoing nature of the vocation to the vowed religious life. It is particularly intended for those who have committed themselves to this form of life. The ideas in this division presuppose that the call to religious life is also a call to growth as a religious. It is assumed that the subject has successfully fulfilled the entrance requirements and undergone a satisfactory formation period, been accepted by the order and the community and made final profession. This division is especially intended for such a religious at a time when, due to changes and ambiguity, the meaning of his vocation has come into question. He still feels he has found his vocation but is struggling to establish meanings that will give it new life for him. He is afraid his vocation is slipping through his fingers, that he has lost, or is losing his grasp on it.

The prospect of growing to a deeper appreciation and acceptance of my vocation brings up the question of the possibility of temporary vocation. I, as a vowed religious, may feel quite confident that the life I have chosen is the right life for me to be living for the time being. But how do I know that it will still be the life for me ten or twenty years from now? Would I not be better off to remain open to other possibilities to which God may call me later?

There are a number of possible answers to the question of temporary vocation. At one extreme is the answer that vocation is by definition permanent and "temporary vocation" would imply that God changes his mind. At the other extreme would be the denial of any permanence in God's call. He only calls man one day at a time and is free to alter whatever pattern I may think I see in his actions and inspirations. A more satisfactory answer is found by making the distinction between having a vocation and <u>knowing</u> one's vocation. In this case it is the subject who changes his mind. He thought he had discovered a way of life which suited him and in which he could realize his ideals. He embraced that form of life and committed himself to it in good faith. At some time in his attempts to grow as a religious, he may be confronted with indications that he has chosen a life that is not altogether compatible with his temperament and character. He discusses the matter with mature persons who know him well and it is agreed that religious life is probably not the best suited for his full spiritual development. This might be called a temporary vocation but it is better thought of as a temporary misinterpretation of vocation. Even in such a case, it seems that the best way for the person to decide whether or not the religious life is his vocation is by living that life faithfully while he questions its appropriateness for himself.

The question of temporary vocation is usually based on some particular <u>concept</u> of vocation. In the context of the <u>experience</u> of vocation, the question of temporality is less important. If I have experienced a call to the religious life and responded to that call it seems that any genuine new vocation should be an outgrowth of that call, not a departure from it. Thus, whatever I may think about the permanent or temporary nature of vocation, while I am committed to the religious life I should attempt to grow spiritually <u>as</u> a <u>religious</u>. This involves fidelity to the demands of that state.

One of the possible dangers in religious life is the attempt to build too large an edifice on a foundation that is not strong enough to support it.

271

The foundation must grow in proportion to the edifice. In this respect, the architectural analogy does not hold. When putting up a building, the foundation must be complete before the actual building can be begun. In the spiritual life, the foundation need only be strong enough to support the building in its present stage of development. The example of a tree would be somewhat more accurate. The roots grow at the same time as that part of the tree that is above ground. The roots need not have formed a complete fully developed system in order for the tree to sprout above ground. At first they need only be strong enough to support a tender sprout. But they must continue to develop as the trunk and branches grow. If the root system stops developing the tree may never reach maturity, or the trunk and branches may continue to grow to proportions that the roots can no longer support them. In that case the tree will topple over.

In the development of the spiritual life of the vowed religious there are certain elements which are foundational. They are the roots which support spiritual development. They must continue to grow and deepen throughout life. Other elements are less foundational, though equally important. They could be compared to the trunk, branches and leaves of the tree. They are the more visible elements. The fruit seems to emerge more directly from there.

In this division we will consider some of the foundational presuppositions upon which the growth of religious vocation is based. These presuppositions must be strengthened and deepened. These considerations will be followed by the study of some of the practices by which the religious expresses his assent to the ongoing vocational attraction.

CHAPTER IX

I AM CALLED TO GROW

AS A VOWED RELIGIOUS

If I am to grow as a religious, my life must be solidly based. Several elements will be considered in the first section of this chapter which are often taken for granted but may be lacking or deficient. My religious vocation must be based on genuine religious experience. I must preserve and deepen my capacity for such experience. I also have to preserve the specifically Christian nature of my life. Spiritual growth is a gift, a sharing in the risen life of Christ following a participation in his death. I have to live within the bounds of my limitations, accepting myself as I am but willing to follow the Lord's call when it beckons me to tasks that I feel (perhaps rightly) are beyond my competence. Finally, I need to retain a realistic view of what God is asking of me so as not to live in a state of complacency. Each of these elements will be considered in turn. Then we will study some of the practices of the religious which are based on these presuppositions.[150]

---

[150] It might be noted that practically all that is said in this division can be applied to a Christian living in the world as a married or single person. The division could have been limited to the elements that are peculiar to religious, such as the vows of poverty, chastity and obedience. My decision to treat the more fundamentally Christian elements was made for practical reasons. When a religious begins to question the meaning of his vocation it usually indicates some dissociation between the values he esteems and the way he is responding to them, or expressing that response. Either the person is losing contact with the values that

I. PRESUPPOSITIONS

Religious Experience [151]

It may seem superfluous to speak of the need for the vowed religious to continue to develop his religious sense. Cannot that be taken for granted? After all, he is a Catholic, not a pagan! How can he not be capable of, and deeply involved in, religious experience?

Unfortunately, it seems quite possible that a religious can "settle in" to a relatively secure and comfortable situation. While it may be a frugal and demanding life, he at least has what he needs, he has the respect and esteem of others,

---

religious life expresses or he still retains his esteem for those values but finds no adequate way to express them in his outward situation. In either case, the first step seems to involve gaining a deeper, more concrete grasp on those values and ideals upon which religious life is based.

[151] The material in this section consists of reflections on the contents of the previous divisions from the point of view of vocational development. Further reading on these themes can be found in the following sources: Robert S. Ellwood, Many Peoples, Many Faiths (Englewood Cliffs, N.J.: Prentice-Hall, Inc., 1976), pp. 1-26, 336-339: Rudolf Otto, The Idea of the Holy (London: Oxford University Press, 1971): H.C. Rumke, The Psychology of Unbelief (New York: Sheed and Ward, 1962): Huston Smith, The Religions of Man (New York: Harper and Row, 1965), pp. 1-13, 350-355: Evelyn Underhill, Practical Mysticism (New York: E.P. Dutton and Co., 1943): Engelbert J. van Croonenburg, Gateway to Reality (New York: Seabury Press, 1971), p. 6, (Summer 1962), are also relevant. The articles are "The Phenomenology of Religious Experience" by Roman Guardini (pp. 88-92), "The Psychology of Religious Experience" by Jean Guitton (pp. 93-96), and "The Philosophy of Religious Experience" by Johannen Lotz (pp. 97-100).

he has a theological perspective that gives satisfying answers to his questions about the meaning of life and he knows what sort of behavior is expected of him. It is not difficult to slip into complacency. Why should he leave himself open to the Wholly Other, the unpredictable, uncontrollable God, who dwells in inaccessible light? Why risk what he has worked so hard to master? He has God reduced to a doctrinal system, a moral code and a set of religious practices. His religious life began with a vague perception of the Holy which attracted him even while it disconcerted and disturbed him. He responded to the mysterious attraction and came to an explicit knowledge of God and his ways of dealing with man in scripture, the sacraments and the doctrine of the Church. He has further felt the mysterious attraction to dedicate his life to God and has given his assent to that attraction. He has expressed his assent by embracing the religious life. From ambiguity and vagueness his life has moved toward clarity and explication. Should he now move back in the opposite direction?

I am not suggesting that he should move back to his starting point but that he should never totally leave that beginning. Scripture, doctrine and theology should not replace the mystery of God. The mystery should surge up anew in the midst of the explanations.

An example may help clarify this. I was visiting some friends last spring. They had an eight-month-old boy who was absolutely fascinated by trees. His little mouth dropped open in wonder whenever we walked under a tree and he gazed in awe at this wondrous mystery. For an infant this attitude is fine. But as he grows older, he will have to learn to see the tree differently. He will have to come to a more explicit knowledge of the tree, a more pragmatic, materialistic view, if he is to live a successful life. When he reaches the tree climbing age, he will have to learn that it is a long way from even the lower branches to the ground. He will have to learn that the smaller branches cannot support him. When he is learning to ride a bicycle he will have to learn that trees do not move out of the way and that the trunks are very hard. In biology class he will have to learn about things that do not appear to the observer; sap circulation and photosynthesis. The tree cannot always be <u>just</u> mystery for him. But it should retain some mystery however complete his practical knowledge of it is. It may be that the quality of mystery cannot emerge and be appreciated as long as there is fear and insecurity in the practical aspects of the relationship. If, due to a few accidents, I develop a fear of trees, I will no longer be able to accept the tree for what it is, to let it be. It is no longer a thing of majestic beauty; it is a threat, a danger. I must be careful of it.

Another possibility is that the practical relationship to trees may develop and become totalized. A lumberman may be able to see trees only in terms of profit. To be open to their beauty would interfere with his business so he dismisses such an attitude as sentimental.

In personal relations similar problems may arise. In infancy I may gaze on others with an attitude of trust and simple wonder. As I grow I have to learn to relate comfortably to them in a practical way. If I do not they will always be something of a threat to me and I will be afraid to open myself to the deeper mystery that each of them embodies. On the other hand, I may learn to relate in a manipulative way, in a way that views others only as social objects to be used for my own welfare. Either attitude prevents my being open to the other as mystery. I should become capable of relating to others in a practical way while respecting the mysterious uniqueness of each person.

How do these analogies apply to religious life? It is possible that I may never come to a satisfactory relationship with scripture, doctrine or theology. I may not give my total consent to the vows, especially obedience and chastity. Something in me holds back though I may not recognize the fact. As long as I am undergoing some type of interior struggle, as long as I am not comfortable with the bases of my Christian or religious life, it is not likely that I will be able to build on them.

On the other hand, I may "have it all together." I have an airtight network of theological, scriptural and doctrinal arguments that can answer any questions. I am safe from any doubts or anxieties about religion. Others may respect me as a man of "unshakable faith." All this may be little more than an elaborate defense mechanism against the ambiguity and insecurity inherent in the human condition. I may actually be defending myself against God.

If I am to grow as a religious, I have to remain open to the possibility that God may shatter my defenses, my patterns of thinking – any of the things that I take for granted. He is always greater than articulations about him. Giving my life to his service, answering his call to me, must be given priority over persevering in any particular way of life or carrying on any particular apostolate. I have to be always open to the infinite mystery of freedom which he is.

Christian Perspective

While I must be open to the infinite mystery and freedom that God, is, I am not completely in the dark. I know something of his way of dealing with man and man's path to God. But this does not mean that there is a clear path lined out for me and I only have to exert enough will power to stay on it. Each path I think I can perceive leads to the cross where my desire to attain salvation by my own efforts has to die, and I must accept the unpredictable gift of a new life. The one thing I know about my spiritual development, as a Christian, is that it will be different from what I expect. It is not something that I can plan out for myself. Nor is it a plan made by another that I can figure out and understand.

As the Christian life must always be founded on a genuine experience of the Holy, so the life of the vowed religious must rest on a fundamentally Christian foundation. Part of my motivation for entering religious life may be the search for security. If I am to grow in my religious vocation, however, I must eventually abandon that desire and leave myself at God's disposal, asking him to do <u>his</u> will in and through me. I must desire that and nothing in addition to that. The three vows are not merely the laying aside of cares and responsibilities so I can be free for more important things. They are an explicit expression of Christian surrender and should be lived as such. When I take vows, I am giving up something that I know but I am also giving up many things that I do not know. When I give up the joys of married life I know what that means now. But I am also giving up the joys of married life as they would have been twenty years from now without knowing what that would have been like. The same can be said for obedience; I am giving up many desirable projects and ambitions that will someday appeal to me.[152] I am giving up more than I can possibly realize at the time. Nor do I see very clearly what is going to replace what I have sacrificed. I have some idea what will replace it but my idea is inadequate and will prove to be rather childish in the long run. In the beginning I am always making a deal, giving up one thing in order to get something better. Eventually I may reach the stage where I give up what I know is inadequate because it is inadequate, because it is not what I <u>really</u> want. I will not have a clear idea of what I really want but I will be confident that God knows what is best for me.

Ultimately what the Christian and the vowed religious are looking for is the full development of the Christ life within themselves. This can only come about through participation in his passion and death and rising to a new life – his life. When we speak of means and ends, we must always remember that we are unworthy servants, we can do nothing except open ourselves to the gift God wants to give us, to cherish that above all and be content to have nothing else.

<u>God's Love</u>

If I am to grow in my vocation to the religious life I must retain my

---

[152] Something similar happens if I get married. I am choosing one girl in preference to all the other girls I know. But I am also choosing her in preference to all the girls I do not yet know but will someday meet.

capacity for religious experience. That religious experience is not just a primitive awareness of the Holy but a realization that I meet God in Christ by participation in his death and resurrection. What does this meeting involve or presuppose?

A merely intellectual assent to the centrality and efficacy of the Paschal Mystery is not sufficient. I must be able to put that assent into practice in my everyday life. To do this is no easy matter. It will be difficult and painful and must always be so. Otherwise it would not be a sharing in the death of Christ. But it is possible if I have sufficient confidence in God's love for me. Again, an intellectual conviction of God's love is not enough. It must be an experience that I have known with my whole being.

It is very unlikely that I will be able to experience God's love if I have not experienced some kind of human love. It is not enough to have had someone love me. I must have <u>experienced</u> that love as love. I must have accepted it as a gift that this other person gives to me without my being able to do anything to earn or deserve it. He loves what I am, not something I have or do. To experience his love for what it is, I must accept the fact that I am lovable just as I am. It is difficult to accept myself as I am with all the weaknesses and inadequacies that I see in myself. I try to keep them from coming to my attention and especially from being evident to others. It is even more difficult to present myself to others as I am. If I am not satisfied with what I am, how can I expect others to be? In answer to the question, "Why am I afraid to tell you who I am?" one person answered, " I am afraid to tell you who I am, because, if I tell you who I am, you may not like who I am, and it's all that I have."[153] The risk is simply too great; I am entrusting you with that which is most precious to me. I am risking everything. It is only possible if I have a great trust in you.

I can only reveal myself to another if I trust him and I can only leave myself open to God if I trust him. If I am confident that he will accept me, embrace me, love me as I am. If I have entered the religious life to escape from guilt feelings I will have a difficult time trusting God. I may say that I trust him, but what do I mean by that? That I trust him to conform faithfully to my concept of him as a judge who is scrupulously just by worldly standards? How can I expect him to forgive me if I cannot forgive myself? This is not to say that he will not forgive me, but that I will not expect it of him, I will not be able to trust him.

When I first enter religious life my ability to trust may be quite limited. This capacity must grow little by little as the years go by. Occasionally I may be painfully confronted with my lack of trust, my fear of rejection or my burden of guilt. Such experiences can be most discouraging and lead me to the brink of despair. All the books I have read which tell me how the saints thought of themselves as the most useless or sinful of men make no impression on me at times like this. No sermon on the mercy of God gets through me. My illusions about myself have fallen apart

---

[153] Quoted by John Powell in <u>Why Am I Afraid to Tell You Who I Am?</u> (Chicago: Argus Communications, 1969), p. 12.

and therefore all is lost. Such incidents reveal to me that much of what I had thought was love of God was only an attempt to establish an acceptable self-image for myself.

Generally my frame of reference has to change so that all things are seen in the light of God's love. My belief in his love has to be effective. When I realize that some major area in my attitudes has been hypocritical or selfish my whole world need not collapse. It is not as if I had been genuine and wholehearted all along and now all my integrity has disintegrated. It is just that I have suddenly realized what I have been all along. If I can see things in the context of God's love, there is no reason to be so upset. He has known all along what I am and has loved me. Will he now stop loving me just because I also know? Surely not. This all seems very simple when written on paper. But it is very difficult to live it when the bottom drops out of my life.

Fortunately, I do not have to have complete and total confidence in God's love when I begin religious life. I only need enough to get me through each situation. This confidence will grow slowly over the years providing a solid foundation for my spiritual development. I need only enough confidence at each moment to be able to give up whatever the Lord is asking at that particular time. I do not have to be ready for martyrdom until that prospect presents itself. Meanwhile, however, I do have to have enough confidence to get through each day. I may not always breeze through with a smile but I do get through. Each time I make it, a little of my fear will dissolve and the reality of God's love for me will become a little more effective in my life. I will be a little more willing to give up my own desires and let Christ live his own life in me.

Limitations

In order to grow in my religious vocation, I must retain my capacity for religious experience and not allow myself to become encapsulated in mere observances. I must also retain a specifically Christian perspective by recognizing that growth results from an incorporation in the Paschal Mystery of Christ's death and resurrection. Finally, my confidence in God's love for me must expand and deepen so that I may be more willing to give up my own ideas and plans for my life when grace seems to be moving me in another direction.

Another presupposition that must be taken into consideration is the fact of my limitations. While I strive to realize my ideals, I must do so in the context of my limits. I am limited in the number of things I can do and I am also limited in the quality of my performance. We each have our gifts and our weaknesses. I will want to do those things at which I am best. I will want to avoid the jobs in which my performance will not compare favorably with that of others. Possibly there is a stage in my development at which it is necessary to compare my efforts to those of others. That may have a lot to do with learning. But I should grow beyond that stage and be satisfied with having done my best. Once I have done my best what difference does it make if someone else has done better? What difference does it make if someone else is not satisfied with my best?

To grow spiritually, I must have at least some independence from the performance and opinions of others. As I grow, that independence must increase. To be independent of the opinions of others does not mean to despise their opinions. I give them a respectful hearing but I am free not to agree with them if they do not reflect my own originality.

Possibly one of the more difficult things for a religious to do is accept a job that he knows he cannot do well. There is not much personal satisfaction in doing a job to the best of your ability when you know that your best is not particularly good. In such a situation I will usually be all too ready and willing to proclaim my limitations: "Oh, I could never do that; I am just not the type." It is true that I should not try to do things that are beyond me. But it is also true that I should not try to avoid things merely because they may result in my looking bad or having to experience my limitations.

The value of an assignment or task does not lie in what it has to offer my ego by way of satisfaction. The value does not lie in the job's potential for enhancing my prestige or self esteem. This is obvious to all of us when we hear it said. No religious would question it. But how deep is the conviction? Suppose I am asked to do a job that I know I cannot do well. Perhaps others in the community can do it better but are not willing or are not available for one reason or another. I claim to want to do God's will and no more than that, to be totally his, to let Christ live his life in me. The degree to which that is true will show up when I am asked to do something that has nothing else to offer. As long as there is something else, some prestige, some nourishment for my self image, I cannot be sure of my intention.[154]   I may be doing the job because it is the right thing to do, but I may also be doing it because of what is in it for me. Usually, of course, my motives will be mixed. The point is that the religious is not free to limit his activities to the areas of his choice. True love cannot be determined by the satisfaction that accompanies my work. It appears when I am to do something that does not appeal to any self-centered motives.

<u>True Love</u>

We have been looking at some of the presuppositions that must be taken into account if growth in the religious vocation is to be possible. The religious must have an adequate capacity for religious experience and openness to the fact that he will find God through participation in the Paschal Mystery. Only a confidence in God's personal love for him can make this possible. His growth as a religious is not determined by his success or reputation, but by his doing his best, however inadequate his performance may be by his own standards or those of others.

---

[154] Of course, the desire to be "sure" of the purity of my intention is itself a problem. Why should I want to be so sure? Obviously, because it would enhance my self esteem or alleviate my guilt or something like that. The important point is that I not kid myself into thinking that I am doing things only for God because I am enjoying them. Perhaps I am limiting my activities to the things I enjoy. Or I may not be admitting to myself that I am really a little bitter about some of the things I may have to do.

The value of my religious life is not gauged by visible standards. But there may be indications that all is not well. It was said above that motives of generosity are put to the test when all self-centered motives are absent. When all is going well, when I have a job I like and am working with people whose company I enjoy, when the weather is nice and my superiors understand my needs, I feel that my love for God is growing daily. Then things change. I am assigned to a job I do not care for, one that does not make use of my abilities. The people I am working with are difficult; it is cold or rainy and everyone thinks I should be happy in this situation. Now how do I feel about my love of God? Chances are it will seem pretty cool and feeble. This is, of course, understandable. Does this mean that my love fluctuates with the vicissitudes of life? Can I judge the depth and intensity of my love by how I feel, how energetically I pursue my work and, especially, how much love I feel for those around me?

We all know the answer to the question. Jesus said, "As often as you did it for one of my least brothers, you did it for me." [Matt. 25: 40] We have heard this interpreted as meaning that the amount of love that I have for the least is the measure of my love for Christ. The "least" does not mean the poorest, most underprivileged person in the world. It means the one whom I value the least, the one who is least in my estimation.

When I am judged by this standard I can no longer kid myself. I am judged by the dedication and loyalty that remains when all motives of self-interest fail. There is nothing wrong with my love for those who appeal to me. There is nothing wrong with enjoying the type of work that suits me. But these are not the true measure of my love. My motivation is strongly influenced by the satisfaction they offer me. There is nothing wrong with that. I need a certain amount of satisfaction to keep me going – probably more than I am willing to admit. I should be grateful for that satisfaction. But somewhere in everyone's life is the one person who goes against the grain. He is usually not very far away.

In our days there is much concern for the underprivileged in the "third-world" and all sorts of minority groups. This is certainly good in itself. It is a worthy cause and is generally recognized as such. My interest in such a cause may reflect a genuine concern for those who are suffering. But is it real Christian love? It may be. But it may also be a project that appeals to me because it makes me look and feel like a loving Christian. But am I really loving the poor or am I loving my own feeling of holiness?

The best way to keep from falling victim to such an illusion is to keep in mind the criterion that Christ gave: How genuine is my love for the person I find most difficult to love? How interested am I in his welfare, in his genuine happiness? This is different from my interest in straightening him out, putting him in his place or giving him enough rope to hang himself. At best, these latter interests express a desire to shape his welfare according to my own ideas, not according to his unique potentialities and needs. At worst, they express a genuine hatred disguised as interest. Of course, there may be all sorts of psychological obstacles that prevent a more favorable attitude towards him. But what am I making of the attitude that I have now? Am I giving him the benefit of the doubt, admitting that it is mostly myself that is to blame for my attitude? If I am not; if I am insisting that it is all his fault, that it would be foolish to be open and generous with such a person, then I should at least admit that my love for God is not very strong.

If I cannot help my attitude towards others, I can at least admit it for what it is. That is better than trying to hide from my hostility by being kind and generous in situations where virtue is easily practiced. A realistic attitude that does not allow me to deceive myself is not only the safest but the most accurate appraisal of where I stand before God.

The foregoing presuppositions are like the roots or foundations which support the spiritual life which I am trying to develop as a vowed religious. They are basic attitudes, criteria and abilities which must support my religious practices in order for them to bear fruit. One of the fruits the practices should bear is the continual strengthening of the roots or foundations. Having studied some of the more important presuppositions we will now look at some of the primary practices by which the vowed religious seeks to deepen his spiritual life.

II. PRACTICES

In times of change, such as those in which we now live, a certain amount of anxiety is inevitable. This is especially true when there has previously been a long period with relatively little change. Before the Second Vatican Council the course of religious life seemed fairly predictable. Rules and customs changed only slightly and slowly at that. There were departures from religious life but they were not highly publicized. In a matter of a few years all that changed somewhat drastically. Extensive changes were introduced and many religious left amid much publicity. Many of those who remained found themselves severely shaken by the events. They had been good religious, faithful to all their exercises. What had happened to them? What can be done to prevent their being so shaken again? The purpose of this section is to provide some suggestions that may prove helpful to the religious who wishes to grow more deeply in his vocation. It is hoped that some attention to them will provide him with a fruitful response to the assent he has already given to God's call as well as open him to future attractions and invitations of the Holy Spirit.

Fundamentals

The first general practice to be recommended is fidelity to the fundamentals of vowed Christian religious life. In a time of change many possibilities open up for the religious. Some of them are quite valuable, some less so. It is not my intention to give criteria which will distinguish the more valuable from the less valuable.[155] I wish, rather, to make some suggestions that will help the religious to strengthen his vocation by participation in the fundamental and permanent element of religious life.

The first practice that comes to mind is participation in the Eucharist. It is principally in the Eucharist that I, as a Christian and a religious, become more deeply incorporated into the Paschal Mystery. But the Eucharist is available daily. It can tend to become routine and even boring. I have read so many books that try to bring it's meaning to life. Guitar Masses, dialogue Masses, outdoor Masses, all offer a little sensible stimulation for a short time. But there is only so much you can do with the Eucharist. Meanwhile there are all sorts of other interesting things going on: inner city work, campaigns for social justice, Eastern methods of meditation – things like these seem to be "where it is at" in the modern world! Perhaps. But such activities are modes of expression and modes of expression will not be solid basis

---

[155] For this purpose, a good many valuable insights are provided by Adrian van Kaam, The Dynamics of Spiritual Self Direction (Denville, N.J.: Dimension Books, 1976).

for a religious life. I must have something to express. What is needed is a deep spiritual union with God. Such union cannot be acquired by external activity however worthy the activity may be. It is not something new or something different that I must do. I must do the basic things in a new way.

In regard to the Eucharist, this means finding its meaning for myself at a deeper level. I must overcome the urge to look for new activities, new apostolates, new workshops as a final solution. Nor is a new theological approach to the Eucharist the answer. These things may be of some help. But what is really needed is the personal recognition of what the Eucharist is - a sacramental uniting of my life with Christ's in his death and resurrection. This mystery is much deeper than I can realize at a glance. I must stay with it; I must allow the realization of what this sacramental union means to grow in me. I must be faithful to it, that is, believe in its power, trust in it, put my hope in it. I believe that the Eucharist will bring me more fruit than workshops and social rights protests. These activities have no Christian value if they are not also a share in the Paschal Mystery. I should be able to relate everything in my life to this mystery. As I gradually learn to do that, I will come to see the centrality of the Eucharist. It will not crowd out other activities, but will inspire them and permeate them with its own meaning. Thus my life will become more closely bound to a central point to which I can relate whatever workshops, apostolates or meditation methods I may become involved in.

There are other fundamental elements in the Christian religious life to which I should remain faithful even though they may seem dry and fruitless. The Sacrament of Reconciliation is one. In times when there is so much emphasis on self-realization there is a danger that I may lose contact with the fact that I am always a sinner. I may still pay lip service to the fact of my fallenness, but do I really experience it? Is it difficult for me to apologize to another for having been sarcastic, selfish or insincere? Do I usually just skip the apology and restore good relations by being a little extra nice the next time I see him? This can be a way of undoing my wrong (at least as far as my guilt feelings are concerned) without really admitting to myself that I was wrong. In the sacrament, I must express my realization of my fallenness verbally. I have to come right out and say it. Again, this may involve faith and patience. I do not commit any real sins – sins I could almost be proud of! Confession would be easier if I did. But telling someone of the little meannesses, the petty duplicities – confessing them is really humbling. It would be easier to just say to myself that I have not done anything worth telling and skip the sacrament for this week – or this month. Pretty soon I may be skipping it for this year.

The Church has given us the Sacrament of Reconciliation for a purpose. I cannot lightly put such a sacrament aside as not having any fruit for me. I must find its fruit. I must be faithful to the sacrament, honest with myself and confident that fidelity will be conducive to my spiritual welfare regardless of how futile the practice may seem for a time.

There are other practices in religious life that can be seen in the same light. Prayer and spiritual reading are two good examples. After many years in religious life I may look back and ask myself what do I have to show for it all. I expected some kind of experience of holiness. Prayer has, in general, been pretty dry and reading has been somewhat boring. Others do not seem to have that trouble. If these years have borne fruit, why do I not feel something? A more pertinent question might be why do I expect to feel something? The obvious answer is: because I am not willing or able to get by on faith. I believe more in my feelings. I am not willing to enter into the darkness and obscurity by letting my own desires, ideas and images die. I am not willing to surrender myself to the Paschal Mystery, to the mercy and love of God.

Ultimately, any failures in the Christian life seem to come back to this same basic point: I have my own plans for how my life should go; my own desires interfere with my inner urge to surrender to the Lord. Such a general statement is true but may seem too broad to be of practical help. One way it can be applied specifically is in the matter of the fundamental religious practices. Do not abandon them, however, little satisfaction may be found in them. Do not let them take second place to newer, more modern practices. The new practices should, rather, be seen in the context of the fundamental spirituality of the Church and take their meaning from it.

Workshops, meditation techniques, special liturgies and so on all have their place. But they will only be of value to my spiritual growth if they are articulations of fundamental spirituality. Meanwhile I must always be sure they do not distract me from the centrality of the fundamentals.

The Present Moment

What has just been said about the centrality of fundamental religious practices may sound like a conservative approach. In one sense this is true. The approach centers on the conservation of my vocation. But I try to conserve my vocation as a foundation for future growth, not as an heirloom to be kept in a glass case. Holding on to the past I look forward to the future. But that is best done by living in the present.

In this book we have considered the influence of a person's past on his vocational attractions. We have also considered the effects of his ideals and his plans for the future – what he is striving for. There is a danger of losing contact with either one of these two temporal poles.

I may become bogged down in discouragement and lose my grip on my ideals. Finding nothing to look forward to, I do a lot of thinking about the past, how good it was in the old days. I preserve a store of memories to carry me along through the boredom of the present. I confine my relationships to those who lived those days with me and understand. I can relate to others if they are interested in hearing about my world of the past but I cannot get interested in their plans or ideals. I may become a prophet of doom implicitly hoping that religious life will collapse so that I can leave without feeling that I have abandoned my vocation. I will be able to say that I was faithful but religious life abandoned me.

The other possibility is that I will lose sight of the past. "Thank goodness the old days are gone for good! All that stuff we learned in the novitiate has finally been thrown out and we now face a wide-open world! The shackles of the past have been discarded at last!" Besides losing contact with the healthy traditions of religious life, I am probably trying to deny my own limitations when I make such statements. I do not like to look at my past and see how little progress I seem to have made. I feel better looking at all the possibilities of the future. I spend my life imagining situations, making plans, wishing, hoping, wanting for the future and regretting the past.[156] Thus the resources of the past, as well as the possibilities of the present, go to waste.

I can only unite the past and future in the present. To live in the present moment does not mean forgetting about my ideals. If they are ideals which I hold with any conviction, they will be effective in my life even when I am not consciously thinking about them. My past also is effective since it has made me what I am.

---

[156] G.K. Chesterton has an interesting essay entitled "The Contented Man" in which he maintains that the person who is constantly bemoaning the past never really lived the events about which he is complaining. The essay can be found in G.K. Chesterton, A Miscellany of Men (London: Methuen and Co., 1930), pp. 254-260.

But the person that I am can only act in the present. Only here and now can I find God today. Living in, and responding to, the present moment is the best way to combat discouragement. While it may seem that such a view narrows my horizons, it actually only confines them to the real situation I am in. This does not mean being indifferent about the future. Making plans for the future is often part of the responsibility which I must meet in the present moment. [157] Suppose I am making plans for a retreat in which I will be participating next month. There are a certain number of practical things to be taken care of. But what of spiritual preparation? Often this may consist of thinking about how fervent I am going to be, how attentive to the stirrings of the Holy Spirit. I am trying now to live a situation that will not come for a month. I should, rather, be concerned with my present attitudes: What are they? Am I bored with life, with its trivial events and its petty inconveniences? The best preparation I can make for the retreat may involve facing that boredom and trying to work it out. What do I expect of life? What is my attitude towards the Eucharist, prayer, my community? Why am I unable to find anything interesting in my world? These are not rhetorical questions. They have answers and the answers are not always obvious. But the answers will not be found by flights of the

---

[157] A good treatise on living in the present can be found in Jean-Pierre de Caussade, Abandonment to Divine Providence (Garden City, N.Y.: Doubleday, 1975), pp. 36-58.

imagination into the future in which the problem will presumably not exist. It does exist now and it is part of my way to God at the present. Neither can it be solved by recalling and dwelling on past times in which life was exciting. In trying to work out the causes of my present state, I may often refer to past situations in which I had similar feelings. But such reflections are always in the service of my present living, not an escape from it.

Self-Reflection

The manner in which I reflect on my life is important.[158] There is, first of all, the danger of too intense an approach. I may find my first experiences of self-discovery fascinating. This can lead to a curiosity that is satisfying but not spiritually fruitful. With the great emphasis on psychology today there is a desire to be aware of all the reasons why I behave the way I do. This can lead to introspection that only increases tension and focuses my attention on myself. The attempt to know all my motives reflects a subtle form of pride. It shows a lack of trust in my nature; I think my emotions, my co-ordination, my responses will work better if I control them from my own ego center. I want to get nature under my control. I am not willing to trust that which I cannot fully understand, even when what I do not understand seems to be functioning well. I should have a healthy interest in my physical and psychological functioning but I should also be careful not to interfere with them.

---

[158] For a good treatment of the process of reflection see Adrian van Kaam, <u>In Search of Spiritual Identity</u> (Denville, N.J.: Dimension Books, 1975) pp. 172-196.

I do not have to understand everything. I should trust my nature until there is some indication of trouble.

Besides excessive introspection, there is the possibility of a self-conscious type of reflection.[159] I try to reflect on my responses even while I am responding. This has been referred to as "remembering the present." I am trying to do two things at once. Here again, I am trying to direct my experience; I do not trust spontaneity. It is true that I cannot simply surrender myself to every impulse that comes along. There are some situations I should try to avoid. But when I am in a particular situation, having a conversation for example, I should give my attention to the other person and respond to him. I should not be attending to my responses as I make them, wondering what kind of image I am projecting or what kind of impression I am making.

Self-reflection, to be genuinely fruitful, should not coincide with the experience upon which I am reflecting. After the experience, I look back upon it and ask why I felt this particular movement of anger or confusion or what that particular response really meant. I need not inquire into every detail, only those that seem to express feelings that I do not understand. A good example of this is the

---

[159] This type of distortion is described by Dietrich von Hildebrand in Transformation in Christ (Garden City, N.Y.: Doubleday, 1962). On page 50 he writes, "There is a type of person whose glance is always turned back upon his own self, and who is therefore incapable of any genuine conforming to the spirit of an object. If, for instance, he is listening to some beautiful music, he at once develops an awareness of his own reaction, and thus loses the possibility of a genuine response to that beautiful music." Von Hildebrand is criticizing this attitude as an obstacle to true conscious participation in the music rather than an obstacle to reflection. Actually, it is an obstacle to both.

"embarrassing question." Somebody asks me a simple question and I feel a brief onrush of emotion. I give a long, explanatory answer which leads the conversation to another topic. If this tactic works, I usually simply forget the incident. Something was touched that I do not want to face. Maybe it is not really important, maybe it is.

Probably the most important point in regard to such embarrassing moments is to recognize them for what they are. They indicate that I am not completely at peace with myself in some area of my life. That should not come as any great surprise. Nor should it be a cause for worry. I should be grateful that some problem has come to my attention. That is already progress. The question then becomes: what do I do about this situation which I do not completely understand?

The first step is to be as specific as I can about the problem. What kind of questions bother me in this way? What are my feelings? What would my feelings be if I gave this answer: what would they be if I gave that answer? In what other situations do I feel this same discomfort? Such questions should be asked in a broad context. They should be asked in the light of the presuppositions we have discussed above. I must be at least implicitly aware that God's love is greater than my weaknesses and imperfections, that Christian growth takes place by way of a process of death and new life, and that I will never be without some shortcomings. I must try to understand what St. Paul meant when he said:

> Therefore I am content with weakness, with mistreatment, with distress, with persecutions and difficulties for the sake of Christ: for when I am powerless, it is then that I am strong. [II Cor. 12: 10]

I must be content with what I am for the time being. I wish to become something other than that, but I do not try to be anything other than what I am at the present moment. I take what I am and present it to the Lord.

> We can do nothing better than press on into the sight of God. The more deeply we understand what God is, the more fervently we shall want to be seen by Him. We are seen by Him whether we want to be or not. The difference is whether we try to elude His sight, or strive to enter into it, understanding the meaning of His gaze, coming to terms with it, and desiring that His will be done. [160]

Besides exposing my weakness to God, it may be helpful to confide it to another person who is prudent and trustworthy. Just the revelation of my weakness helps to make it more real to me. It is easy for me to say that I am being honest with myself and honest with God. If I am not able to communicate my weaknesses to another there may be a reasonable doubt whether I am really facing them.

Self-reflection should not be limited to negative experiences. I should also reflect upon my positive responses. What is it about this person, this homily or this suggestion that elicits such a favorable response from me? From such a reflection I may come to know something of my ideals or values that I may not have recognized explicitly before. These positive experiences should also be discussed with another. Expressing them helps me to keep such experiences rightly situated in relation to the rest of my life. There is, of course, also the possibility that the one to whom I speak

---

[160] Romano Guardini, <u>The Living God</u> (New York: Pantheon Books, 1957), p. 35. The entire Chapter, "God Sees", pp. 28-36, is well worth reading.

may be able to provide some insights that escape me.

Keeping a notebook or journal of my reflections is also a good idea. Writing down my thoughts helps to make them concrete while they are still fresh. It challenges me to clarify my feelings in a way that I might not do just by thinking. It also provides me with a record of my past responses and the things that have affected me at other periods of my spiritual life. [161] Self-reflection and notebook keeping may often raise questions that demand attention. I come to see conflicts between my ideals and my actual behavior, between the desires I profess and the desires that seem to really motivate me. This conflict, if I face it honestly, is experienced as an invitation to further self-knowledge. Such an attraction is a continuation of my vocational experience. It raises the question: which way do I want my life to go? Do I want to repress the conflict and go on as if everything were alright? Or do I want to face the problem and try to purify my motives? The realization that there is a conflict is an invitation to the latter solution. If I give my assent to the invitation, I will have to express that assent somehow. One way in which I might express it is by seeking spiritual direction.

---

[161] A good presentation of the values of keeping a spiritual notebook can be found in Susan Annette Muto, <u>A Practical Guide to Spiritual Reading</u> (Denville, N.J.: Dimension Books, 1976), pp. 26-33. In this section, the author is discussing the value of journal keeping in relation to spiritual reading. But most of the material can easily be adapted for use in a spiritual notebook which might include reflections on events of daily life.

Spiritual Direction

The term "spiritual direction" can be understood in several ways. It is ordinarily thought of as a relationship in which one person directs, guides and advises a second person in the interests of the latter's spiritual growth. It is in this sense that I will be using the term. It is, however, worth noting the other valid uses of this term. The liturgy is a form of spiritual direction since, through the readings of the liturgical cycle, we are invited to a deeper personal union with Christ. Spiritual reading has the same directive character. Papal and ecclesiastical documents supply general directives as do the rule, vows, constitutions and guidelines of a particular religious order. The events of everyday life have a directive value as do my reactions to those events. All these things supply directives that I can take into consideration in trying to discern God's will for me. [162]

The religious has more directives in his life than the average layman. But having directives all around me is not enough. I must know how to appraise and evaluate them. I must respond to them. If I have more advantages I also have greater responsibility. To fulfill that responsibility I may occasionally have to seek help or advise from another. There are two possible extreme positions open to

---

[162] One further use of the term "spiritual direction" is worth noting. Adrian van Kaam in The Dynamics of Spiritual Self Direction (Danville, N.J.: Dimension Books, 1976) uses the term in reference to the unique transcendent destiny to which each man is called. "Direction" in this sense does not mean guidance or supervision. It means the orientation or course along which my spiritual emergence should take place if I am to reach that destiny.

302

me. I may be timid and scrupulous, running to a spiritual director to ask his opinion on every decision, even the most minute. Or I may go to the opposite extreme. I may see myself as a self-made man who can stand on his own two feet and does not need help from anyone. If the first possibility is more repulsive, the second is probably more dangerous.

There are, fortunately, other possibilities. There is the possibility of occasional recourse to the spiritual director. If I have been a religious for several years, I do not need advise on everything I do. To a great extent I can get along on my own experience, prudence and wisdom. But there are always times when I may question my wisdom in a particular situation. I may have to make a decision in a matter concerning something in which I have strong conflicting feelings. Even if I am not particularly looking for advice or suggestions, I may profit from the opportunity to present the situation and my dilemma regarding it to another person. If the one to whom I speak happens to know me fairly well, the conversation is more likely to be profitable to me. Thus there is some advantage in keeping in touch with one particular person on a regular basis even though I may not be continually in need of formal spiritual direction. Merton describes the meaning of spiritual direction as:

> ... a continuous process of formation and guidance, in which a Christian is lead and encouraged in his special vocation [italics in the original], so that by faithful correspondence to the graces of the Holy Spirit he may attain to the particular end of his vocation and to union with God.[163]

---

[163] Thomas Merton, Spiritual Direction and Meditation (Collegeville, Minn.: The Liturgical Press, (1960), p. 5.

When some problem does arise in my life, it is much easier to talk about it in the context of a relationship that has been established for that purpose. To have to start a new relationship in the midst of a difficulty is doubly hard. A common reaction is to weather the storm and resolve to arrange for a spiritual director later. Once the problem is solved I no longer feel the need for a director and the resolution is forgotten until the next crisis.

If I have a director whom I see on a regular basis – monthly, for example – it may seem that most of our talks are somewhat routine. There are usually no big problems and things go smoothly. Direction seems somewhat fruitless. Is it really worth the trouble? Is this really spiritual direction? Does this really have anything to do with furthering my spiritual life? Is it of any value? Merton goes on to say:

> However if we are wise, we will realize that this is precisely the greatest value of direction. The life that is peaceful, almost commonplace in its simplicity, might perhaps be quite a different thing without these occasional friendly talks that bring tranquility and keep things going on their smooth course. How many vocations would be more secure if all religious could navigate in such calm, safe waters as these! [p. 42]

The religious should not live a fearful, conservative life, worrying about all the possible dangers that might befall him. But the very possibility of dangers is a call to him to be prepared for them. It is another of the little attractions that I must follow. I am defending what I have for the sake of future growth. I am reminded of the fragility of my spiritual life and I take steps to protect it.

What Merton says of spiritual direction might be said of all the exercises and practices we have been discussing in this section. Looking back on life things seem to have moved pretty slowly. All the Eucharists, the confessions, the hours of prayer both public and private, the spiritual reading and the external activity, all this does not seem to have borne as much fruit as it should have. But I should never lose sight of the question Merton poses: what if I had <u>not</u> been faithful to those things? What if I had decided long ago that they were not really helping me and had given them up one at a time? Where would I be now? What would have become of my vocation? It is a sobering thought.

Conclusion

I began this book with an account of my own experience of being called. As the book ends, the process of being called is still going on. The call is no longer an invitation to enter into a new state of life or undertake a new course of action. The call is now an invitation to an ever-deeper entry into the real meaning of the original experience. At the time I entered religious life I thought I knew what I was doing and I thought it was the right thing for me. I still think so, but looking back after some years I realize there was more to it that I had thought at first. With each new meaning I discover in my vocation I am invited to accept that new meaning and incorporate it into my life. Each new meaning is a new aspect of my vocation. To this new attraction I must give my assent if I am to continue to grow spiritually. That assent will become embodied in my actions and decisions, thus deepening my contact with the whole meaning of my call. As this happens I will grow toward human fulfillment. I will also become more fully available to religious experience and more deeply convinced of the reality and power of the Paschal Mystery in my life and in the world.

For a complete listing of all your religious
vocations options contact:

Vocations Placement Service
6311 NW 47 Ct.
Coral Springs, Fla. 33067
www.VocationsPlacement.org
Toll free: 800-221-1807
E-mail: station1@vocationsplacement.org
Fax: 954-344-9231